D0205537

The Tale
of the Tribe

The Tale
of the Tribe

. . .

EZRA POUND AND
THE MODERN VERSE EPIC

. . .

Michael André Bernstein

PRINCETON UNIVERSITY PRESS
PRINCETON, NEW JERSEY

Published by Princeton University Press, Princeton, New Jersey
In the United Kingdom: Princeton University Press,
Guildford, Surrey

Library of Congress Cataloging in Publication Data will be
found on the last printed page of this book

Publication of this book has been aided by
The Andrew W. Mellon Foundation

This book has been composed in VIP Bembo

Clothbound editions of Princeton University Press books
are printed on acid-free paper, and binding materials are
chosen for strength and durability

Printed in the United States of America by Princeton
University Press, Princeton, New Jersey

For
DINA BERNSTEIN

remember that I have remembered

ACKNOWLEDGMENTS

• • •

One of the pleasures of working on this book during the past six years has been the number of obligations and debts incurred in its composition. Without the generous encouragement of friends and colleagues, I might never have completed such a project, and without their steadying advice the final text would have suffered immeasurably. The list of names included here is only a partial and fragmentary record of all those upon whose counsel I have relied, and my gratitude to everyone involved extends well beyond the formal expressions appropriate to an acknowledgment.

To Richard Ellmann, Alex Zwerdling, Thomas Parkinson, Ronald Bush, A. Walton Litz, Paul Alpers, Robert Hollander, James A. Powell, Herbert Marks, Victoria Yablonsky, Robert Owen, Jeanne Wolff von Amerongen, Paul Let, George Butterick, and James Laughlin, my sincere appreciation for having made the book possible.

I am also glad of this opportunity to thank The American Council of Learned Societies, The Canada Council, The Committee on Research of the University of California, Berkeley, and the Departments of English and Comparative Literature at the University of California, Berkeley, for granting me both the free time and the funds to work on this study.

The staff at Princeton University Press and especially Mrs. Arthur Sherwood, Literature Editor, and Miss R. Miriam Brokaw, Associate Director and Editor, encouraged my work from its beginning and I very much appreciate their support.

Chapter Five, "Identification and Its Vicissitudes," appeared, in a different version, in *The Yale Review*, and I am grateful for permission to reprint it here.

For authorization to quote from their works, I am indebted to the publishers and Literary Estates of Pound, Williams, and Olson.

Reprinted by permission of the New Directions Publishing Corporation and Faber and Faber Ltd.: Ezra Pound, *The Cantos*, copyright 1934, 1937, 1940, 1948, © 1956, 1959, 1962,

Paterson, copyright © 1946, 1948, 1949, 1951, 1958 by W. C. Williams; excerpts from "A Study of Ezra Pound's Present Position" as published in *Massachusetts Review*, Vol. 14, No. 1, Winter 1973, and from a letter by Williams as published in "The Eighth Day of Creation" by P. Mariani in *Twentieth-Century Literature*, Vol. 21, No. 3, copyright © 1973 by Florence H. Williams.

Reprinted by permission of Beacon Press: William Carlos Williams, *I Wanted To Write a Poem*, copyright, 1958 by W. C. Williams.

Reprinted by permission of George Butterick and The University of Connecticut Library: excerpts from Charles Olson's writings printed in *Olson*. Reprinted by permisson of George Butterick and the Charles Olson Estate: *The Distances* by Charles Olson; *The Maximus Poems Volume Three* by Charles Olson.

Reprinted by permission of Jonathan Cape Ltd.: Charles Olson, *Letters for Origin* (A. Glover ed.) copyright 1969 by Charles Olson; *Mayan Letters* (R. Creeley ed.), copyright 1953 by Charles Olson; *Maximus Poems IV, V, VI* copyright 1968 by Charles Olson.

Reprinted by permission of Jargon/Corinth Books: Charles Olson, *The Maximus Poems*, copyright 1960 by Charles Olson.

Reprinted by permission of Four Seasons Foundation: excerpts from *Additional Prose* (G. Butterick ed.), copyright 1961, 1962, 1964, 1965, 1967, 1968, 1969, 1974 by the Estate of Charles Olson.

TABLE OF CONTENTS

• • •

TABLE OF ABBREVIATIONS
for the Works of Ezra Pound

. . .

ABC of E: *ABC of Economics*, London, Faber & Faber, 1933.

ABC of R: *ABC of Reading*, New York, New Directions, 1960.

C: *Confucius: The Great Digest, The Unwobbling Pivot, The Analects*, New York, New Directions, 1969.

CC: *Confucius to Cummings*, New York, New Directions, 1964.

CWC: *The Chinese Written Character As A Medium For Poetry*, San Francisco, City Lights Books, 1963.

GB: *Gaudier-Brzeska*, New York, New Directions, 1960.

GK: *Guide to Kulchur*, New York, New Directions, 1970.

J/M: *Jefferson And/Or Mussolini*, New York, Liveright, 1970.

L: *The Selected Letters of Ezra Pound 1907-1941*, ed. D. D. Paige, New York, New Directions, 1971.

LE: *Literary Essays*, ed. T. S. Eliot, New York, New Directions, 1968.

Per.: *Personae*, New York, New Directions, 1971.

PM: *Patria Mia*, Chicago, R. F. Seymour, 1950.

P/J: *Pound/Joyce*, ed. Forrest Read, New York, New Directions, 1970.

SC: *Social Credit: An Impact*, London, Peter Russell, 1951.

SP: *Selected Prose 1909-1965*, ed. William Cookson, New York, New Directions, 1973.

SR: *The Spirit of Romance*, London, J. M. Dent & Sons, 1910.

Trans: *The Translations of Ezra Pound*, ed. Hugh Kenner, New York, New Directions, 1963.

The 1975 New Directions edition of *The Cantos* is used throughout this book. References are given in the text as: (LXXI:421) to designate Canto LXXI, page 421.

*The Tale
of the Tribe*

THE TALE OF THE TRIBE

> "I hold that a long poem does not exist. I maintain that the phrase 'a long poem' is simply a contradiction in terms. . . . If at any time, any very long poem *were* popular in reality—which I doubt—it is at least clear that no very long poem will ever be popular again."
>
> —Edgar Allan Poe,
> "The Poetic Principle"[1]

> "A heroic poem, truly such, is undoubtedly the greatest work which the soul of man is capable to perform."
>
> —John Dryden,
> "Dedication Of The Aeneis"[2]

In 1920, Georg Lukács published a critical study entitled *The Theory of the Novel*. The subtitle of this work, "A historico-philosophical essay on the forms of great epic literature," announces Lukács' decision to treat the *novel* as the fundamental form of epic literature in modern writing. Subsequently, he justifies this decision, explaining:

> The epic and the novel, these two major forms of great epic literature differ from one another not by their author's fundamental intentions but by the given historico-philosophical realities with which the authors were confronted. The novel is the epic of an age in which the extensive totality of life is no longer directly given, in which the immanence of meaning in life has become the problem, yet which still thinks in terms of totality.[3]

The conviction that verse could no longer deal adequately with "the extensive totality of life" (while the novel was now regarded as uniquely suited to attempt such a task) was by no means original with, or restricted to, Lukács. Rather, he is representative of a widely shared attitude: a narrowing of the sphere regarded as "appropriate" for verse, which any poet seeking to equal the breadth of scope and subject matter of great novelists was compelled to confront. In 1917, when Ezra Pound began to publish his long modern verse epic, *The Cantos*, he was distinctly nervous about the problematic nature of his undertaking, and in the unrevised version of Canto I, he speculates whether it would not be wiser to "sulk and leave the word to novelists."[4] As late as 1922, after he had already completely revised the poem's opening and published the first eight Cantos, Pound's correspondence reveals a man still anxiously defending the ambitious intentions of his work-in-progress: "Perhaps as the poem goes on I shall be able to make various things clearer. Having the crust to attempt a poem in 100 or 120 cantos long after all mankind has been commanded never again to attempt a poem of any length, I have to stagger as I can." (*L*:180)

Underlying both Lukács' critical pronouncement and Pound's initial self-doubt is a questioning of the essential nature of poetic discourse, of the formal limits within which the special language of verse must move if it is to remain faithful to its fundamental character as poetry. The question is really one of "decorum" in the full classical sense, an attempt to discover anew which modes of literary presentations are intrinsically most suitable to the different areas of human experience. By the end of the First World War, a verse epic was not so much a form as an oxymoron, an anachronism that seemed to violate what many poets as well as critics had come to regard as the characteristic structure and horizon of poetic discourse.

Edgar Allan Poe's strictures against the long poem in "The Poetic Principle" (1848) exercised a profound influence throughout the nineteenth century, especially upon the decisive figures in the development of modern French verse—Charles Baudelaire, Stéphane Mallarmé, and Arthur Rimbaud—but, in their own writings, Poe's argument was taken up as only one aspect of a fundamental upheaval in the connection between language as a literary, poetic artifact and the world of quotidian reality. At bottom it was the representational nature of artistic language that was challenged, the traditional conception of verse as a mimesis of some external, and consequently independent, event. For Mallarmé the poetic text was neither the discoverer nor even the celebrant of previously existent values: it was their sole originator, at once the source and only locus of meaning. The words of a poem, an incantation and hieroglyph, were absolutely divorced from their usage in the mundane world, and art, rather than offering an articulated duplication of reality, was seen as itself conferring the only reality, the only authentic and absolute form of being attainable. Mallarmé's most cherished project, the impossible "Grand Oeuvre," "doué d'infinité jusqu'à sacrer une langue,"[5] offers an illuminating antithesis to the ambitions of epic verse. Rather than expressing the fundamental struggles and beliefs of a society, the "Great Work" would absorb the entire, anarchic raw material of human life into its own depth, transforming it into a sacred text, self-sufficient and autonomous. The words of such a poem would themselves contain (or rather "be") the noumenal meaning absent from the concrete realm of human activity, and the relationship between text and values would be not one of embodiment but rather of absolute *identity*.

No single volume, of course, ever fulfilled the demands of so rigorous a program, and Mallarmé himself confessed that all of his efforts were but tentative steps towards the unrealized "Great Work." However, there was also a quite different limitation to his poetics, a limitation to which Mallarmé was largely indifferent but which became one of the major dilemmas of subsequent poets. The metaphysical elevation of verse, its radical separation from the sphere of daily life, had, as its logical corollary, made it virtually a contradiction in terms for a poem to treat directly the specific events of its age, to include details of historical confrontations or to comment upon the changing codes by which society was governed. In fact, the special claims made for poetic discourse rendered suspect *any* attempt to find a common basis whereby the judgments expressed in verse would be relevant to other human affairs. Before the nineteenth century, as

Michel Foucault has described, there existed a "reciprocal kinship between knowledge and language. The nineteenth century was to dissolve that link, and to leave behind it, in confrontation, a knowledge closed in upon itself and a pure language that had become, in nature and function, enigmatic—something that has been called, since that time, *Literature*."[6] After the success of the Symbolist writers, the discourse of poetry became increasingly "more differentiated from the discourse of ideas, and encloses itself within a radical intransitivity . . . it addresses itself to itself as a writing subjectivity. . . ."[7] The celebrated injunction with which Ludwig Wittgenstein ended his *Tractatus Logio-Philosophicus*, "Wovon man nicht sprechen kann, darüber muss man schweigen"[8] (what we cannot speak about we must pass over in silence) would only have pleased Mallarmé, since the border, now so absolutely demarcated, where ordinary discourse reached the limits of its competence, also locates the threshold where true poetry, "l'explication orphique de la Terre,"[9] begins—its subject matter, syntax, and form constituted exclusively by "what we cannot speak about" in the shared idiom of communal speech.

Thus, it was left to that other discourse, possessing what Lukács called an "indestructible bond with reality *as it is*,"[10] to portray the actual world as concretely experienced in the lives of individuals and whole societies. In France, at least, the new epic "comedy" was to be human, not divine, and, more important, it was conceived as a series of novels, written in the language of contemporary historical judgment and characterization, that is, in prose.

· · ·

In order to assure the incantatory power of the *word*, the advocates of a "pure" poetry had deliberately abandoned the *world* "to novelists." The new French verse was purged of the deadening, accumulated weight of neo-classical or romantic rhetoric, the possibilities of more flexible rhythms were explored, and, especially in the work of Baudelaire, new themes and areas of consciousness hitherto considered intrinsically sordid and "unpoetic" were rendered accessible to artistic treatment. Yet the inner world of a poem was increasingly confined to that of a single, intensely felt perception, to a moment of absolute insight or emotion crystallized into a timeless pattern. Often such poetry became totally self-reflective, its subject the inner process of its own creation, thereby leaving a purely formal structure intentionally emptied of all "outside" content. The natural *model* for this conception of poetry was music, the art whose "language" is most purely abstract and devoid of any external reference. For Mallarmé himself, the greatest threat to the pre-eminence of verse came from music, and he was determined to find a way of achieving "la transposition, au Livre, de la symphonie."[11] The characteristic *form* of all such verse was the brief, highly wrought lyric. In England, Walter Pater, for all his frequent appeals to "life," echoed both Poe and his French heirs in stressing the aesthetic primacy of the single lyric: "lyric poetry, precisely because in it we are least able to detach the matter from the form, without a deduction of something from that matter itself, is, at least artistically, the highest and most complete form of poetry."[12] The purpose of this poetry received its most famous definition in Mallarmé's sonnet, "Le Tombeau d'Edgar Poe:" "Donner un sens plus pur aux mots de la tribu."[13] It was this same phrase that T. S. Eliot was to adapt, with a characteristic and quite un-Mallarméan sense of *moral* urgency, in his own meditation upon the poet's craft in the "Little Gidding" section of the *Four Quartets*: "Since our concern was speech, and speech impelled us / To purify the dialect of the tribe."[14]

In the *Guide to Kulchur* Ezra Pound announced, "There is no mystery about the Cantos, they are the tale of the tribe—give Rudyard [Kipling] credit for his use of the phrase" (*GK*: 194). Pound himself clearly liked the phrase as well, for he quotes it again in his correspondence to explain that his poem must succeed in making all of its diverse elements come alive "as reading matter, singing matter, shouting matter, the tale of the tribe" (*L*:294). Surprisingly, in spite of Pound's acknowledged borrowing from Kipling, the significance of a "tale of the tribe" has never been explored and its precise source has been left undiscovered. Traditionally, the words have been regarded as only another version of the Mallarméan exhortation to "donner un sens plus pur aux mots de la tribu," and yet between the two statements lies the entire gap separating the "poésie pure" of *Un Coup de Dés* from the modern verse epic, *The Cantos*.

• • •

In an address delivered at the Royal Academy Dinner in 1906, Kipling tells of "an ancient legend" in which a man who had accomplished

> a most notable deed . . . wished to explain to his Tribe what he had done. As soon as he began to speak, however, he was smitten with dumbness, he lacked words, and sat down. Then there arose—according to the story—a masterless man, one who had taken no part in the action of his fellow, who had no special virtues, but who was afflicted—that is the phrase—with the magic of the necessary word. He was; he told; he described the merits of the notable deed in such fashion, we are assured, that the words became alive and walked up and down in the hearts of all his hearers. [15]

Gradually the tribe realized that only through the power of words "will our children be able to judge of the phases of our generation." [16] Since the survival of its shared values, and thus of its very existence as a coherent society, depended upon the permanent record of the group's decisive achievements, upon "the tale of the tribe," [17] a great moral and political as well as artistic responsibility fell upon the "man . . . with the necessary word." At the fundamental level of articulating the common aspirations, ethical beliefs and unifying myths of a people, "the Record of the Tribe is its enduring literature." [18] It was through the teller of this "record" that the deeds of warriors, priests, and men of action were set down, providing a storehouse of heroic examples and precepts by which later generations would measure their own conduct and order the social fabric of their lives. It is this conception of an artist's task to which Pound paid homage in borrowing Kipling's phrase, and, for all their differences in temperament and beliefs, it is this same conception that he hoped to embody in composing *The Cantos*.

The most radical difference between the "tale of the tribe" and the "mots de la tribu" lies in the antithetic notions of language implied by each phrase. Although Kipling speaks of the "magical" power of words, their magic resides precisely in the power to crystallize history, to make actual events live again in the minds of future readers. Language is not an absolute, transcendent force, but rather the most enduring and powerful means of *representing* a specific occurrence in the world, an occurrence which, by itself, already contains a significant meaning. Far from being absolutely autonomous and divorced from daily reality, the "tale of the tribe" is intentionally directed towards that reality, and is expressly fashioned to enable readers to search the text for values which they can apply in the communal world. Such a work is an artistic transcription of and meditation upon actions, and will, in turn, become a stimulus to future deeds. The ideal relationship between history and the tale, therefore, is one of perfect interpenetration. As the experiences of the community give rise to a text, that text in turn becomes instrumental in shaping the world-view of succeeding ages, so that, in the words of the tale, past *exempla* and present needs find a continuous and unbroken meeting-ground. From the anthropologist Leo Frobenius, Pound took over the notion of *Sagetrieb*, the "theory that man has an inborn urge to use poetry as a means of giving expression to and interpreting his past."[19] Pound's fundamental conception of an epic poem was precisely the *Sage* (literally "saying" or "speech") of his own historical era, the ἔπος (speech, or tale) of a tribe that had itself inherited all of man's previous legends and accomplishments as constitutive elements of its own consciousness. In Canto XCIV Pound declares: "This is not a work of fiction / nor yet of one man" (708), thereby indicating that, as is true of Kipling's tribal spokesman, the materials of his poem, the specific subjects included in the fabric of the text, are communal property, and that the situations represented therein embody the accumulated labor of successive generations. In a sense, even Pound's repetitive use of foreign phrases, his narration of incidents taken from a multitude of diverse sources, represents a unique attempt in modern literature to find a structural parallel for the interweaving of different dialects, of fixed epithets and stock situations, which Milman Parry revealed as underlying the oral diction of Homeric verse: "For the character of this language reveals that it is work beyond the powers of a single man, or even of a single generation of poets."[20] Canto XCIV was printed in *Thrones* in 1959, forty-two years after the hesitations and uncertainties that marked the initial three Ur-Cantos. During this long span, two of Pound's most critical as well as attentive readers, William Carlos Williams and Charles Olson, each began his own version of a modern verse epic, *Paterson* and *The Maximus Poems*. Both these texts were fundamentally influenced by the example of *The Cantos*, and both Williams and Olson were determined to learn from Pound's poem while avoiding the structural, ideological, and thematic weaknesses which they felt had seriously compromised it.

Although the particular success of each of these works is still a subject of considerable debate, the existence of a continuing tradition of modern epic verse, a tradition whose first and most significant document remains *The Cantos*, can be clearly demonstrated. The unfolding of that tradition and the scope of three individual solutions to the problem of contemporary epic poetry is the subject of the following study.

· · ·

The principle underlying a classification can never be postulated in advance. It can only be discovered *a posteriori*.

—Claude Lévi-Strauss, *The Savage Mind*.[21]

Thus far, the term "verse epic" has been employed without any attempt at a rigorous definition. I am aware that my own reliance upon the phrase is likely to create considerable resistance in readers who, fearing the implicit claims of such a term, would be far happier with an intrinsically looser (and largely uninformative) label such as "long poem." Yet, the idea of a modern verse epic, for all its apparent lack of precision, is extremely useful in trying to understand the nature of Pound's work, giving us a measure by which to locate his particular intentions, and a framework within which to examine his technical strategies. There are, I think, two distinct, although related, problems involved in using the concept of an epic throughout this book. First, what is meant by the work "epic," and how does Pound's poem satisfy the conditions specified for such a designation? And, second, what is gained by calling *The Cantos* a "modern verse epic" that is not available with the obviously more modest designation "long poem"?

In a strong sense, of course, to establish any single, rigid set of criteria defining the nature of an epic is bound to seem reductive since, for Ezra Pound as well as for his literary ancestors, the nature of an "epic" was a question, a problem to be explored through specific texts, rather than an established poetic form with a generally acknowledged set of conventions. One of the dominant goals of *The Cantos*, a concern governing the work's internal order and historical stance, is just such a quest for the necessary structure of a new epic, a structure that would emerge in the literary articulation of the poem itself and not in its adherence to external criteria. Thus, although the Homeric epics and the *Divina Commedia* exerted an immense influence upon Pound's conception of his work, to read *The Cantos* largely as an attempt to adapt their techniques to the contemporary world would leave unanalyzed the specific structural difficulties and thematic intentions of that poem. An adequate understanding of the particular sense in which Pound conceived of his poem as an "epic" can arise only from a scrupulous analysis of the text; while, at the same time, it is primarily by studying the work from the vantage-point of its ambition as a modern epic that the numerous obscurities in its structure and argument become comprehensible.

Revealingly enough, all the problems encountered here in trying to define precisely what an epic is only recapitulate, in miniature, a debate characteristic of literary history from its beginning. Recent specialized studies demonstrate a continually changing interpretation of what constitutes epic verse, an urge felt by succeeding ages to redefine the meaning of an epic according to their own aesthetic and intellectual needs.[22] Even in Aristotle's *Poetics* only two of the twenty-six sections are devoted exclusively to the epic, and it is too often forgotten that his discussion of the epic is governed as much by the examples of Choerilus and Antimachus as by Homer. (Milman Parry has shown that Aristotle's understanding of "heroic metaphors," for example, applies far more convincingly to these later *written* epics than to the oral narrative of *The Iliad* and *Odyssey*.)[23] To search among the other canonic texts of classical criticism for a stable definition is equally frustrating since, as E.M.W. Tillyard observed, "throughout antiquity a wide range of poems was commonly regarded as 'epic.' Generally speaking, hexameter poems were called 'epics,' whether they were heroic in character (as the *Iliad, Odyssey*, the Cyclic Epics, the *Argonautica, Aeneid, Pharsalia, Thebaid*), or didactic (Hesiod, Empedocles, or Lucretius), or commemorative of religious mysteries (Orphic poems, *Theogony* of Hesiod)."[24]

Extended debates on the nature, purpose, and language of the epic really began only with the sixteenth-century Italians who reversed Aristotle's preference and, in their hierarchy of literary genres, elevated the epic over tragedy. Even among Renaissance theoreticians, however, the absence of any significant unanimity of judgment out of which a strict definition of the epic might have evolved is startling, considering how often the word is used as though its meaning were self-evident. Nonetheless, one general principle, formulated by Torquato Tasso in his *Discorso Primo*, is crucial for an understanding of Pound's treatment of history in *The Cantos*. Tasso insists upon what is basically an affective or intentional distinction between the epic and tragedy; in his view, the principal emotion aroused by an epic should be admiration for some distinguished achievement, or noble character-trait, rather than the pity and fear ("l'orrore e la compassione") proper to tragedy.[25] Pound fully shared this conviction, and, as will become apparent, some of the attitudes which have troubled readers of *The Cantos* derive from the poet's quite intentional decision to avoid the characteristic world-view and psychological effects of tragedy. On the whole, however, the legacy of the Italian, and even of the classical, critics did not continue to exert a dominating influence after the eighteenth century. The outstanding epic works of the past remained both powerful models and primary sources of inspiration, but the use to which they were put, and the specific manner in which traditional themes and techniques were adapted, varied enormously with each poet. In France, for example, the nineteenth-century epic was, in the words of one study, "a very indeterminate form," ranging from conventional heroic narratives to long, philosophical treatises-inverse (*Vision d'Hébal, Prométhée délivré*, etc.).[26] In England, during the same period, poems which also possessed the length and wide-ranging concerns associated with epic verse (*The Prelude, Don Juan, Sordello, The Dynasts*, etc.) shared virtually no other significant structural characteristics, and, unlike their French counterparts, were rarely perceived as epics by either their creators or audience.

The conclusion that arises from any comparative historical survey is, perhaps dishearteningly, that no one constellation of fixed attributes, no set of necessary and sufficient elements, can be isolated that would allow us to determine by a purely formal analysis whether or not a poem is an epic. One solution would be that, rather than seek a single, limited set of attributes, each of which must be present in all epics, we could think of these poems sharing what Wittgenstein called a "family likeness." Many entities, in the argument of *The Blue and Brown Books*, are quite properly grouped under one general category without necessarily sharing their particular features in any specific instance. As Wittgenstein says, "they form a family the members of which have family likenesses. Some of them have the same nose, others the same eyebrows and others again the same way of walking; and these likenesses overlap. The idea of a general concept being a common property of its particular instances connects up with other primitive, too simple, ideas of the structure of language."[27] Yet such a "solution," although helpful, is by itself rather unenlightening. I think that Kipling's explanation of "the tale of the tribe" offers a more stable foothold, and I want to offer a series of propositions characterizing epic verse, propositions based upon an admittedly uneasy combination of *a priori* conditions and *a posteriori* conclusions drawn from specific texts:

(a) The epic presents a narrative of its audience's own cultural, historical, or mythic heritage, providing models of exemplary conduct (both good and bad) by which its readers can regulate their lives and adjust their shared customs.

(b) The dominant voice narrating the poem will, therefore, not bear the trace of a single sensibility; instead, it will function as a spokesman for values generally acknowledged as significant for communal stability and social well-being. Within the fiction of the poem, the dominant, locatable source of narration will not be a particular individual (the poet), but rather the voice of the community's heritage "telling itself."

(c) Consequently, the proper audience of an epic is not the *individual* in his absolute inwardness but the *citizen* as participant in a collective linguistic and social nexus. Whereas a lyric is addressed to the purely private consciousness of its hearer apart from all considerations of his class, circumstances, or social bonds, the epic speaks primarily to members of a "tribe," to listeners who recognize in the poem, social (in the broadest sense, which here includes political) as well as psychological, ethical, emotional, or aesthetic imperatives.

(d) The element of instruction arguably present, if only by implication, in all poetry, is deliberately foregrounded in an epic which offers its audience lessons presumed necessary to their individual and social survival. The epic, that is, must contain both clearly recognizable models of "the good" and an applicable technique, methodology, or behavior pattern by which that good can be concretely realized and imitated.[a]

---

[a] I have called my four characteristics an uneasy mixture of *a priori* criteria and *a posteriori* features, inductively derived by considering what numerous specific examples of the form have in common. Although such a way of reaching a definition is unorthodox, it is also methodologically necessary, as is the subsumption of my own characteristics under Wittgenstein's notion of "family likeness." That is, no single epic need demonstrate *all* of these characteristics; neither does the presence of *one* of these features assure that a given poem is an epic. In a Kantian sense, the epic is an Idea which specific texts incarnate more-or-less successfully, each in its own way and under the pressures of the contingent, historical circumstances of its composition. Phe-

If one is willing to grant my characterization at least a provisional, heuristic value, the most immediate gain in considering *The Cantos* as an epic is that the category is now shown to possess a recognizable, even if rather elastic, meaning, whereas "long poem" tells us nothing beyond the bulk of the volume in question. Moreover, and this consideration is at least as crucial as the four general criteria I have posited, by agreeing to regard a poem as an epic (or, in the case of the texts I will discuss, as three different *attempts* at an epic) the reader's horizon of expectations is affected: the responses which previous examples of the genre will have developed become available to guide an initial reaction to the new work. These expectations are, of course, also known to the poet, who can then deliberately manipulate them, can satisfy, thwart, or even seek to "correct" and improve upon the conventions of epic decorum. In all these instances the tradition of epic verse has provided a series of pre-texts with which any new poem aligns itself, pre-texts that also directly influence the author's own understanding of how this poem should be structured and what features it must include. To decide to write an epic situates a certain contract between author and reader, one that defines the text's and the audience's mutual responsibility and generates an intentional framework within which the particular exchange, poem/reading, can proceed.

If we now return to Lukács' pronouncement in *The Theory of the Novel*, it becomes clear that it is not so much the possibility of writing an epic per se that is being challenged (although this is itself a crucial question to which we will, of necessity, keep returning), but rather of *poetry*'s adequacy to the task. In spite of the many nineteenth-century poetic experiments, by World War I it was clear to most critics that the novel had replaced verse as the proper medium for narrating "the tale of the tribe." The exemplary literary study of an entire age emerged in works such as *La Comédie Humaine, War and Peace*, or *Bleak House*, and not *The Dynasts* or *La Légende des Siècles*. Advocates of a "poésie pure" could point to the

___
nomenologically, the epic is a project, an intentional structure to be isolated and distinguished from other intentional structures such as the lyric or the novel.

relative failure of contemporary poems with epic ambitions to justify their own belief in the necessity for an absolute and self-sufficient lyric form. Only prose, with its language still linked to the world of communal *praxis*, was considered able to encompass concrete political and social details successfully within a work of art.[b] Furthermore, it was exactly those details which, since the beginning of the nineteenth century, had become increasingly recognized as indispensable to any proper understanding of a society. The decisive changes in the discipline of history, its concentration upon the forces of economics and of specific social structures in determining the causes and significance of events, inevitably affected author and critic in their judgment of what constituted the elements needed to substantiate any valid interpretation of an epoch. The nineteenth-century epics, with their sweeping, symbolic visions of mankind's progress (*La Légende des Siècles*) and their numerous historical inaccuracies (*Sordello*), might be considered satisfying aesthetic creations, but they could not attempt to match the novel's richly textured analysis of contemporary reality. Nor is it a question of "realism" in any narrow sense;

[b] Such a description may seem to embody, as I am well aware, a distinctly limited understanding of the specific technical and imaginative preoccupations of the major nineteenth-century novelists. Clearly, for prose writers like Henry James, Flaubert, or Turgenev, the *literary* problems of the novel were of paramount significance. More particularly, the relationship between the language of prose fiction and the "objective facts" of social reality was, in their eyes, neither transparent nor untroubled. Yet the issue at stake here does not, in any essential way, depend upon a rigidly mimetic or even representational notion of language. Rather, the codes at work in a "realistic" novel correspond to (which does not mean are synonymous with) the nexus of interpretive structures through which we also "make sense" of quotidian experience. Moreover, the two systems reinforce one another and are subject to compatible revisions. (As our notions of psychology or history change, for example, our view of the *vraisemblance* of a fictional character's behavior or of his milieu is inevitably modified. Conversely, fictional works themselves help to shape the ideas of a society which is the prerequisite for their existence.) For the present discussion, however, it is sufficient to recognize that to Pound, one crucial index of the artistic excellence of his favorite novelists was their creation of a form and language adequate to the portrayal of the modern world. However restricted Pound's reading of the novel may appear, it is nonetheless an integral element in his thinking about the task confronting a modern verse epic.

rather, the way in which history was represented differed profoundly in the two literary modes. The past, for the writers of nineteenth-century verse epics like Victor Hugo, could serve as an implicit comment upon present conditions, but such a commentary, because of the text's refusal to include anything but the most archetypal and universal historical factors, remained almost entirely abstract. Even when the poet's intention was most clearly to use historical *material* as an elaborate judgment upon contemporary life, the absence of anything recognizable as a historical *analysis* (which would, of course, have meant the presentation of details considered suitable only to prose) vitiated the specific authority of the narration about both the past (the poem's apparent theme) and the present (the poem's actual concern). It is as if, for all its seeming diversity of forms, the nineteenth-century verse epic, even in France, the one country whose poets regularly continued to produce self-conscious examples of the genre, had never really departed from Le Bossu's famous definition in the *Traité Du Poeme Epique* of 1675, "un discours inventé avec art, pour former les moeurs par des instructions déguisées sous les allégories d'une action importante, qui est racontée en vers d'une manière vraisemblable, divertissante et merveilleuse."[28]

For two generations of readers tutored both by the theoretical developments in historiography and by the concrete and increasingly cataclysmic upheavals of their own societies—upheavals beginning with the Franco-Prussian War and culminating in the virtual self-extinction of the European imperium in the trenches of World War I—such a poetics was clearly not the place to seek an understanding of history. Marx's lifelong praise of Balzac, the conservative Catholic-Royalist, for the depth of his insight into the emerging structure of post-Napoleonic French society, is well known and has become a *locus classicus* of left-wing criticism.[29] Less often cited is an observation by William Butler Yeats, an artist one might have expected consistently to affirm the priority of verse over prose: "Balzac has brought me back, reminded me of my preoccupation with national, social, personal problems, convinced me that I cannot escape from our *Comédie humaine*."[30] When it came to seeking perceptions from literature about modern "national or social" problems, both men immediately refer to a novelist; in both instances, the possibility that a poetry existed which could deal with these themes authoritatively is not so much challenged as simply passed over, the negative answer long since taken as self-evident.

Lukács' treatise had, of course, only claimed the priority of prose in the handling of one, albeit crucial, subject matter. From the presuppositions of *The Theory of the Novel*, however, it is only a short step to the more unnerving (and simplistic) question posed by Edmund Wilson in his 1934 essay entitled, suitably enough, "Is Verse a Dying Technique?" Wilson articulates his fundamental argument with characteristic boldness, "It is simply that by Flaubert's time the Dantes write their visions as prose fiction instead of as narratives in verse."[31] He then proceeds to state the reasons for poetry's uncertain prospects in a sentence that assumes as a truism much of the development in nineteenth-century poetics whose background I have thus far sought to illustrate: "The horizon of the verse writer has narrowed with the specialization of the function of verse."[32] The curious aspect of Wilson's analysis is that it came so late, that by the time it was printed numerous poets, and in English especially Ezra Pound, had already begun to make his description an anachronism, had started to answer his essay with works that belied its gloomy prophecies.

•   •   •

"The stylistic reform, or the change in language was a means not an end."

(*CC*:315)

Although there were many aspects of the Symbolist heritage which the young Pound rejected—he especially deplored what he called Symbolism's "mushy technique" (*GB*:85)—initially he seems to have shared its skepticism about the possibility of a successful modern verse epic. In 1909 he defined an epic as "the speech of a nation through the mouth of one man,"[33] but almost at the same time he took pains to describe the *Divina Commedia* as a "lyric" or "a cycle of mystery plays" (*SR*:161). Later in the same work, Pound attributes the limitations of Camoens' *Os Lusíadas* in part to its author's desire to write an epic when the time for such an endeavor was no longer propitious. "An epic cannot be written against the grain of its time: the prophet or the satirist may hold himself aloof from his time, or run counter to it, but the writer of epos must voice the general heart" (*SR*:228).

From his earliest years in England, Pound had longed for a kind of verse that would offer ". . . something greater, / some power, some recognition, / Some bond beyond the ordinary bonds / of passion and sentiment / And the analyzed method of novels."[34] But the very fact that the poem-fragment from which these lines were taken ("Redondillas or Something of That Sort") was abandoned in 1911 indicates that, at this date, he had not yet found a suitable language, structure, or narrative technique which could give form to his longing. Even as Pound's own poetry began to include ever more passages of social observations, he maintained his suspicion of both the artistic desirability of *any* kind of extended verse narration— "Am at work on a long poem. Which last two words have an awful sound when they appear close together"[35]—and about the specific possibility of successfully narrating "the tale of the tribe": "But the man who tries to express his age, instead of expressing himself, is doomed to destruction" (*GB*:102).

Nonetheless, by the 1930s, Pound was unhesitatingly describing *The Cantos* as an epic, offering in 1933 his famous definition, "an epic is a poem containing history" (*LE*:86). This is a definition he was to repeat with only minor modifications for the rest of his life. Somehow, between the hesitancies of 1909 and the self-confident definitions of the 1930s, Pound had grown to accept the necessity, not just of a "long poem," but of one which would make history—the tale of the tribe—rather than Sextus Propertius' private inspiration ("ingenum nobis ipsa puella facit")[36] its principal concern. The motives for so radical a change are by no means self-evident, and yet it is essential to understand them in order to make sense of Pound's intentions in *The Cantos*.

The first and most crucial impetus underlying Pound's attempt to make a seemingly outworn genre new, to resurrect the epic poem, has already been extensively described. He sincerely feared that unless poetry could successfully challenge the novel in the breadth of its representational powers, it might become as irrelevant and out-of-date as "the art of dancing in armour" (*LE*:55). His debates on the proper mode and subject matter of poetry throughout the years immediately before and after World War I, keep taking up and trying to answer the same issue of poetry's survival to which Edmund Wilson called attention in his 1934 essay. What my discussion has not answered, however, is a quite different problem: if the novel is already so successful in providing a modern prose epic, what reason beyond ensuring the survival of verse can there be for challenging its authority? (The obvious response, that Pound was, after all, a poet, and a singularly ambitious one, while undoubtedly true, is hardly adequate: the very intensity of his ambition would have forced him to find a more securely grounded justification.) What, in other words, is uniquely true of poetry that not only makes a successful competition with the novel possible, but even necessary for the well-being of the entire community? Why, when it can read the *Comédie Humaine, L'Education Sentimentale*, and *Ulysses*, does the tribe still need a modern verse epic?

In a 1934 review of Laurence Binyon's translation of Dante, Pound makes the same judgment we have already encountered in Lukács and Edmund Wilson, the affirmation that "definite parallels" can be found between the great Medieval poet and Flaubert (*LE*:211). He does not go on to suggest the nature of those parallels, but from his other, separate references to both writers it is clear that the power to express a coherent and highly critical image of their age prompted the association. Although Pound is scrupulously aware of the technical mastery with which Flaubert constructed his texts, he regarded that mastery as much in moral-political terms as in aesthetic ones: to him, the novels are "pages of diagnosis" (*LE*:297), they are the true tragedies of nineteenth-century bourgeois culture. Pound's opinion of James Joyce, repeated over many years and in numerous essays, is couched in remarkably similar terms. He never really regarded *Ulysses* as a recreation in modern terms of *The Odyssey*. Instead, the novel appeared to him as a great modern comedy, a Rabelaisian satire on the banality and shabbiness of contemporary life. Pound saw the references to Homer as a private aid which had helped Joyce to compose his novel, but which do not enter a reader's consciousness in any significant way. Already in "The Paris Letter" of June 1922 (*The Dial*), Pound wrote: "The correspondences with Homer are part of Joyce's medievalism and are chiefly his own affair, a scaffold, a means of construction, justified by the result and justifiable by it only" (*LE*:406). And by 1933 he was repeating the same observation in still stronger terms: "The parallels with the *Odyssey* are mere mechanics . . . Joyce had to have a shape on which to order his chaos. This was a convenience . . ." (*P/J*:250). Though many Joyceians would disagree with Pound, for our purposes it is important only to realize the qualifications inherent in his enthusiasm for *Ulysses*. He admired the novel immensely, but largely as a satire, as the ultimate step in the refinement of a narrative method adequate to record the ignoble character of its age. Although he grants that Joyce had, ". . . for the first time since 1321, resurrected the infernal figures" (*LE*:406), Pound does not consider *Ulysses* an example of mythic recurrence. He never mentions any positive values which Joyce's book might embody. The novel, to Pound, is all irony and artifice and not the means of discovering "what sort of things endure, and what sort of things are transient; what sort of things recur; what propagandas profit a man or his race; . . . upon what the forces, constructive and dispersive, of social order, move" (*PM*:68), which he had established as his own goal. In *Guide to Kulchur*, Pound even used the same word, "diagnosis" (96), for *Ulysses* which he had previously applied to Flaubert. "Ulysses," he writes, "is the end, the summary, of a period" (*GK*:96), adding elsewhere, "Joyce's influence in so far as I consider it sanitary, is almost exclusively Flaubert's influence, extended" (*P/J*:252). At no time, however, were either Joyce or Flaubert credited with more than a negative, critical ability. The articulation of a *solution* to the social quagmire their prose reflects, the portrayal of readily imitable models of "the good" by which readers can regulate their society, is, in Pound's eyes, not to be found within the pages of even the greatest novels.[c]

Pound's "defense of poetry" never assumed the form of a single, coherent essay; instead, its elements are contained in numerous asides scattered throughout his writings. The true cornerstone of his justification *pro arte sua* is contained almost as an afterthought, hidden away in a footnote to his long essay on Henry James:

> Most good prose arises, perhaps, from an instinct of negation; is the detailed, convincing analysis of something detestable; of something which one wants to eliminate. Poetry is the assertion of a positive, i.e. of desire, and endures for a longer period. Poetic satire is only an assertion of this positive, inversely, i.e. as of an opposite hatred.
>
> This is highly untechnical, impressionistic, in fact almost theological manner of statement; but is perhaps the root difference between the two arts of literature.
>
> Most good poetry asserts something to be worthwhile, or damns a contrary; at any rate asserts emotional values. The best prose has been a presentation (complicated and elaborate as you like) of circumstances, of conditions, for the most part abominable or, at mildest, amenable.
>
> (*LE*:324)

Thus, according to Pound's "almost theological" conviction, both prose and verse can portray the negative aspects of life, but only poetry is genuinely capable of articulating a vi-

---

[c] This discussion is, of course, not intended to deny the enormous technical influence of Joyce's novel upon Pound while he was revising the Ur-Cantos. Ronald Bush, in *The Genesis of Ezra Pound's Cantos* (Princeton, 1976) has given a detailed and convincing analysis of how Pound's conception of his initial drafts changed under the month-by-month impact of the chapters Joyce mailed from Paris, but it is equally true that Pound never regarded *Ulysses* as a challenge to the potential authority of verse. Pound was able to learn from Joyce's work without fearing that *Ulysses* had usurped his own domain or answered the need for a new "tale of the tribe."

sion of beauty, of crystallizing the possibility for a better existence, and therewith of providing an impetus for the attainment of that good. If the novels are "diagnoses," the greatest poems contain, along with diagnostic elements, "the art of cure," a "hygiene" which "reminds one that something is worth while" (*LE*:45). Because Pound did not believe in the autonomy of literary discourse, because he was convinced that the words of a fictional text both reflect and help shape the society within which it is created, he was unwilling to abdicate the full range of either literature's "diagnostic" or potentially "curative" powers. And only poetry, he felt, could create the language necessary to register all the real needs of a community, could keep alive concepts and intuitions otherwise lost to the tribe's public vocabulary (*SP*:359–362). Pound was certain that "in the long run human intelligence is more interesting, and more mysterious than human stupidity, and stays new for longer" (*ABC of R*:163). The presentation of an *active* human intelligence, as opposed to the passive registration of social and psychological determinants (Frédéric Moreau, Leopold Bloom, etc.) was, so Pound felt, the special contribution only poetry could bring to literature. The casual tone with which he usually introduces these claims disguises the daring shift in the position he had seemed to maintain. Now he asserts that it is poetry which is more richly directed towards man's future horizon of expectation. By both naming the present ailment and indicating the necessary direction of a cure, poetry, not prose, can exercise the broadest and most beneficial function for humanity.

Although Pound calls his belief that poetry is uniquely able to offer "cures" as well as "diagnoses," "highly untechnical [and] impressionistic," he does offer at least two arguments in support of his intuitions. The first is that because verse is more concise than prose, "There is MORE in and on two pages of poetry than in or on ten pages of any prose" (*GK*:121). Ideally, poetry can present the crucial elements of the tribe's heritage in a memorable (and memorizable) form, can crystallize its truths in a series of striking images or lines that, like the fixed situations and epithets of oral epics, permit the audience to retain their significance when the text is no longer at hand. (This ambition helps to explain the use of certain repeated economic slogans, "shorthand" terms like "Metathemenon" or "hoggers of harvest" which, as M. L. Rosenthal rightly observes, create "lyric refrains" out of political, fiscal and social perceptions.)[37]

Pound's second argument is far more complex, depending as it does on poetry's greater ability to include "the mythological exposition" among its techniques. He states that "People need poetry: that prose is NOT education but the outer courts of the same. Beyond its doors are the mysteries" (*GK*:144-5). Only poetry with its roots in the language of mythological narration, a discourse which "tries to find an expression for reality without over-simplification, and without scission" (*SP*:87) can obey the injunction, "When you don't understand it, let it alone," the "copy-book maxim whereagainst sin prose philosophers" (*GK*:127). The difficulty with this line of reasoning is that it requires of the final text a constant and precarious balance between the two codes: the historically analytic and explanatory elements (the "prose tradition" of the great novels recaptured for verse) and the mythological, intuitive insights, the religious revelations of universal truths (traditionally the rightful domain of verse). If either code begins to displace the other, the poem as a whole risks fragmentation or intellectual incoherence. And as we shall see, one of the major dilemmas in *The Cantos* arises directly from the tension between the historical and mythological codes, arises, that is, when the two types of perception no longer harmonize towards a single, comprehensive understanding. Irrespective of Pound's particular success in satisfying the demands of his own theory, however, his reasons for embarking upon so immense an undertaking as a modern verse epic are both internally consistent and intrinsically worthy of, not only our respect, but, more important, our full critical attentiveness. To dismiss *The Cantos* because of their very ambition, to label Pound's attempt as *a priori* doomed to failure ("wrong from the start") seems to me both ungenerous and illogical. Worst of all, such a stance has, as its unacknowledged presupposition, precisely that narrow, restricted understanding of poetry's horizon which it was, perhaps, Pound's single major contribution to modern literature to overthrow.

· · ·

In 1913, in his Imagist manifesto, Pound had already announced that poetry must succeed in the "direct treatment of the 'thing' whether subjective or objective" (*LE*:3). Although it seems a long way from "A Few Don'ts by an Imagiste" to the problem of creating a modern verse epic, in a sense the challenge of *The Cantos* was precisely to make the tribal heritage itself that "thing," to create, in verse, an exemplary testament for his own age in which the hitherto distinct demands of aesthetics, religion, and history could be reconciled and satisfied; to record, in other words, not just the moments of insight attained by a solitary and unique consciousness, but rather (in terms of Eric A. Havelock's description of Homer) "a sort of encyclopedia of ethics, politics, history, and technology which the effective citizen was required to learn as the core of his educational equipment."[38] Or as much of that *summa* as Pound's own abilities and wisdom could encompass and his epoch permit. It is these two qualifications to which the rest of this study will now seek to give a more precise content.

A · THE CANTOS

"The life in me abolished the death of
  things,
Deep calling unto deep."
                    —Robert Browning,
          The Ring and the Book, I.520-521

CHAPTER ONE

. . .

A POEM
INCLUDING HISTORY

"The task to be accomplished is not the conservation of the past, but the redemption of the hopes of the past."
Max Horkeimer & Theodor Adorno[1]

But the lot of 'em, Yeats, Possum and Wyndham
had no ground beneath 'em.

Orage had. 不   [pu = not]

(XCVIII:685)

In his essay, "Ez and Old Billyum," Richard Ellmann refers to these lines and restricts his commentary to a single, ironic sentence: "Orage stood on the firm ground of Major Douglas' economics."[2] Clearly Ellmann intends to allow Pound's own extravagance to mock its author, and his laconic dismissal itself "stands on" the assurance that all except for a few "credit cranks" (Pound's own term)[3] will find the poet's judgment not worth serious consideration. Later in this chapter, I will examine the function of Pound's fiscal doctrine as an integral development of his conception of history, but first there is a more general type of question that needs to be asked. How different would Ellmann's reaction have been if, instead of an advocate of Social Credit and newspaper editor, Pound had named a Catholic philosopher, Marxist economist, or Oxford historian? Any one of these might express similar reservations about Yeats, Eliot, and Lewis without incurring an instant dismissal of his criticism. Similarly, Pound's conviction that these writers and personal friends whose contempt for contemporary decadence he largely shared, and whose literary texts he admired, presented only a personal, religious,

or aesthetic "ground" for their views and that such a foundation was in many ways insufficient, is neither cranky nor
prima facie absurd.

In one of his letters to Olivia Shakespear, Yeats wrote: "I
have constructed a myth, but then one can believe in a
myth—one only assents to philosophy."[4] Pound, on the other
hand, for all his faith in the power of myth to evoke "belief,"
was never willing to sacrifice the "ground" of intellectual assent; indeed, to do so would have entailed surrendering precisely the analytic element of "the prose tradition" which he
intended to recapture for verse. Pound wanted to give his epic
a "grounding" in a system that was more than purely individual and intuitive; rather than condemn or praise by authorial fiat his desire was to provide the reader with a sufficient
(and craftily selected) "phalanx" of historical, literary, and
economic "particulars" to compel an intellectual as well as
aesthetic agreement. Poets like Mayakovsky, Neruda, and
Brecht would have applauded the ambition, even while condemning the viewpoint. Long before the term *engagé* became
a literary commonplace, Pound wrote, "It is my intention . . .
to COMMIT myself on as many points as possible. . . . Given
my freedom, I may be a fool to use it, but I wd. be a cad not
to" (*GK*:7). It is not the smallest of the many ironies in
Pound's career that the contemporary political order in which
he sought the locus of an objective truth should have removed
him from virtually all sources of intelligent support. Yet
among the reasons why he has exerted such a strong influence
upon three generations of poets (especially in the United
States), is the seriousness of his attempt to find some rational,
political dispensation that would fulfill his ethical and aesthetic needs, his struggle to create a poetic form which includes the *reasons* for the author's judgments among its *materia
poetica*. Someone else might have used less "eccentric" (and,
in several instances, undeniably sinister) criteria. The point
remains though, that poets as different in temperament as
W. C. Williams, Hugh MacDiarmid, and Allen Ginsberg have
returned to *The Cantos* again and again, not only because of
the text's numerous triumphs of rhythm and imagery, but
also because, as a model for an extended poetical treatment of

history in which the data of scientists, anthropologists, and statesmen could figure, *The Cantos* are, quite simply and literally, unique.

Of course it is a truism that the desire to write a poem with social and ethical implications is not limited to the author of *The Cantos*. All serious poets are, in Pound's phrase, "contending for certain values" (LXXIX:485), but their strategy is usually fundamentally different from the one adopted by Pound. To take an obvious counter-example: many readers have seen in *The Waste Land* a uniquely powerful record of the post-war European sensibility, one obviously not restricted to those sharing its author's individual and strictly private *malaise*. *The Waste Land* clearly did succeed, quite against Eliot's subsequent and rather disingenuous explanations of the poem's genesis, in presenting the *Weltanschauung* of a culture, but its artistic structure is far closer to a *psychomachia* than to the "tale of the tribe." *The Waste Land* does include "representatives" of the world it is portraying, but the ladies in the pub, or Mr. Eugenides the Smyrna merchant, are only *types* of modern decadence; they are "typical" of their kind, and their historical existence is irrelevant. Similarly, the use of literary "tags," classical parallels, and, more explicitly, the religious force of "What The Thunder Said" shows us a world from which we have declined, and the distant possibility (or, more accurately, pre-conditions) of a regeneration. There is no historical analysis of, or context for, such a fall; the Waste Land is a spiritual and psychological, not a geographic or political, demarcation. For all its seeming specificity of detail, Eliot's poem presents a vision of a world which the reader accepts for aesthetic, moral, and psychological reasons. There is no attempt at either a logical or historical argument; the poem convinces by the force of its language and, unlike an epic, is intended for the individual reader as a private man, not for the chief magistrate or "citizen." Finally, *The Waste Land* contains no "party" program or claim to a "literal" truth, and this discretion has made the poem acceptable to men of widely different beliefs. Visions are open to many interpretations and only implicitly contain an imperative to action. There is a strong presence of gods and goddesses in *The Cantos* and yet

Pound's poem is not "a vision." Instead, it is an attempt at an all-embracing historical and aesthetic synthesis, a poem that praises or attacks well-known men and institutions, that proposes an economic explanation of civilization's rise and fall, and contains an explicit series of specific recommendations to both ruler and ruled. Like Dante's *Divina Commedia, The Cantos* demand to be taken as literally and historically true.

I realize that this last description will raise numerous doubts. Not content with claiming in the Introduction that Pound intended his poem to compete with and ultimately surpass the novel, I now want to argue that he was equally determined to endow *The Cantos* with at least the same *degree* (which is not identical to the same *kind*) of authority as that possessed by a historian's text. Indeed, to a very large extent the two ambitions are intertwined, since it is exactly the novelist's ability to present the social history of his age (with, in Pound's eyes, an accuracy and penetration equal to any historical study) that he so greatly envied. To advance the seemingly irrefutable argument that Pound's philosophical, economic, or political causes are woven into the fabric of his verse as poetry not history is true only as a description of how *we* tend to read his text, of *our* willingness to make a radical disjuncture between aesthetics and politics, but it assumes as an unquestioned *donné* an understanding of the two categories that Pound deliberately meant to subvert. Perhaps the easiest way contemporaries (as well as future generations for whom the immediate issues engaged by the text are no longer politically relevant) can agree to consider works of art with a pronounced polemical component worthy of study is to restrict claims for their significance to ahistorical and aesthetic criteria. In reading *The Cantos* such a decision may even appear especially charitable, but it offers no assurance that our "charity" will not undermine an accurate grasp of the text's own intentions. The aestheticization of *The Cantos* is, of course, one of the most characteristic critical strategies employed by Pound's admirers. Daniel Pearlman, for example, thinks that "It is time for the *dehistoricization* of Pound." He fears that "critics who historicize Pound inevitably *politicize* him" and offers, as a solution, "that the 'history' in the *Cantos* is deliberately idealized and mythical, a string of *exempla* used to flesh out Pound's ruling ethical-philosophical ideas."[5] As will become evident throughout this book, I regard such a "defense" as fundamentally inadequate. History and politics are both present in *The Cantos*—indeed, their presence is one of the poem's greatest strengths as well as a source of grievous weaknesses—and it is more damaging to Pound's intentions to deny their relevance than to confront openly their implications.

The fact that no historian, *qua* historian, would accept many, let alone all, of Pound's judgments, while undeniable, is also an irrelevant counter-argument, since Pound fundamentally distrusted the methodology, aims, and often even the intellectual honesty, of most professional historians. Their presumed disagreement would establish only that: (1) Pound had a very different understanding of history and historically accurate writing; (2) he was a very mediocre historian; or (3) conventional historians ignore what is most essential about their own subject. Any such disagreements, however, do not in the least disprove that Pound intended to write a poem which would to a large extent supplement, and at times even supplant, books normally accepted as "histories." Among the reasons he so often points us towards those texts to whose arguments he is willing to grant authority, is a desire both to acknowledge his sources in a manner characteristic of all historians and to establish a corpus of "safe" texts, of books that may be trusted amidst the swarm of other, either ignorant or corrupt, claimants. Determining the usefulness of standard texts, deciding their degree of factual reliability and analytic insight is, after all, one of the more conventional ambitions of any new history book. Kung supposedly "cut 3000 odes to 300" (LIII:273), and *The Cantos* are full of similar weedings-out in the domain of historiography and art. In the words of Canto LXXXIX, three types of wisdom are essentially interrelated and will, ideally, be united in one text: "To know the histories / to know good from evil / And know whom to trust" (590).

When Donald Davie, quite correctly, I believe, censures Pound's historical juxtapositions at the end of *Thrones* as "the notorious 'whig interpretation' of English history in a sort of parody version for grade-school,"[6] he is being far more honest than most of the poem's admirers by acknowledging that *The Cantos* do advance a quite specific "interpretation" of history. Davie's argument, in effect, assigns Pound to my second category, describing him as a wretchedly bad historian, subject to all the autodidact's simplifications and eccentricities. However, if we return to explore another possibility—that Pound was proceeding from a fundamentally different conception of what constitutes a valid historical narrative—we will, I think, be able not so much to "justify" particular arguments in *The Cantos*, as to understand better the poem's characteristic *mode* of argumentation and the structures within which its historical material is inscribed.

While critics have debated the intellectual responsibility of Pound's judgments and questioned the artistic strategy by which these are presented in *The Cantos*, during the last twenty years there has been remarkably little controversy surrounding the actual content of those judgments. Studies by writers such as Hugh Kenner, Clark Emery, Donald Davie, and Christine Brooke-Rose, as well as countless individual articles and monographs, have done decisive and groundbreaking work in explaining the central core of Pound's beliefs, and there has been no serious challenge to their summary. This is in part a tribute to the thoroughness of his explicators, but it is also in large measure a comment on the presentation of values in *The Cantos* themselves. Pound is simply not ambiguous or "difficult" in the same way that Flaubert or Joyce have been so considered. It is impossible to imagine debates about the author's own stance, about the degree of his approval of or irony towards crucial characters and episodes, arising around *The Cantos* as still mark discussions of *Madame Bovary* or *Ulysses*. Instead, Pound's difficulties are a matter of surface and structure. Problems arise from the wealth of references to different intellectual realms and cultures, and from the manner of their presentation, rather than from any ambiguous stance towards the subject-matter itself. My own attention in this chapter will therefore be focused less upon the thematic content of the poem's historical argument than upon its structures, upon the narrative principles according to which the historical data is presented, and the criteria by which the intellectual authority of the historical code is to be validated.

If, as Pound wrote in *The Spirit of Romance*, "The study of literature is hero-worship" (v), then the modern epic could be defined as the continuation of hero-worship by different means. In one sense, of course, Pearlman is quite right: the historical narrative in *The Cantos is* meant to provide a series of *exempla* of good and bad behavior. But this is done in order to determine what specific *political*, economic, and religious practices most benefit mankind, and to instruct both ruler and ruled in their proper roles. And, crucially, the material must unfold in such a way as to enforce the rational and intellectual, as well as the emotional or aesthetic, agreement of its audience. For this agreement to be obtainable, it is logically necessary that the actual historical incidents selected for inclusion, and the judgments made about such incidents, be placed within a framework of argumentation whose validity can be confirmed from *outside* the text as well as from within its own pages, that a set of autonomous verification criteria be established to which an "independent" appeal can be made. That framework underwent modifications as Pound's own understanding of his task evolved during the many years of the poem's composition, but one can isolate two fundamental structures upon which Pound relied throughout *The Cantos*. The first of these might be called the "Inductive or Ideogrammic Method" and the second "Confucian Historiography." Traditionally, critics have followed Pound's own arguments and seen these two structures as essentially interdependent. However, a careful analysis reveals that each one receives its justification from a quite different conception of history and narration; each contains its own distinct advantages and limitations, constituting certain domains for textual inclusion while, at the same time, precluding others. Moreover, the two structures are by no means always mutually reinforcing, and a great deal of the uncertainty that has marked discussions of Pound's historiography arises directly from the disjunction between *The Cantos*' different narrative principles.

•   •   •

"If, as Hegel argues, the whole is what is true, then it is so only if the force of the whole is absorbed into the knowledge of the particular."

—Theodor Adorno[7]

Pound's first, and certainly most explicitly articulated, convention of "emploting"[8] the historical material derives from his conception of the inductive technique of the scientist allied to the principles, as he understood them, of the Chinese ideogram. Although these two sources do, in fact, combine to validate one general technique, there is considerable value in first scrutinizing each one separately before tracing the results of their interaction.

From the two "heroes of science" to whom Pound frequently refers, the German anthropologist Leo Frobenius (1873-1938)—"The white man who made the tempest in Baluba" (XXXVIII:189)—and the Swiss-born Harvard teacher and naturalist Louis Agassiz (1807-1873)—"Agassiz with the fixed stars" (XCIII:625)[9]—Pound inherited the idea that a true scientist proceeds by an "act of collecting and arranging a mass of isolated facts, and rising thence by a process of induction to general ideas."[10] Only the scrupulous assemblage of concrete, observable details, the comparison and examination of specific minute features ("Agassiz and the Fish"), can give rise to insights possessing a universal validity while remaining untainted by the abstraction and vagueness of all purely theoretical generalizations. Moreover, if Agassiz' teaching helped to persuade Pound that a "scientifically" correct conclusion could be based solely upon the careful scrutiny of individual specimens, it also assured him that, in Ian Bell's words, "Historical fragments whether as fossils, cave-paintings, or torn papyrus provide . . . the 'luminous detail' which gives privileged access to geological, racial and cultural characteristics."[11] By combining Agassiz' emphasis on the empirical amassing of natural facts with Frobenius' notion of *Kulturmorphologie*, the conviction that all the essential characteristics of a particular civilization are discernible from a very restricted number of its artifacts, Pound was able to fashion an epistemology that gave him two crucial and dearly sought advantages. First, it permitted him to think that the most fundamental truths, even about as multiple and various a subject as human culture, could be grasped (and hence also communicated) by means of individual and even fragmentary "luminous details."[a] Then, it confirmed his intuition that the careful juxtaposition of isolated facts was no mere "poetic shorthand" but the rigorous application of the best "method of contemporary biologists" (*ABC of R*:17). In other words, the poetic technique which Pound had been developing since his days as an Imagist, the ability to "present an intellectual and emotional complex in an instant of time" (*LE*:4), could validly be extended to present "a historical and cultural complex" as well; it was now possible, as I suggested in the Introduction, for Pound to include history itself among the "objective" subjects treated in terms of Imagist and Vorticist aesthetics.

Although a detailed discussion of the ideogram as a linguistic *sign* is the concern of a subsequent chapter, the ideogrammic *method* as a means of structuring the narration of a huge mass of heterogeneous details needs to be included here, largely because Pound himself regarded it as a literary homologue to Agassiz' and Frobenius' scientific principles (*ABC of R*:20). In making this connection, Pound was only being faithful to Fenollosa's own claims. *The Chinese Written Character as a Medium for Poetry* insists that the ideogram, and by extension all true poetry, "agrees with science and not with logic" (28). That is, the Chinese sign is built up out of a series of root perceptions, each of which retains, through a kind of visual onomatopoeia, an intimate link to a natural process. The defense of the ideogram throughout *The Chinese Written Character* is based upon its supposedly closer relation-

---

[a] Cf.: "an expert, looking at a painting . . . should be able to determine the degree of tolerance of usury in the society in which it was painted" (*SP*:323).

ship to nature than our arbitrary, conventionalized system of alphabetic writing. Like Agassiz, Fenollosa entertained a thoroughgoing distrust of any generalization not based upon an accumulation of observed particulars. But in the ideogram Fenollosa felt he had found a system of writing that in itself already prohibits the expression of rootless abstractions and compels a keen awareness of concrete, natural facts. Finally, the ideogram does not reflect natural states (in the sense of discrete, *static* conditions) which Fenollosa regards as fictions interposed between our perceptions and the real world by our language-system of atomistic nouns and verbs combined according to a logic of abstract, syllogistic predication. Instead, the ideograms represent natural relations, "meeting-points" of actions and organic forces (*CWC*:10). Ideogrammic composition resembles Pound's ideal vortex, generating a unity in multiplicity, that does not, like some of his early imagist poems, crystallize a static aperçu, but rather offers "a radiant node or cluster . . . from which, and through which, and into which, ideas are constantly rushing" (*GB*:92). Again, however, the appeal of the ideogrammic method as a technique for structuring an enormous amount of historical data arises because, like Agassiz' and Frobenius' inductive procedures, it lets the poet present single details which, by being combined, will *naturally* suggest a particular argument or interpretation, thereby establishing the text's governing fiction: it is up to the reader to "draw his own conclusions"; the poet is only presenting objectively verifiable "evidence" for a "case" upon which the reader-"jury" must pass the final verdict (XLVI:233).[b] The poet, in other words, does not invent any-

---

[b] If this technique seems conclusive proof that Pound was not trying to assume the function of historian, that he was using historical material purely *qua* poet, it is worth noticing that Theodore Zeldin's massive two-volume study of *France 1848-1945* (Vol. i, "Ambition, Love and Politics," Oxford, 1973; Vol. ii, "Intellect, Taste and Anxiety," Oxford, 1977) uses much the same procedure. Zeldin's books are certainly intended as history, and yet he approaches the same topics from many different vantage-points, combining and selecting new aspects without formally tracing the connections or offering any grand synthesis. Zeldin's description of his own procedure could have come directly from the *Guide to Kulchur*, it is so close to Pound's own arguments for the validity of the ideogrammic method of composition: "I

thing (*vide* Milman Parry); like any epic bard he merely arranges what is already there, apparently letting the tribe's own history narrate itself for the edification (judgment) of its hearers, the truth of the narration guaranteed by the poet's strategic refusal to assume the role of sole, originating source of articulation.

As an example of how this structure "goes into action," we might consider a typical account: the presentation of late Medieval and Renaissance Italy in *A Draft of XXX Cantos*. Pound's goal is to weigh the strengths and limitations of this pivotal epoch in Western history, to indicate its contribution to our cultural heritage and to evaluate which of its characteristics could still be incorporated usefully into the modern world. However, he neither proposes an explicit historical thesis, nor states a formal series of conclusions. Instead, following the Agassiz/Fenollosa model, he presents a number of vividly selected episodes culled from contemporary records of various Italian principalities and ruling families (chiefly the House of Malatesta, Este, Mondrefeltro, Medici, and Gonzaga, as well as the deliberations of the Venetian Council). From these particulars, a picture emerges of an era splendid for its patronage of the arts and encouragement of individual *virtù* (two qualities Pound found sadly lacking in the England and U.S.A. of his own day), but limited by savage, internecine warfare, individual sexual and emotional excesses, ruthless competition for political power, and a profound social instability due to the absence of any unifying central authority.[c] Just as Sigismundo Malatesta constructs his Tempio

---

prefer juxtapositions, so that the reader can make what links he thinks fit himself" (Vol. II, p. 1157).

[c] In this connection, it is fascinating to see how the pressure of Pound's own historical situation made him revise his judgment of earlier eras. Ronald Bush has demonstrated how the shock of World War I and the further disillusionment of the Treaty of Versailles helps to explain the markedly more bitter tone introduced by Pound in his revision of the "Ur-Cantos" (Bush, *op.cit.*, p. 247). In 1915, Pound still disagreed with Dante's idea that a single empire was a necessity. Indeed, he felt that the absence of any unified central authority directly benefitted culture since "it did result in the numerous vortices of the Italian cities, striving against each other not only in commerce but in the arts as well" (*LE*:220). By 1919, however, in his essays for *The New Age*,

out of whatever material is at hand and whatever artists he can
employ, so Pound builds his presentation not just of Sigismundo himself, but of the entire era, out of a series of brief,
memorable incidents. He transposes quotations from Sigismundo's correspondence, papal missives, ambassadors' reports, and the recorded conversations of contemporary witnesses directly into *The Cantos*, thereby showing, for the first
time in over a century, that poetry can actually *incorporate*
prose, that the modern verse epic is a form sufficiently strong
to absorb large chunks of factual data into its own texture
(something the nineteenth-century verse epic had always
avoided), without ceasing to be poetry. As Richard Sieburth
rightly notes, Pound's quotations treat language itself as an
"object of representation," using the words of historical characters "as documents" freely transposible into his epic.[12] The
seemingly unobtrusive moment in Canto VIII, when the first
series of historical letters is introduced into *The Cantos* and the
personality of Sigismundo is shown by juxtaposing his prose
instruction concerning a painter he wishes to engage (29) with
a lyric poem he writes for Isotta degli Atti (30) *without privileging either medium*, represents one of the decisive turning-points
in modern poetics, opening for verse the capacity to include
domains of experience long since considered alien territory.

For Pound, the externally verifiable character of the
"luminous details" assures his text a degree of truth fully
commensurable with that offered by any conventional history. By allowing the conclusions to arise "inductively" in
the reader's mind from the mass of details assembled by the
poem, *The Cantos* can claim to be more "scientific" than
standard histories, which Pound thinks sacrifice the local
truth of an event for some abstract, universal formula. Yet
such a mode of narration also involves grave limitations, both
theoretically and in the kind of presentation it enforces, limi-

---

Pound was already moving towards a willingness to sacrifice such fructifying
"competition" for the political stability of a unified *imperium*. Still later, in
Canto LVIII, written at the height of Pound's infatuation with Mussolini, the
poet even defines TO KALON ("beauty," according to the dictionary) as
"order" (318; cf. also *J/M*:128).

tations which seriously undermine the poem's capacity to tell the tale of the tribe.

The epic, as I have argued, must function as a spokesman for values considered essential for communal stability. Yet, in practical terms, Pound's technique can be effective only if enough pertinent information is provided for an overview to be discernible. Thus, in the presentation of Malatesta or John Adams, the text supplies the reader with "a sufficient phalanx of particulars" (LXXIV:441) to maintain the fiction of an inductive procedure. In the last cantos of *Thrones*, however, we are meant, among other themes, to follow the development of the English principle of individual freedom and property rights from the Magna Carta (1215) to Sir Edward Coke's (1552-1634) defense of those liberties against monarchial encroachment and common neglect. In theory, the mode of presentation is identical to that of *A Draft of XXX Cantos*, but now the details provided are so scanty, their interconnection so uncertain, that it is hard not to second Davie's harsh strictures against this simplistic and teleological reading of English history. In linguistic terms, to apply Roman Jakobson's categories, Pound's "inductive" assemblage of historical particulars from widely scattered eras follows a basically *metonymic* progression (as opposed to the *metaphoric* structure of the ideogram), one which, unless carefully controlled, can so overwhelm the reader that he is "crushed by the multiplicity of detail unloaded on him in a limited verbal space, and is physically unable to grasp the whole. . . ."[13] Paradoxically, specificity indiscriminately applied loses all its specific nature. To connect a mass of sufficiently diverse "particulars," only the most banal and abstract links can be posited, and the element of history itself, the truth of each "local truth," is lost.[d]

[d] Pound's decision to present his argument as much as possible through the actual words of his historical characters can sometimes lead to needless confusion when issues of factual reliability and moral judgment are at stake. For example, two of Pound's most trusted sources are *The Diary of John Quincy Adams 1794-1845*, ed. Allan Nevins, New York, 1928, and Thomas Hart Benton's *Thirty Years View*, New York, 1854-56. Yet John Quincy Adams' diaries refer to Benton as a notorious liar, and list the major character traits of another Poundian hero, President Martin Van Buren, as "obsequiousness . . .

A second paradox is that Pound's technique works convincingly only if his conclusions fall within the range of historical judgments with which the reader is already familar. Thus, *The Cantos'* view of Renaissance Italy (except for the exemplary role assigned to Sigismundo Malatesta) is, if anything, terribly old-fashioned, agreeing in almost all its larger assumptions with classic studies such as Jacob Burckhardt's *The Civilization of the Renaissance in Italy* (1860). It is this closeness to orthodox assumptions that lets the reader successfully combine Pound's "particulars" without the poet's needing to provide any detailed argument. But, when the text says that "Wellington was a jew's pimp" (LX:248) who led a Rothschild-financed conspiracy against Napoleon, or, less offensively, that "Byzance lasted longer than Manchu / because of an (%) interest-rate" (XCVIII:690), Pound may or may not be correct, but in the absence of a precise refutation of more normal explanations the reader is as free to accept or dismiss these "historical" opinions as he would be with the articulation of any purely private revelation.

The value of ideogrammic fusions to convey a historical argument is equally dependent upon the precise nature of the details brought together. Fundamentally, the ideogrammic technique has the effect of creating a new type of *metaphor*, one which permits the presentation of historical judgments by combining disparate factual elements to suggest some fundamental but hitherto unobserved relationships between existent phenomena: "Relations are more real and more important

---

sycophancy . . . profound dissimulation . . . duplicity . . . fawning servility" (*Paideuma*, 6.1, Fall 1977, pp. 218, 225).

Of course, it is perfectly reasonable of Pound to admire certain qualities and perceptions in one man without seconding all his judgments, or refusing to find good in that man's political opponents. The difficulty is that since Pound never steps in to tell us how far any single, privileged source can be trusted, nor why both Adams and Benton can be regarded from our vantage point as honest witnesses, while considering one another unscrupulous liars, we are given no real assistance in "know[-ing] the histories / . . . and . . . whom to trust" (LXXXIX:590). Pound's desire to allow his sources to speak for themselves, which is often so effective as a poetic technique, is here responsible for a rather serious problem in establishing the logic of his historical argument.

than the things which they relate" (*CWC*:22). The difference between the inductive assemblage of numerous particulars on the *same topic*—e.g., the Italian Renaissance—and the unexpected combination of the essential characteristics of *different subjects* into a new unity is the principal linguistic distinction between the inductive and the ideogrammic technique. Pound, of course, uses both principles, thereby giving *The Cantos* the metonymic construction Jakobson says characterizes "the realistic author" and the metaphoric "process . . . of romanticism and symbolism."[14] I have chosen to analyze these techniques separately for reasons of clarity, but it is fascinating to see that even on the level of fundamental linguistic patterning, Pound incorporated the two structures usually kept apart, one considered suitable primarily for prose, the other for verse.[e]

Thus, for example, in the middle of Canto LV we come across the lines:

> Honour to CHIN-TSONG the modest
> Lux enim per se omnem in partem
> Reason from heaven, saith Tcheou Tun-y
>   enlighteneth all things
> Seipsum seipsum diffundit, risplende
>
>   (298)

Chin-Tsong (Shên-Tsung) was one of the Chinese Emperors (reign: 1068-1086) of whom Pound approved because of his able administration and adherence to the Confucian ideal of the just ruler. The next line as well as part of the last one is a variation of Robert Grosseteste's (c. 1170-1253) statement in his treatise *De Luce*, "Lux enim per se in omnem partem se

---

[e] Logically, the ideogrammic method is also different from principles of metamorphoses, although critics have often discussed them together. Metamorphosis implies some universal *forma*, some constant element which finds expression in a multitude of changing guises, as Aphrodite can appear to the poet in a wide range of incarnations from the traditional terrible goddess to the barefoot girl of Pisa, or as the essence of Jannequin's sixteenth-century bird-song chorale is still present in Gerhardt Munch's modern violin transcription. With the ideogrammic juxtaposition, on the other hand, the emphasis resides in the new insight that emerges from the combination of two or more apparently unrelated elements.

ipsum diffundit," and means "For light, of its own nature, shines (diffuses itself) in all directions." Grosseteste was one of Pound's favorite Medieval "Light Philosophers," a thinker whose work he had already associated with both Provençal poetry and the Italian *dolce stil nuovo* in his "Cavalcanti" essay (*LE*:158-161). Tcheou Tun-y (Chou Tun-i) was a noted Confucian scholar and philosopher (1017-1073) who wrote a commentary on the *I Ching*. The theory here attributed to Tcheou Tun-y is one dear to Pound, neo–Platonism, and Confucianism: the natural relationship between heaven and earth is one of essential harmony; the cosmos is governed by a divine reason—cf. Erigena's "Authority comes from right reason" (*GK*:75)—which, like Plotinus' *nous* or the light of Dante's *Paradiso*, shines ("en-lightens") throughout the created universe. Finally, Pound completes the quotation from Grosseteste, but with a characteristic intensification. The repetition of "seipsum, seipsum" (itself, itself) suggests a cry of joy, as if both the light and the illuminated world are together shouting out their de*light* at the beauty of the divine process. Then, Pound adds a single word "risplende" from Cavalcanti's great canzone, *Donna mi priegha* where the full context reads, "Risplende in se' perpetuale effeto" (*LE*:164), that is, Love "shineth out / Himself his own effect unendingly" (XXXVI:177). Pound's sudden interjection of Cavalcanti's term is especially appropriate, not only because of the connection he saw between the *Donna mi priegha* and the *De Luce*, but because it recapitulates the sense of *shining*, of luminous clarity, that informs all of the different texts here united. Cavalcanti, that is, *names* the actual source of all light as Love, thus showing, in a very Dantean union, that Divine Love and Reason are ultimately one, the single source of all growth and fruition.

I have chosen this passage to illustrate Pound's ideogrammic technique at its most successful. The lines brilliantly fuse discrete perceptions, making them constituent elements of a new unity. Just government, a respect for nature and the laws of cosmic harmony, Medieval light philosophy, and the clarities of the best lyric poetry are synthesized without sacrificing their individual identity. The total "ideogram" defines the type of sensibility Pound believes must be present in a truly humanized society, a sensibility dependent for its success upon the rightful union of the best elements in a number of quite different historical traditions. The full range of such a sensibility is not available from any one culture alone—"It can't all be in one language" (LXXXVI:563)—and the great advantage of Pound's technique is precisely its inclusiveness, its ability to present a new "factive" metaphor to educate the tribe.

And yet, only one Canto earlier, Pound twice demonstrates the chronic limitations of ideogrammic juxtapositions:

and HAN was after 43 years of TSIN dynasty.

> some fishin' some huntin' some things cannot be changed
> some cook, some do not cook
> > some things can not be changed.
> > > (LIV:275)

From external sources, one can learn that the lines about cooking refer to the domestic arrangement among the poet, Dorothy Pound, and Olga Rudge, but it is impossible to find any new insight arising from these components. John J. Nolde's recent suggestion that "perhaps Pound was simply referring to the fact that during Ch'in times each subject of the empire was given an assigned task"[15] is merely clutching at straws in the hope of finding some significance in Pound's arbitrary juxtapositions.

A few pages later in the same Canto, we read:

And the kings of Si-yo, that are from Tchang-ngun to the Caspian
> came into the Empire
to the joy of HAN SIEUN TI
> (Pretty manoeuvre but the technicians
> watched with their hair standing on end
> > anno sixteen, Bay of Naples)
> > > (LIV:279-280)
[anno sixteen = 1938, the sixteenth year of Mussolini's rule]

This passage juxtaposes the submission of the frontier Tartar-kingdoms to the Han, an act symbolized by their prince, Tchen-yu's visit to the Han capital in 51 B.C., with a description of the ceremonies honoring Hitler's state-visit to Mussolini in 1938. (The welcome, which Pound saw in a newsreel, included a group of submarines diving and then surfacing simultaneously.)[16] At best one could argue that the equivalence established by the relationship—Mussolini/Han : Hitler/Tartars—is a sign of how much more Pound admired the Italian Duce than the "barbaric" Germans, his championing of "Mediterranean sanity" over "hysterical Hitlerian yawping" (*J/M*:127). But by 1938 Hitler was already the senior partner and dominant voice in the Axis alliance, whose visit could in no way be regarded as a submission, so that even this attempt to recuperate the passage lacks any historically plausible basis.

It is important to notice that, methodologically, both of the texts criticized are structured according to the same principles as the striking success quoted from Canto LV. The difference is that the elements ideogrammically fused in LIV are so irrelevant to the events they supposedly illuminate that the weakness of the technique becomes glaringly obvious. Pound himself praised the ideogrammic method because of its ability to present "one fact and then another until at some point one gets off the dead and desensitized surface of the reader's mind, onto a part that will register" (*GK*:51). What this explanation passes over, however, is that the authority of the ideogram depends largely upon the value of the compound thus formed, upon the *degree* of objectively significant relationship between the single elements. By itself, the ideogram cannot justify, let alone validate, any particular narrative sequence, nor can it, as has often been claimed, assure a meaningful interpretation of history itself. Critics have spent a great deal of energy debating the extent of Pound's understanding of Chinese writing, as well as questioning the epistemology according to which an extended piece of writing can be likened to an image fully visible in one glance (Lessing's *Laokoon* redivivus). Instead of contributing to what seems by now a rather exhausted polemic, I want to point out another decisive and hitherto unremarked restriction upon the ideogram, a restriction which holds true even within the framework of Pound's own conception of the Chinese written character.

Pound's sources defining the ideogram all agree that the terms of the pictorial relationships are certified by the entire culture which employs them. It is the *community* of written-speech users throughout the culture's linguistic history that has shaped the ideogram's configuration and validated its accuracy. The justice of any ideogrammic juxtaposition is determined by the linguistic competence of the whole tribe, and, as is true of the fixed epithets of oral epics, any particular use of that form depends upon a long history of tribal selection and confirmation. In the case of Pound's new ideograms (his juxtapositions and combinations), there is no voice but his own to give them authority. The patterns he discerns may be accurate and enlightening, or they may be arbitrary and trivial, but, unlike those of the Chinese ideogram, the responsibility for their fashioning and the proof of their justice must be assumed by the poet himself. By comparing his technique to the Chinese written character, Pound sought a narrative convention which would permit the presentation of specific historical and cultural patterns as if they were objectively true, as if their pertinence were, like the connections established in Chinese compounds, "naturally" guaranteed. Pound was thereby enabled to become only one of the "characters" in his own poem ("E.P."), rather than the text's principal speaker. He was also at liberty to generate an, in principle unlimited, number of original historical theses by juxtaposition and combination alone (i.e., without any analytic proof or rigorous historical argument). But, as another chapter will show in greater detail, these advantages are gained only at the risk of unintentionally deconstructing the very historical texture the ideogrammic technique is intended to establish. To quote one of Pound's favorite examples: according to Fenollosa the ideogram for "red" consists of the combination of signs representing

ROSE	CHERRY
IRON RUST	FLAMINGO

(ABC of R:22)

Fundamentally, the problem with the ideogrammic method is that on numerous occasions (e.g., when the components are themselves complex terms) either the text gives us too little indication that "red" is the intended signified (the "some cook, some do not" passage), or it tells us this means "red" without adequately substantiating its own interpretation from the given particulars (the Tartar-Han : Hitler-Mussolini visit). Whenever such a breakdown in readability occurs, *The Cantos*, to appropriate Erigena's dictum, cease demonstrating the "right reason" from which the text's entire "authority," both as poem and as historical narrative, derives. At such moments, the reader is left alone, no longer participating in the tale of the tribe, but confronting, instead, the fragments of a single man's isolated and arbitrary will to order.

·   ·   ·

> "The ontological basis of history is the relation of men with other men, the fact that the individual 'I' exists only against the background of the community. . . . When men and social groups study history, they . . . are looking primarily for *values and ends*."
> —Lucien Goldmann: *The Human Sciences and Philosophy*[17]

In discussing the inductive / ideogrammic method, I have emphasized that, in essence, Pound was taking over techniques of verse composition he had already mastered in the creation of single lyrics and attempting to apply them to the narration of history. At the same time, he continued searching for some principle of historiography by means of which he could articulate a coherent and *sequential* account of a historical process, a principle that would give him a fixed code of judgment against which an entire chain of specific events could be tested. As the philosopher Siegfried Kracauer has remarked, "Obviously the chances for bards to develop into scientists would appreciably increase if it could be shown that human affairs are governed by laws that bear on the relationships between repeatable elements of historical reality."[18] Confucian historiography, Pound felt, had uncovered just those "laws," and from the classics of that tradition he himself could derive both a verification system and a new narrative technique.

Even in our own Occidental tradition, until quite recently one of the conventional justifications for the study of history was its utility as a source of exemplary models, offering illustrations of the efficacy of certain shared beliefs, modes of political conduct, and social relationships in establishing communal and individual prosperity. Such a belief constituted the fundamental purpose of historical studies in Confucian thinking and, paradoxically, still seems to dominate Chinese historiography under its modern government. Confucian history, however, differs from any contemporary beliefs by maintaining that it was solely the character and will of the rulers that determined the nature of the society. The Confucian ruler imposed form and order on events from above, almost like a classical author's control over the "plot" of his text. Because Pound fully shared this conviction, *The Cantos* would ideally serve as a type of modern *Il Principe*—"Gli uomini vivono in pochi" (*GK*:266)—advising those in power how best to exercise their authority for the common weal. More than any other philosophical system, Confucianism explicitly argued that social justice was within reach of any state if only its administrators would follow the lessons of Kung and the history classics. Mencius stresses this point repeatedly: "The great man alone can rectify the evils in the prince's heart. When the prince is benevolent, everyone else is benevolent; when the prince is dutiful, everyone else is dutiful; when the prince is correct, everyone else is correct. Simply by rectifying the prince one can put the state on a firm basis" (Book IV, Part A, 20).[19] Or, in Pound's own translation of the *Analects*, "He said: Honest men govern a country a 100 years, they could vanquish the malevolent and get rid of the death penalty. I mean these precise words" (Book 13, XI; *C*:250).

The precise number of those in power, whether a single wise prince like Pietro Leopoldo in nineteenth-century Italy, or a collective body such as the U.S. Senate, is unimportant. The significant feature of this doctrine is that the legislator(s) can by rectitude alone assure a harmonious social order.[f] In an

---

[f] Cf.: "This is not to say I 'advocate' fascism in and for America, or that I

age when, as Alex Zwerdling has written, "The qualities of heroism . . . have become almost totally unpredictable because they depend on the individual, private code of the writer,"[20] the benefit, to Pound, of placing large portions of his text under the aegis of Confucian ethics and historiography—a system with a clearly defined code of values and an assurance of the social efficacy of that code—was obviously immense. It was Confucianism's claim to a demonstrable social *praxis* that made it a more appealing model than, for example, the Thomistic and Franciscan Catholicism which had provided Dante with a coherent moral and religious schema, but contained, in Pound's eyes, little that could be applied in establishing a politically just society on earth.

Pound believed that Confucianism had been tested and proven true in the concrete sphere of Chinese history. He introduces his translation of *Ta Hio* ("Great Learning") with a note that makes this connection quite explicit:

> Starting at the bottom as market inspector, having risen to be Prime Minister, Confucius is more concerned with the necessities of government, and of governmental administration than any other philosopher. He had two thousand years of documented history behind him which he condensed so as to render it useful to men in high official position. . . . His analysis of why the earlier great emperors had been able to govern greatly was so sound that every durable dynasty, since his time, has risen on a Confucian design and been initiated by a group of Confucians. China was tranquil when her rulers understood these few pages. When the principles here defined were neglected, dynasties waned and chaos ensued. The proponents of a world order will neglect at their peril the study of the only process that has repeatedly proved its efficiency as social coordinate.
>
> (C:19)

---

think fascism is possible in America without Mussolini, any more than I . . . think communism is possible in America without Lenin. I think the American system *de jure* is probably quite good enough, if there were only 500 men with guts and the sense to USE it . . ." (*J/M*:98).

Although a more detailed discussion of how Pound integrated Confucian ethics with his other religious beliefs belongs in a subsequent chapter, one could summarize the Confucian element in *The Cantos* as his most determined attempt to show a concrete, historical embodiment of his intuitions, to prove by specific examples that a worthwhile state can be established on the basis of an ethic unencumbered by Judaeo-Christian notions of man's innate sinfulness, and by the related assumption that life on earth is a pilgrimage to, or preparation for, some other, higher existence. Orthodox Confucianism is, perhaps, unique among the world's major creeds in concentrating its attention exclusively on the details of this life, without thereby becoming a form of materialism, or losing a sense of something sacred and permanent underlying all human experience. Moreover, Confucianism must have been especially appealing to Pound for the high social duty it assigned to the poet-sage, designating him as the vital preserver of the tribe's cultural heritage and the rightful instructor of princes. If, as Pound says in *Terra Italica*, "Civilizations or cultures decay from the top" (*SP*:55), Confucian doctrine clearly stated that it was up to the poet-sage to apply the corrective where it would be most effective, i.e., to the "top" members of society. The possibility of a poet's directly contributing to the public good occupies a central place in Confucian historiography and provides sufficient impetus, in the words of a letter Pound sent Robert Creeley, "to learn ENOUGH so that if yu ever do get near anyone who has hand on control-levers you can TELL the buggah WHAT ought to be done."[21g]

In the Introduction, I drew attention to Tasso's distinction between the epic and tragedy; Pound also felt that admiration for the potential accomplishments of human will, rather than pity and fear for mankind's inherent limitations, must domi-

---

[g] I suspect that it was the example of Confucian historiography which finally helped Pound to overcome the sense that an artist is "too far ahead of any revolution, or reaction . . . for his vote to have any immediate result" ("The Exile" in *The Exile*, I, Spring, 1927, p. 91). Chinese history seemed to reveal that the voice of the poet-sage could indeed have a profound and immediate political consequence.

nate the epic. As we shall see later, both Confucian and neo-Platonic philosophy emphasized the innate moral perfectibility of *man*. Confucian historiography, however, also showed the political perfectibility of the *state*, the chance for a just and harmonious social order if the ruler's will were finely tempered enough. Ever since T. S. Eliot's strictures against the "Hell Cantos," critics have reproached Pound for lacking a tragic sense.[h] Of course, *The Cantos* eventually did contain a strongly personal and tragic dimension, but it is equally true that, as an epic, the poem was committed to a radically different conception of human destiny. There is no sense in *The Cantos* that political chaos, social injustice, and individual misery are inevitable; the poem's governing historical assumption is that such tragedies are avoidable, that a social remedy does exist for most human woes. Charles Olson saw that Pound's real subject is "one long extrapolation, canzone on WILL," that his interest is "Politics—not economics. . . . And validly. For (1) politics is a context as wide as nature, and not only what we call 'politics'; and (2) its essence is will. Which latter—will—is what E P cares abt. . . . Will contradicts tragedy, insists upon cause & effect in the face of stupidity. . . ."[22]

The emphasis upon "will" shows that every circumstance is changeable, that man can transform his condition by the strength of his own labor. *The Cantos*, in effect, offer a vision of a fully "human history," a history subject to man's control, and thus provide what Olson saw as a major methodological breakthrough in modern verse. And, paradoxically, it was Confucian historiography, perhaps the world's oldest con-

[h] Samuel Hynes, in *The Auden Generation*, London, 1976, seeks to contrast the attitudes of Auden and his circle with those of the previous generation of poets. He says, for instance, that Christopher Isherwood's *Goodbye to Berlin* shows hell in a radically new way, "And what makes it 'thirtyish is that it can define hell in political terms" (p. 355). This distinction is valid only if *The Waste Land* alone is held up as the characteristic model of "twenties writing." Yet Pound defined his Inferno just as much "in political terms" as did Isherwood, and it has always seemed curious to me that, on the one hand, Pound is reproached for politicizing his "spiritual" realms, and, on the other hand, remains overlooked when such politicization is suddenly regarded as acceptable.

tinuing tradition of historical interpretations, which provided Pound with this "modern" breakthrough.

If Pound believed that "an epic is a poem containing history," it was not until he began exploring Confucian historiography that he ventured a definition of history itself. Significantly, his most succinct explanation occurs in the midst of the Chinese Dynasty Cantos, when all of the foregoing discussion is condensed into a single aphorism: "History is a school-book for princes" (LIV:280). Much of the text of the Chinese History Cantos is a condensation and adaption of Père Joseph-Anne-Marie de Moyriac de Mailla's *Histoire Générale de la Chine* (13 vols., Paris, 1777-1783), itself a translation of the *T'ung Ch'ien Kang Mu*, a compilation of Chinese history originally prepared by the Sung Dynasty scholar Chu Hsi (A.D. 1130-1200). John J. Nolde, to whose account of the *Histoire Générale* I am indebted, calls it "the best known and most highly esteemed history of the Empire,"[23] and Pound's extensive reliance upon a text whose modern historical value is severely limited, but which occupied a position of overwhelming authority in Confucian thought, is evidence of how welcome such an authority was to a poet trying to find a fixed code by which history could be both judged and narrated.

Pound, as we have seen, stated that the purpose of an epic was to learn "what sort of things endure, and what sort of things are transient; . . . upon what the forces . . . of social order move" (*PM*:68). De Mailla offers almost the same reasons for studying history, therewith confirming the essential link between Pound's definition of an epic poem and the Confucian history text: "L'histoire des anciens nous sert de miroir pour connoître ce qui éleve et détruit la fortune des hommes."[24] The duty of the Confucian historian-sage is to aid his people by placing those "mirrors" before the eyes of the ruler, a conception of historiography to which Pound was to remain faithful throughout the writing of *The Cantos*.

While Confucian historiography is, from a modern perspective, certainly lacking in objectivity or rigor, it is important to realize that its goals were always explicitly more ideological and didactic than analytic. The *Shu King* or "History Classic" (traditionally credited to Kung himself, although contemporary scholarship disputes this attribution), served, in essence, to justify the conquest of the Shang by the Chou Dynasty (1122 B.C.) and to legitimize the new regime's claim to authority—"Our dynasty came in because of a great sensibility" (LXXXV:543).[25] According to Herrlee G. Creel:

> The cornerstone of the ideology of the Chinese state is the conception of the Mandate of Heaven: the idea that the ruler of China holds a sacred trust from the highest deity which permits him to rule so long as he does so for the welfare of all the people—but . . . if he fails in that trust, Heaven will appoint another to rebel and replace him. This was the keynote of the propaganda by which the Chou sought, ultimately with complete success, to reconcile those they had conquered to their rule: it became the basis of the constitution of the Chinese state. Each succeeding dynasty claimed to hold the Mandate of Heaven; when the last dynasty was overthrown in 1912, this was called "ending its Mandate."[26][i]

Thus, Confucian historiography incorporated from the beginning a curious (and very Poundian) mixture of conservative and revolutionary tendencies. As the official doctrine of a regime anxious to confirm its new authority, it encouraged the virtues of obedience and civil order, and gave a divine sanction to Imperial power. At the same time, its theory of the "Mandate of Heaven" meant that if the Emperor became corrupt and the government politically irresponsible, then its violent overthrow and replacement by a new and more worthy dynasty was not only permitted, but inevitable. However, since the Chou's right to hold power was justified only by their *restoration* of the discarded virtues of earlier rulers and not by the acknowledged formulation of original

---

[i] That Pound was familiar with the politico-theological concept of the "Mandate of Heaven," or "Celestial Decree," as it is sometimes translated, is made clear in one of his comments on why the Adams family lost its political influence in American government: ". . . if [Eliot] would consider the dynasty of the Adamses he would see that it was precisely because it lacked the Confucian law that this family lost the Celestial Decree" (SP:321).

policies—"All there by the time of I Yin / All roots by the time of I Yin" (LXXXV:543)[j]—history was conceived not as a series of changing circumstances requiring new techniques of government, but as a closed arena in which a fixed set of already known qualities and practices would assure success. Accordingly, the Confucian historian-sage had little interest in any categories that vary with specific conditions (e.g., particular technological or demographic developments, changing economic circumstances, etc.) and restricted his analysis of historical causality to the ruler's degree of obedience to Kung's precepts. One aspect of the specific relevance of the Chinese History Cantos to the poem's development is well defined by Daniel Pearlman, "The dynastic cantos rise as a fully articulated counter-myth, clothed in concrete historical detail, to challenge the myth of Western decay that was presented in equally full historical costume in the first thirty cantos, and as usury in the transitional cantos that followed."[27] However, to Pound the value of the *Shu King* and the *Histoire Générale* is its *truth as history*, not merely as myth. The "Western tradition" failed precisely because it lacked any permanent foundations of statemanship such as China possessed, and even if, as Pearlman writes, both epochs are "presented in full historical costume," the narrative principles governing each are quite different, accurately reflecting the difference in the historical outlooks underlying the two sequences.

To many readers, the Chinese Dynasty Cantos seem a wearying list of endless genealogies and names, reviving painful memories of the "begat" lists of Bible instruction. These cantos contain virtually none of the colorful incidents and dramatic personalities that marked the portrayal of Western

[j] I Yin was an advisor of T'ang, the first Shang Emperor (reign 1766-1753 B.C.), who encouraged his master to overthrow the corrupt H(s)ia Dynasty. After T'ang's death, I Yin continued as chief minister and moral guide to the second Shang ruler, Tai-kia (reign 1753-1720 B.C.). In Canto LXXXV, these words are presumably spoken by Wu Wang who overthrew the Shang in 1122 B.C. when they in turn had grown corrupt and fallen away from I Yin's precepts. The speech emphasizes a conservative revolution, i.e., the establishment of a new dynasty that is entitled to rule by restoring the very ideals and just practices upon which the ousted regime had itself based its "mandate."

Europe in *A Draft of XXX Cantos*, or of Revolutionary
America in *Eleven New Cantos*. But although this lack may
make the text less immediately compelling, its function is to
illuminate the limitations of government based on purely individual *virtù*, to make us see the communal stability that results when an invariable code of just rule is firmly established.
We may, as readers, miss the vivid portraits of men like
Sigismundo Malatesta, but within the logic of the poem it is
necessary to introduce a radically different and higher model
of historical possibilities. "The full historical costume" of the
two sections, that is, differs to the precise degree that the narrative style of Confucian historiography is distinct from the
"method of luminous detail," or that the ideology of Confucianism rejects the Western principle of individual self-
assertion.

The narrative in Confucian historical writing proceeds
along two discrete *paradigmatic* axes, one of effective, the other
of evil or incompetent, rulers. History itself is constituted as
an enormous ground in which representatives of the good, of
order and stability, do battle with those who embody evil or
socially disruptive tendencies. The names within each group
are meant to be interchangeable, offering a set of possible substitutions for one another rather than any *syntagmatic*, linear
progression. For example, Pound can write that, "Shun's will
and / King Wan's will / were as the two halves of a seal / . . .
Their aims as one" (LXXVII:467), and again, "From Kati to
Jang Hi / two ½s of a seal" (XCVIII:690), in spite of the fact
that Shun (or Chun) was a semi-legendary culture hero whose
reign, in the *Annotated Index*, is given as 2255 B.C., while King
Wan (or Wên Wang, Duke of Chou and father of the first
Chou Emperor) lived from 1231-1135 B.C. Similarly, the
Egyptian Pharaoh Kati (Nebkeure Akhtoi: 2252-2228 B.C.)
has no historically discernible connection to the relatively recent Chinese Emperor, K'ang Hsi, whose reign lasted from
A.D. 1662-1722. However, because the historical criteria of
evaluation are themselves so universal (consisting largely of
justice in taxation, respect for the arts and religious customs, a
lack of court or civil corruption, and an orderly administration), such seemingly ahistorical parallels can be presented

with perfect inner consistency. Each ruler is assigned his place in the paradigm exclusively by his degree of adherence to these few criteria. Individual temperament, for example, is important only in so far as it aids or hinders the Emperor in faithfully adhering to the already defined conditions for administrative rectitude, and this standard is clearly intended to counterpoise the personal eccentricities and political excesses of the Italian ruling houses presented earlier.

Pound's admirers have regularly "excused" his historical errors in the Dynastic Cantos by citing the poet's almost exclusive reliance upon De Mailla. (Pound's uncritical adoption of his sources' Confucian/Jesuit polemic against the rival Taoist and Buddhist philosophies is only the most notorious instance.) And yet, the decision to transpose large sections of the *Histoire Générale* represents a deliberate choice and often a very difficult poetic exercise. Logically, therefore, Pound's conviction of the general merits of Confucian historiography must have *preceded* his adherence to any particular aspects of the doctrine. Only a system akin to Confucian historiography in the economy of its organizational and evaluative structure could have given him a narrative technique able to present *in a temporal sequence* (something the ideogrammic, or inductive, method cannot, by itself, indicate) several thousand years of continuous political and social history from a unified vantage point. Moreover, by adopting the very historical criteria of the culture under examination, Pound could claim that the text's judgments and condensations were not his own arbitrary impositions, but rather the conclusions established and validated by millennia of concrete, historical experience. Pound's intention is less to chronicle Chinese history for its own sake than to enrich his epic with a systematic, historically "objective" series of *exempla* of propitious and destructive social practices, principles of political conduct which, he felt, could be imitated even by a modern, Occidental government. The *Histoire Générale* already contains a complete "tale of the tribe," which Pound was able to integrate into his own, larger narrative, both as a correction to the bias of other histories and as an instigation to his contemporary audience, the "tribe" for whose edification all the historical material in *The*

Cantos exists. In the process, he again demonstrated that his own verse form was now sufficiently flexible, his poetic technique assured enough, so that even the most massive prose history was not beyond *The Cantos'* absorptive capacity. By the time of the Chinese Dynasty Cantos, the challenge of the novel had been in large measure met, and a poetic equivalent to its range of narrative capacities clearly established.

Many of the most significant attractions the Confucian view of history held for Pound have been discussed, and I shall take up the vexing problem of its relationship to other ethical and religious systems such as neo-Platonism or Taoism in the next chapter. But there remains a central aspect of Pound's historical beliefs which has been mentioned only indirectly thus far, an aspect more intimately linked to the principles of *The Cantos'* historiography than traditional criticism has been eager to acknowledge. That aspect, to return to the quotation from Canto XCVIII which opened this chapter, is Social Credit monetary theory, the "ground" which the editor of *The New Age* possessed and which Yeats, Eliot, and Wyndham Lewis all apparently lacked.

· · ·

"I don't see that anyone save a sap-head can now think he knows any history until he understands economics."

(*LE*:86)

"No, I am not a social crediter, I passed by that alley."
—Rome Radio Broadcast, 1942[28]

It is a curious phenomenon that many readers who have attacked Pound's emphasis on economic theories in *The Cantos* object not just to the actual content of his beliefs, but to the very presence of such a subject in a poem. Yet, Pound's proposition, affirming the need to include economics in any historical analysis is a truism which no one today would challenge. The underlying premise of these criticisms is that verse should not, indeed cannot, aspire to the level of historical explanation and hence has no need for the mundanities of commerce and money. But precisely because Pound was determined, in Michael Alexander's words, not to "acquiesce in the silent expropriation of the public realm from the range of emotions proper to a poet,"[29] he had to include economics in his epic. Without an analysis of the concrete details of real life, of which economics is the most immediately visible and quantifiable general indicator, *The Cantos* would be no more a tale of the tribe than was Hugo's *La Légende des Siècles*. The poem, that is, would have lacked exactly those elements which might substantiate its ambition to be a genuinely *modern* verse epic.

Nonetheless, Pound hesitated a long time before locating in economics the central agent of historical causality. The first thirty cantos contain almost no "fiscal explanations," attributing events to the idiosyncracies of personality, religious bigotry, or misdirected sexuality. For example, the Albigensian Crusade, in which most modern historians discern a clear political and economic motive—the jealousy of northern France against the richer and more successful communities of Languedoc and Provence—is presented in *The Cantos* purely as an example of general Christian fanaticism allied to the sexual frustration of one of the "Crusaders," Bernart de Tierci (XXIII:108-109). The fact that Pound sees no economic basis in a historical episode that would seem ideally suited to justify one—versus his later explanation that "The Civil War [was] rooted in tariff" (LXXXIX:596)—indicates how slowly he came around to accepting the necessity of including such explanations in his poem. The theme of fruitful versus destructive sexuality, already announced by the Circe/Aphrodite opposition in the opening canto, remains one of the poem's major thematic concerns, but it ceases to be granted any explanatory authority for public, political events by the end of *A Draft of XXX Cantos*. Nonetheless, female beauty—and, by implication, human sexuality—is not formally "cleared" of the earlier suspicions until Canto XLVI, when two of the Greek epithets, ἑλανδρος, ἑλέπτολις ("destructive of men," "destructive of cities," from Aeschylus' *Agamemnon*, lines 687-8), initially applied to Helen of Troy and Eleanor of Aquitaine, are transferred to Geryon, Dante's and Pound's embodiment of Usury.[30]

Aurum est commune sepulchrum. Usura, commune sepulchrum.
helandros kai heleptolis kai helarxe
Hic Geryon est. Hic hyperusura.

(XLVI:234-235)

Pound here even coins a new epithet, *helarxe* ("destructive of
government") to indicate the extent of Usury's *social* disrup-
tiveness. (The passage also demonstrates how Pound's
method of narration by juxtaposition can let him indicate a
new argument or a change in perception with a startling
"economy" of means, simply by combining previously familiar components in a new configuration.)

At one point Pound suggests that it was the pressure of
economic coercion regularly faced by both himself and by his
fellow artists that initially prompted his concern for economics: "What drives a man interested almost exclusively in
the arts, into social theory or into a study of the 'gross material aspects' videlicet economic aspect of the present? . . . I
have blood lust because of what I have seen done to, and attempted against, the arts in my time. . . . The effects of social
evil show first in the arts . . . " (*SP*:228-229). At other moments, Pound explained his drive to investigate the "gross
material aspects" of society by a need to understand the causes
of the World War and the disastrous Treaty of Versailles. But,
whatever the proximate cause (the concern was, like most of
Pound's other interests, "overdetermined"), the emphasis on
economics enabled him to speak for *more* than an artistic
fraternity, to engage society's fundamental mechanisms directly, and thus to contend for values whose significance was
immediately visible, generally applicable, and undeniably central.

Yet, once we accept Pound's right, even his responsibility,
to include economics in his epic, the reasons for his specific
doctrines and allegiances still remain unexplained. In addi-
tion to his numerous pronouncements on fiscal theory (especially in the *ABC of Economics*, the articles written for *The
New Age*, and the six "Money Pamphlets"), his theories have
been extensively analyzed in Earle Davis' *Vision Fugitive: Ezra*

Pound and Economics (Lawrence, Kansas, 1968), and William Chace's *The Political Identities of Ezra Pound and T. S. Eliot* (Stanford, 1973), as well as in many individual essays by explicators of Pound. Davis, Chace, and Brooke-Rose also offer a useful summary of what "orthodox" contemporary economists thought of C. H. Douglas and Silvio Gesell, thereby indicating that, at the time of their actual formulation, Pound's explanations were by no means as "eccentric" as judgments reached over twenty years later confidently assert. There is, by now, little value in again summarizing the careful research of others, but the close relationship between Pound's historical and his economic principles as governing codes in *The Cantos* still requires considerable analysis.

Hugh Kenner astutely remarks that "economics interests [Pound] less than Money itself."[31] However, this critical dissociation of terms is also somewhat misleading, since to Pound the question of money was, in fact, *the* root issue of economic theory and practice, its neglected cornerstone and the one area in which reforms were guaranteed to have the greatest direct social impact. I have already quoted his remark that Social Credit did not constitute the full extent of his economic beliefs. Gesell's idea of *Schwundgeld* or "perishable currency" as a means of enforcing the rapid circulation of money, and Mussolini's "corporative" reorganization of industry into guilds, or associations, of employers and employees, to administer various sectors of the national economy (1926), formed essential components of Pound's proposed reforms.[32] Nonetheless, the essential premises underlying all of Pound's diverse economic arguments can be isolated and summarized as follows:

(1) The technical problem of *production* has been solved, and the issue today is one of the equitable *distribution and circulation* of society's goods and services. (cf. *L*:253)

(2) It is possible to establish an era of economic prosperity by legislation alone, principally by removing control of credit from private, selfish groups (the chartered banks and the international "usocracy") who manipulate the availability of credit purely for their own ends.

(3) Any ruling power which does not so legislate is either

ignorant (a dupe) or criminal. That is, it is a collaborator (knowingly in some cases, unwittingly in others) of the fiscal conspirators. Since the knowledge of how to establish an economically just state already exists—"economic order is possible and . . . the way to a commonly decent economic order is known" (SP:229)—the usurers must prevent that knowledge's "distribution" by lies, repression, and censorship.

(4) Although the community must reassert its crucial right, "the power to issue money and to determine the value thereof . . . to make purchasing power available in responsibly regulated amounts,"[33] it need not assume the actual ownership of the means of production. Private property is to be preserved as an essential basis of individual freedom, but the state must somehow ensure that everyone is able to obtain such property without being victimized by those who already possess more. People, that is, have a right to property, but its possession should confer no special powers or privileges.

Many details of this program are quite similar to what, in recent years, has been termed "socialism with a human face" (except, of course, for the insistence upon private ownership), and numerous critics have defended Pound by showing how close some of his ideas are to today's liberal or left-wing aspirations. Yet what is unusual about his doctrine is the optimistic conviction that a single, theoretically quite attainable, reform in economic legislation is sufficient to guarantee "a commonly decent economic order." Far more curious, still, is Pound's willingness to project his theory backwards as an adequate explanation of the economic structure of all previous history, his readiness to accept the formula: low interest rates and communal control of credit = public prosperity, for every epoch and stage of economic development. This is puzzling because, while one might agree that in a modern, industrialized society the problem of just distribution and circulation far outweighs difficulties of adequate production, it is hard to understand such a thesis being applied to pre-Industrial Europe or to any community dependent upon agriculture or upon fishing for most of its wealth. There is nothing in either Douglas or Gesell that suggests that their theories could have been implemented in twelfth-century Byzantium or in Colonial Cape Ann. Indeed, Douglas' own "A + B" theorem (cf. Canto XXXVIII:190) uses the production of goods in a *factory* to show the discrepancy between the cost of commodity production in an industrial system (worker's wages, raw materials including machinery, *interest on borrowed capital*, etc.) and the total purchasing power thereby put into circulation: "the purchasing power of the whole people can never catch up with the price of the goods that they bring into being" (*SC*:18). Pound's enormous extension of the historical range of the applicability of Social Credit seems to be largely his own contribution, and stems, I think, not from any reasons dictated by a search for solutions to current economic conditions, but from the internal, structural demands of the poem to which he was so deeply committed.

When Pound wrote, in a 1934 letter to the Paris edition of the *Chicago Tribune*, that "BAD economics are complicated. Good economics are simple"[34] he was not merely reversing the stand of his 1922 "Paris letter" to *The Dial*: ". . . With Dickens, with any provincial writer, there is an 'answer,' which the author and reader know; a touch of kindness, the payment of the instalment due on the mortgage, et cetera; but with Flaubert, with the writer of first magnitude, there is no answer, humanity being what it is, and the given character moving inside its own limitations there is *no* easy way out. . . ."[35]

Rather, Pound's needs as a writer had changed. Whereas Flaubert, in *L'Education Sentimentale*, had been content to deal with one generation—the men of 1848—Pound was attempting to select *exempla* from all of human history while still providing an economic "ground" for his judgments. To satisfy those needs, a "simple" theory had, in fact, become indispensable. Only a monolithic and simple fiscal doctrine could enable him to apply criteria of economic causality to the vast range of history treated in *The Cantos*. Equally important, only Pound's extension of a doctrine such as Social Credit or Gesellism could provide a modern economic justification for the belief, already present on an ethical and political level in Confucian historiography, that one just ruler could, at any time, institute an era of fiscal equity. Pound's different

principles are unified by their common rejection of any notion of a dialectic of forces: society is well or badly governed,
but neither its economy nor its political institutions are themselves subject to a complex of factors requiring an analysis of
the specific productive forces at work in a given setting.[k]

In fact, any detailed study of an entire economic structure is
fundamentally uncongenial to Pound: he seeks out individual
malefactors primarily because, with their removal, he is certain that the general problems will also be resolved.
Throughout the *ABC of Economics* he praises human will and
responsibility as a necessary part of an economic program
and, as William Chace argues, the influence of Major Douglas
consists to a large degree in helping Pound to locate the
specific economic "enemies" of mankind.[36] These "enemies"
are rarely seen as representatives of a historically created social
class acting within a particular economic structure; they are
only parasitic and dangerous individuals carrying out the
same fiscal conspiracy against the common weal throughout
history. Pound's characteristic strategy is to substitute a universal and static schema (government control over the issuing
of money and the percentage of interest tolerated) with, by
way of dramatic illustration, a particular set of heroes and villains (e.g., Andrew Jackson versus Nicholas Biddle), for any
analysis of the fundamental conditions prevalent at a given
stage of economic development. Such a technique does satisfy
one of the epic's traditional functions, since it seems to offer
models of exemplary conduct by which readers can judge and
adjust their public customs. Yet in this instance, Pound's
models are essentially uninstructive. They offer a largely
spurious specificity, one fundamentally irrelevant to the

---

[k] This argument also explains why Pound's celebrated retraction in the
1972 foreword to his *Selected Prose* is so crucial. Pound says:

> re Usury:
> I was out of focus, taking a symptom for a cause
> The cause is AVARICE. (6)

What seems like a mere shift of emphasis is, in fact, a fundamental change of
categories. Usury is a specific *economic practice* controllable by legislation. Avarice, on the other hand, is a *moral fault*, a vice which requires individual self-
correction. Avarice unlike usury, cannot be abolished by government decree
or police action.

evolving economic circumstances of any modern society. Pound's habit of neglecting complex causality, preferring instead to portray a few, "representative" figures, is typical of his writing long before Social Credit themes ever entered *The Cantos*. Even as his particular list of villains changed, Pound remained, to the end, "as eager to recommend a specific remedy as he is to find a specific cause."[37]

Neither Pound's "scientific" method of assembling and juxtaposing single facts nor the principles of Confucian historiography has a structure able to accommodate complex and multiple economic determinants in their presentation of historical causality. In neither theory is there anything specifically *historical* connecting or differentiating particular eras. There are concrete, isolated instances (the "factive" personality of a specific ruler, the creation of a memorable art work, or piece of legislation, etc.) whose "scientific" validity for judging an entire era is confirmed by the Agassiz/Frobenius principles. There are also the permanent, unchanging rules of statecraft established by Kung and verified by Confucian historiography throughout centuries of human experience. But there is no mediation between the two narrative and interpretive conventions. There is history in *The Cantos*, but no historical process, no dialectic to show the complex interpenetration of the specific and the general. Basically, Pound's method of presenting historical material is organic, but the underlying philosophy is static, and only an economics as fixed and static as his theory of history itself could ever have been integrated successfully into the structure of *The Cantos*. Pound's monetary doctrine isolates a limited set of fiscal measures and grants it both universal validity and immediate, local applicability, thereby providing an economic constant able to span the text's different epochs and still test the "fiscal sanity" of any single moment.

The terms of Pound's monetary theory, in other words, are designed to complement perfectly both the principles by which the historical material of the poem is presented and to provide the crucial link needed to connect Confucian historiography with the Agassiz/Fenellosa "inductive method," two otherwise quite distinct narrative conventions. It is difficult to imagine any other modern economic doctrine able to serve a remotely similar function, and, irrespective of Pound's many extratextual and perfectly sincere reasons for championing Social Credit or *Schwundgeld*, I think it is true to say that had he never read Douglas or Gesell, he would still have had to invent something remarkably similar to their theories in order to give *The Cantos* an internally consistent economic "ground."[1]

This observation is, of course, not intended as a justification of the doctrine's accuracy, nor does it entail a blindness to its limitations. It makes clear, however, that Pound struggled far more to unify his diverse ideas than is often acknowledged, that his poem, for all its multiplicity of forms and references, does slowly unfold a discernible intellectual structure. Ultimately, the problem with the insertion of Pound's fiscal theories into *The Cantos* is not their disruptive effect on a series of moving lyric passages and dramatic portraits, nor their "eccentricity" amid otherwise comprehensible views. Rather, it is because the economic arguments are so natural an outgrowth of his historical principles and narrative techniques

[1] A clear example of Pound's willingness to shape his theoretical premises to suit the needs of his poem is found in the special role attributed to agriculture throughout *The Cantos*. As we shall see in the next chapter, both Confucian ethics and Enlightenment political economy see farming as the foundation for a just and prosperous state. Pound stresses the same theme in *The Cantos*, but in his strictly economic texts he never assigned so privileged a status to the cultivation of the land. In "A Study of Relations and Gesell," for example, he criticizes "Gesellites" for not realizing "that land is progressively less important, meaning less important *now* than before we had farm machinery . . ." (*SP*:281). Pound adds that, "on the whole the agriculturalist is a *Producer* and the world's problems today do not lie in production" (*SP*:282). This discrepancy can be understood when one realizes that, for his epic, Pound sought to isolate only those aspects of an explanatory system which could be applied to all of his historical material. And, since so much of *The Cantos* deal with pre-Industrial societies, the poem's economic "ground" had to be based upon agrarian principles, even though such a strategy seems to have given the text an internal economic coherence at the price of making the proposed solution irrelevant to modern industrial practices. Critics who discuss Pound's economics have not, I believe, sufficiently realized the extent to which he deliberately narrows the terms of his own analysis to suit his poem, and as in many other areas, they tend to confuse the prose essays with Pound's practice in *The Cantos* themselves.

that they disconcert, exposing inadequacies that might otherwise have been easier to ignore. Pound himself insisted that "Every man has the right to have his ideas examined *one at a time*."[38] This is undeniably both a generous and a valid view, but it indicates the way one can *read* and learn from an author, not the manner in which that author conceived his ideas in the first place, nor the conventions by which he tried to make his text cohere.

At a time when one group of commentators still feels that *The Cantos* were written one unrelated idea at a time, while another assumes that indicating connections between themes is equivalent to confirming their truth content, it is, perhaps, neither ungenerous nor invalid to show that both in the inclusiveness of its ambition as a "poem including history" and in the "errors and wrecks" (CXVI:796) which limit that success, Pound's epic did mark out its own logically consistent, but intellectually desperately restricted, axes of coherence. Need one still add that "the defects inherent in a record of struggle" (GK:135) are often far more instructive than the monuments of a too safe victory?

·   ·   ·

> "For forty years I have schooled myself, not to write the economic history of the U.S. or any other country, but to write an epic poem which begins 'In the Dark Forest,' crosses the Purgatory of human error, and ends in the light, 'fra i maestri di color che sanno.' For this reason I have had to understand the nature of error."
>
> (*SP*:167)

Pound, as the lines from *An Introduction to the Economic Nature of the United States* quoted above make clear, insisted that he was not writing an economic textbook but an epic poem. Yet, he explicitly states that a successful epic must understand *why* man is trapped in the "selva oscura" of the contemporary world, why the clarity of Dante's "joyous realm" has not been realized on earth. The contemporary epic poet must develop a historical and economic analysis, not merely out of a personal sense of social obligation, but because his poem, in order to be a modern "tale of the tribe," demands it. One of Yeats's "own choice and perfect lyrics" (LXXXII:524), or even an aesthetic and theologically grounded critique of post-war civilization like *The Waste Land*, can succeed perfectly without formulating a systematic historical analysis, but an epic excludes a theory of history only at the risk of sacrificing its entire *raison d'être*.

Yet the two narrative codes I have isolated—the inductive/ ideogrammic technique and the principles of Confucian historiography—both entered Pound's vocabulary relatively late. As Ronald Bush has shown, "In [Pound's] collected and uncollected prose, no programmatic use of the term 'ideogram' or 'ideograph' appears until 1927."[39] Bush goes on to demonstrate that in numerous essays written *after* Pound's edition of Fenollosa, the poet maintained a decidedly ambiguous attitude towards the modern applicability of what he continued to call "ideographic representation." Not until 1927 does the term "ideogram"—then defined as "heaping together the necessary components of thought" (*ABC of E*:37)—assume something like its later status. However, by 1933 the ideogram had become the cornerstone not only of Pound's critical method but of his epistemology as well. And it is in the very text, the *ABC of Economics*—in which the ideogram is first given its privileged role—that Pound also first mentions Agassiz by name and establishes the parallel between Agassiz' scientific method and the Chinese written character.

Pound had been drawn to the technique of composition by juxtaposing vivid particulars (called the "method of luminous detail" in the 1911-1912 essays, "I gather the Limbs of Osiris") long before either Agassiz or Fenollosa entered his thinking. Even in the *ABC of Reading*, Pound reprinted as an "exhibit" in the back of the book a series of texts first published in 1913 with the note, "Examples of ideogrammic method used by E.P. in *The Serious Artist* in 1913 before having access to the Fenollosa papers" (96). Similarly, in the tribute to Gaudier-Brzeska, written in 1916, he already speaks of the importance for modern art of an "arrangement of planes" in a manner which prefigures many of his later comments on the ideogram (*GB*:120-121). Each image is described as a type of "plane," and the text's full meaning is revealed only in the relationship or "superposition" of the separate planes. In a rarely quoted passage printed in *The New Age* (August 21, 1919) Pound, for the first time, begins to argue that the interpretation and narration of history itself must also proceed by the principles of assemblage and juxtaposition of particulars, an idea only subsequently associated with Agassiz. "Any historical concept and any sociological deduction from history must assemble a great number of such violently contrasted facts if it is to be valid. It must not be a paradox, or a simple exposition of two terms."[40] The question remains, however: if Pound already possessed all the essential components of what later became the Fenollosa/Agassiz technique, why should he have made so much of these two authorities? Bush, whose analysis of the genesis of *The Cantos* has done much to correct our view of the poet's development, argues that "The ideogrammic method changed *The Cantos* more in theory than in fact."[41] However, beyond seeing the term as a "bone" tossed "to submissive reviewers,"[42] he offers few substantial explanations for Pound's appropriation of the concept. Pound, of course, rarely did anything purely for reviewers, and it is unlikely that he would have filled so many essays and personal letters explaining a terminology in which he found relatively little of personal value.

The solution to this dilemma lies, I believe, in the fact that although Pound intuitively employed many of the poetic techniques he was later to call "ideogrammic composition," he felt that an epic poem required more than an intuitive justification, that some external, *universally valid*, narrative structure was needed to whose authority he could appeal. The "ideogrammic method," Agassiz' "scientific procedure," and Frobenius' *Kulturmorphologie*, were crucial, precisely because they united to offer him the "scaffolding" he thought an epic required without either imposing an anachronistic, theological system—Dante's "Aquinas map" of the universe (*L*:323)—or requiring him to scrap his own earliest aesthetic intuitions. The same is true of Pound's still later reliance upon the monetary principles of Major Douglas or of Silvio Gesell, which, as we have seen, enabled him to "ground" his *already established* theories of history and techniques of narration without enforcing any significant readjustment in either. Pound was being perfectly sincere when he wrote in 1938: "I have not deflected a hair's breadth from my lists of beautiful objects, made in my own head and held before I ever thought of usura as a murrain and a marasmus" (*GK*:109). The intellectual, political, and economic theories he embraced were vital because they could objectify, without ever challenging, the list of "beautiful objects" to which he remained permanently faithful. No matter how many parallels one uncovers between Pound's practices in *The Cantos* and those governing his earlier texts, they have become radically different because of their new function. The ideogrammic method, Agassiz' inductive science and Frobenius' *Kulturmorphologie*, did not so much change *The Cantos* "in theory," as *provide* a theory that made the change from a series of lyrics to a "poem including history" possible. I have emphasized the importance of Pound's epistemological and historiographic beliefs because *The Cantos* are the locus where both unite *as narrative*, where "plot" becomes the realization of theory, and theory the privileged begetter of plot. Morally as well as aesthetically Pound's epic is dependent upon its intellectual structures because it is they which have already decided not only *how* the tale of the tribe is to be told, but also *what* that tale contains. As Hayden White puts it, "Commitment to a particular *form* of knowledge predetermines the *kinds* of generalizations one can make about the present world, the kinds of knowledge one can have of it, and hence the kinds of projects one can legitimately conceive for changing that present or maintaining it in its present form indefinitely."[43]

The polemical vehemence of Pound's critical prose and the exuberance of his enthusiasms has tended to obscure the orthodoxy of many of his actual judgments. Donald Davie is one of the few critics to have noticed how conventional many of Pound's aesthetic beliefs really were, and, although Davie himself does not make this connection clear, a distinctly nostalgic conservatism also marks Pound's attitude toward history and government.[44] Much like Edward Gibbon, Pound seems to long for "a state in which a benevolent prince or oligarchy protected and defended a majority that did not really matter much."[45] As Pound himself wrote, with obvious admiration, "He [Jefferson] governed with a limited suffrage, and by means of conversation with his more intelligent friends. Or rather he guided a limited electorate by what he wrote and said more or less privately" (*J/M*:15) This attitude is also highly revealing of Pound's conception of his audience. The description of an epic proposed in the Introduction specifies that an epic is addressed to the citizen, not to the private individual, but it says nothing about the actual number of its readers. The only requirement is that those readers represent a decisive force in establishing the political and social conditions of the whole society. The poem itself might be read by only an all-powerful Emperor and by the small, educated class occupying the culturally and politically dominant administrative posts, and still exert a profound indirect influence upon the populace. Or it might seek to reach the majority of the citizens, offering them models of a better dispensation and a methodology to reach that goal. The poet's "ideal audience," that is, is determined by his political as well as aesthetic beliefs, and will vary enormously throughout history. In order fully to realize their intentions, *The Cantos* probably needed to reach—and guide—a Jefferson (or, in Pound's case, a Mussolini), capable of ordering the nation by the authority of his judgments. Pound's naïveté about the likelihood of such a situation is part of his entire political outlook, and helps to explain why he never felt the obligation to make his epic accessible to the "tribe" for whose benefit it was, nonetheless, partially written.

Stuart Hampshire has shown that "political philosophers before Vico and Montesquieu conceived the disintegration of societies, and the constant change of their social and political structure, as something accidental to them, and as signs only of their imperfect design; it seemed at least theoretically possible to design a society which would be static, and in a state of equilibrium. . . . The revolution in political thought came with the suggestion that historical change, and the decay of political and social structures, is an essential condition of

human life, . . . and that social systems change into new forms
as part of the natural process of human development.''[46]

In this context, Pound's political theory was decidedly an-
tiquated, but Confucian historiography gave him the foundation needed to "demonstrate" that such a static philosophy of
history could actually be seen working in a concrete setting,
that it was not mere *theoria* but historical *praxis*.[m]

Just as, for example, Pound's fiscal doctrine leaves out
countless factors—ranging from class divisions to the changes
in economic development due to technological, demographic,
or geographic influence—so his historical opinions rarely succeed in raising any of the fundamental issues that have engaged thinkers at least since Rousseau. For all his reliance
upon economics and "specific details," Pound's overview is
still very much the old notion of historical Peaks and Dark
Ages, cycles determined almost entirely by the individual
ruler's degree of enlightenment. The historical evolution of
different forms of government has no real place in Pound's
speculations; ironically, one of the major questions which the
poet's entire interpretive stance has no means even to raise, let
alone resolve, was succinctly formulated by Benito Mussolini's most famous prisoner, Antonio Gramsci: ". . . does one
start from the premise of a perpetual division of the human
race (into rulers and ruled), or does one believe that this is
only an historical fact answering to certain conditions?"[47]

Pound's listing of so many documents and "particulars"
has obscured the fact that he uses them to support and render
concrete a very restricted set of intuitions about the workings
of history. In a sense, Pound, throughout *The Cantos*, is
searching for specific, "provable" facts and experiences that
will give general validity to a number of primary, unques-

[m] Poundian commentators have regularly seen Pound's ideas as somehow
characteristic of the best speculations of the French Enlightenment. Yet, as
Hampshire's discussion makes clear, Pound's political and historical theories
were decidedly pre-Montesquieu. Few of the major *philosophes* would have
accepted the view that an unchanging social system was either desirable or
possible. Diderot, for example, constantly affirmed the necessity for a creative change in all social institutions. Pound, of course, agreed with this view
when it referred to art, but seems to have rejected it (perhaps under Kung's
influence) in the political sphere.

tioned assumptions which generate the whole poem. In writing the epic, his understanding of his own intuitions has, of course, become far more clearly defined, but his treatment of different sources is not in the least "inductive." Pound's narrative method was determined, in a technical sense, by his own pseudo-scientism, by his desire to make the historical conclusions of the poem appear to arise inductively from the "objective evidence" presented. Only such an approach, he felt, would guarantee the authenticity of those conclusions; instead, it has largely resulted in *The Cantos'* being criticized severely for their ambitions, the historical schema being seen as either trivial or incoherent while still sufficiently all-pervasive to mar fatally the work's purely aesthetic aspects. In the event, Pound's understanding of inductive scientific procedure was itself hopelessly subjective and uncertain, and its application to the poem's structure never more than a mystification.[48] All of the work's essential themes (that is, those which did not change in response to the contingencies of his personal life and the historical events occuring during the text's composition) are already fully present in the revised first three Cantos, and the unfolding of historical details only adds density to those primary themes. But, until Pound's discovery of Confucian historiography and of Social Credit economics, and his elevation of the technique of juxtaposing "luminous details" into a scientific and epistemological principle assuring the generation of "objective truth," these themes did not cohere into an epic structure. The explicit and programmatic reliance upon the codes I have described (as opposed to their instinctive and unsystematic use) was indispensable because the logic of his own poetic discourse required such a move. It is, accordingly, impossible to separate Pound's aesthetic intuitions from the rational, codified framework in which they are inscribed, and even the most determinedly ahistorical and apolitical literary criticism will have to take this framework into account.

One could conclude this entire discussion with a curious proposition. Like all works of art, *The Cantos* constantly reveal their own "fictional" structure: e.g., the melodic inventiveness of the verse, the reliance upon heightened language,

and even interruptions like "my authority, ego scriptor can-
tilenae / . . . 11th Jan. 1938, from Rapallo" (LXII:350). Yet, it
is history itself that constitutes the essential fiction of the
poem, and in Pound's epic that fiction must be allowed to
speak as if it were history itself. This desperately precarious
balancing act, in which the world's history is fictionalized,
appropriated with all the thematic license and willful patterning of art, only so that it can re-emerge in the (fictional) text
as "valid" history, constitutes Pound's basic solution to the
problem of a modern verse epic. For all the limitations in the
actual working out of that solution, *The Cantos* did indeed
struggle to restore history to the domain of possible subjects
for contemporary poetics. If what Walter Benjamin writes is
true, that "only a redeemed mankind receives the fullness of
the past,"[49] the astonishing thing becomes how much of the
past *The Cantos* were able to bring into some kind of perspective, not as a stick with which to castigate the present, but as a
field of human endeavor where present and past share a
common (even if too statically conceived) measure of aspirations and disappointments, where the individual cannot be
rescued until the whole tribe—its heritage as well as its
present—is also and simultaneously freed.

CHAPTER TWO

• • •

AN ETERNAL STATE
OF MIND

"Without gods, no culture. Without gods,
something is lacking."
(GK:126)

"Les propriétés des transformations sont
plus dignes de l'esprit que ce qu'il trans-
forme."
—Paul Valéry: "Je Disais
Quelquefois A Stéphane Mallarmé"[1]

If the discussion at the end of the preceding chapter gradually
began to emphasize a curious hybrid of traditionally discrete
discourses—the historical and the eschatological—my reasons
for yoking such unlikely categories was neither the example
of Benjamin's "Theses on the Philosophy of History," nor
the desire to provide an intermediate stage between a section
devoted to *The Cantos'* historical codes and one centered on
the poem's religious beliefs. Rather, *The Cantos* themselves
enforce the abolition of any clear dividing-line, including a
larger and more various group of cosmic principles, traditional deities, and religious philosophies among its "historical
characters" than any major poem since the Enlightenment. In
essence, what I now want to examine is the way Pound's
mytho-poetic imagination interacts with the explicitly historical and didactic narrative of *The Cantos*, the relationship between the structures determining the presentation of history,
and those ordering the emergence of the sacred.

In his much quoted review of *Ulysses*, T. S. Eliot praised
Joyce's manipulation of "a continuous parallel between con-
temporaneity and antiquity" as a new structural technique for
"making the modern world possible for art."[2] Frequently

overlooked, however, is that in the same paragraph Eliot sharply distinguishes between myth and narrative, seeing them not as variants or modifications of one another, but as two antithetical conventions: "*Instead* of a narrative method, we may now use the mythical method" (emphasis mine).[3] Although Eliot's description is only partially adequate to Joyce's actual procedure, he accurately defines one structural device available to a writer seeking a recognizable "scaffolding" for his text. Yet this is a "scaffolding" Pound himself never used: gods, mythic heroes, and a realm of permanent truths all exist in *The Cantos*, but they do not provide a significant structure to the work's unfolding. Charles Altieri offers a succinct description of a very different use of myth, one he regards as characteristic of "post-modern writers," but which I think also fits Pound: "The post-moderns . . . take myth as essentially a condition one lives in, a way of experiencing, and not as a way of ordering and comprehending experience. The sacramentalizing functions of myth, its powers of creating a numinous present, are far more important than its structural and structure creating properties. . . ."[4] In *The Cantos*, the numinous is perceived intermittently and briefly. Paradise is not "artificial," but "spezzato [splintered] . . . it exists only in fragments" (LXXIV:438); *because* it is "jagged" it only becomes manifest, "For a flash / for an hour. / Then agony, / then an hour, / then agony" (XCII:620). "Le Paradis" is always potentially available, but to mortals its manifestations are inherently unstable, and its existence provides no secure framework within which the other moments of purely historical and contingent existence can be rendered comprehensible, or by which an extended poem can be structured. Pound's poem, that is, exhibits what may be called a mythic consciousness, but it does not rely upon a coherent mythic structure to create its form.

Pound, to adopt Ellmann's fine phrase about *Ulysses*, never proceeds "singlemythedly." The constant metamorphoses of the gods interest him as much as any particular incarnations. Like Paul Valéry, Pound seems to have been as curious about "properties of transformation" as about "what they transform." *The Metamorphoses* is probably the least dogmatic of the classic Western texts recounting the endless transformations of the human and divine, and initially, Ovid, the chronicler of the "swift and unanalysable process" (*LE*:431) by which men and gods work upon one another, assumed, in Pound's eyes, as venerable an authority as Confucius. In 1922, Pound directly linked both writers, telling Harriet Monroe that "I consider the Writings of Confucius and Ovid's Metamorphoses the only safe guides in religion" (*L*:183). Throughout *The Cantos*, he draws upon, recreates, and echoes Ovid, and in the *ABC of Reading* he bestows lavish praise upon the Elizabethan translation of *The Metamorphoses* by Arthur Golding.[a] For Pound "the gods exist," (*GK*:125); they can appear to the receptive gaze at any time, and, following the best Ovidian tradition, in an endless number of forms and guises. Ultimately, they offer man a means of palpably beholding a truth without pretending to a full rationalistic understanding of all the different implications contained in one such vision. Each individual appearance of a divine force neither exhausts its potential meaning nor determines the context and shape of its next manifestation. Hence the barefoot girl, "la scalza: Io son' la luna" (LXXVI:453) glimpsed in the Pisan landscape outside the Detention Camp, represents as genuine a sacred revelation as the later, inner visions of Diana, Aphrodite, and Demeter whom she, for a brief moment, embodies.[b] The gods and goddesses themselves are only hypostases of higher unity, and Pound does not hesitate either to

[a] Pound's extensive use of Ovid throughout *The Cantos* has already been thoroughly documented, especially by Sister M. Bernetta Quinn, George Dekker, and Christine Brooke-Rose, and I do not want to recapitulate their research here. However, as will become apparent, I disagree with the argument that Ovidian metamorphoses provide *The Cantos* with a controlling structure. Rather, they offer Pound a *technique* by which he can move from one episode to another, or combine elements from different stories into one composite image, but they do not generate any major patterns of order within the poem.

[b] Since *The Pisan Cantos* are a fusion of memory and present experience, even the most vivid, local figures in this section are often linked to one of Pound's canonic texts. Thus, the barefoot girl Pound watches from the Detention Camp is also the same shepherdess Guido Cavalcanti once encountered (in Ballata IX of Pound's edition): "In un boschetto trovai pastorella / E *scalza*, e di rugiada era bagnata" (emphasis mine). For Guido too the girl is, ultimately, linked to the God of Love: "E tanto vi sentio gioi'e dolzore / Che Dio d'Amore mi parve ivi vedere" (*Trans*:116).

combine the attributes of Aphrodite, Artemis, and Athena, or to "invent" his own, syncretic divinities (Ra-Set). Indeed, one of the elements he so admired in Confucian writing is its strict avoidance of detailed speculation about the transcendent, about what is, to human reason, essentially unknowable.

> And Kung gave the words "order"
> and "brotherly deference"
> And said nothing of the "life after death."
>   (XIII:59)

And although Pound never quotes it, a famous aphorism of Demetrius of Phalerus aptly summarizes the discretion (almost a linguistic notion of "decorum") concerning the superhuman which Pound admired in Chinese philosophy: "About gods, say only that they are gods." However, without any unified dogma of divine revelation and withdrawal, without a coherent and stable religious system from which one can learn *why* the gods act as they do, and *how* we can satisfy their demands or propitiate their anger, a metamorphic, Ovidian series of transcendent encounters is incapable of providing a secure basis for a personal and communal ethic. Pound's syncretistic polytheism, like any unsystematized belief in a number of permanent, universal principles rendered visible through the intermittent appearance of various deities, clearly does have ethical *implications*. Of necessity, however, these are only very general in outline and lack the specificity necessary to enforce a particular ethical *decision* or to aid in selecting among a number of immediate moral and political options. Artemis, Kuanon, and the Divine Clarity of Plotinus' *Nous* may all be different aspects of some absolute human need or transcendent truth, but they have been worshipped in so many different ways as to make it impossible to elaborate an integrated, specific code of conduct from their customary observances.[c] The communal, even "political," aspect of a re-

---

[c] Historically, this has always been one of the major problems of a syncretic religion. Even within the single framework of their Olympian pantheon, for example, the Greeks found it extremely difficult to decide what practices found divine sanction. This moral ambiguity in the mythic tales formed the basis for the Platonic attack on Homer and the poets as sources of wisdom and as models of education.

ligious and ethical system is, of course, central to Pound's attempt to write a "tale of the tribe." To him, a code for personal salvation without clear social ramifications is mere egotism and self-seeking, and not the necessary foundation of a new, cultural *paideuma*.

Unlike the scattered and ambiguous political guide-lines contained in the Greek and Latin myths, or the occasional *dicta* on public policy offered by sages like Apollonius, in Confucian philosophy ethical and religious problems are always linked to concrete issues of public morality and governmental practices. In *Mencius on the Mind*, for example, I. A. Richards notices that, for all its investigations into logic and epistemology, Confucianism is "designed to give intellectual support to a system whose basis is social."[5] Just as Pound's mixture of Social Credit and *Schwundgeld* is the only monetary doctrine which allowed him to "ground" his hope that one just ruler was sufficient to inaugurate an age of communal equity, so it was only in Confucianism that he found a religious and ethical system which could complete, without displacing, all his separate beliefs.

Pound seems to have had a deep awareness of human finitude, of the way an individual's acknowledgment of his own mortality only adds significance to his deeds.

> Thou shalt not always walk in the sun
> > or see weed sprout over cornice
> Thy work in set space of years, not over an hundred.
> > > > (XLII:210)

> > By this gate art thou measured
> > Thy day is between a door and a door.
> > > > (XLVII:237)

At the same time, Pound also recognizes forces ("gods") which transcend any man or epoch. Even the near-pun in the second quotation ("a door" and "adore") indicates that human mortality is a cause, not for despair, but for an intense *worship* of the bounties of life. Confucian silence about an afterlife, its inherent modesty in not over-defining the nature of the Divine Principles, and its articulation of a religiously based political doctrine ("the Mandate of Heaven"), came closer to satisfying Pound's diverse needs than any Western system. Moreover, since it lacked a governing hierarchy such as the Catholic or Anglican Church, there was no established authority to declare "heretical" Pound's incorporation of features he admired in other beliefs while still proclaiming himself an orthodox Confucian. The passage from Canto LV which I analyzed in the previous chapter reveals how easily he was able to link Kung, Grosseteste, and Cavalcanti as sources of "sacred" knowledge. The central place of Kung's beliefs in *The Cantos* is important to the poem's fundamental ethical-didactic intention, not merely because of the many pages devoted to this topic, but as evidence that, rather than making a totally arbitrary amalgam of interesting materials, Pound kept seeking some unified and coherent doctrine sufficiently flexible to encompass his very personal moral and aesthetic intuitions, yet rooted firmly enough in the political history of a nation to establish its validity as a corrective to Occidental thinking and as a model-instigation for new action. Ultimately, no matter what his immediate source, Pound selected only those elements which would harmonize with motifs already present in *The Cantos*. It is the search for a meaningful synthesis of his diverse *exempla*, for a way to give his intuitions global validity, that shapes his use of historical and religious material, and not any pseudo-scientific attempt to imitate an "unbiased" laboratory experiment. As one translator of Mencius explains, "Ancient Chinese thinkers all looked upon politics as a branch of morals. More precisely, the relationship between the ruler and the subject was looked upon as a special case of the moral relationship which holds between individuals."[6]

The inseparability of political, ethical, and religious rectitude stressed in the Confucian classics gave formal expression to Pound's own strongest convictions, and, when combined with the principles of Confucian historiography, helps to explain the seriousness of his faith in Kung's teaching. Moreover, as Peter Makin persuasively suggests, it was in Confucian doctrine, especially in the concept of *li* ("rites") and *wei* ("filiality") that Pound found a reconciliation of the Western opposition between the claims of Reason and those of Authority (cf. *C*:198-9).[7] The certainty that a just ruler ("factive personality") can establish a harmonious kingdom, and the respect for tradition as a source of insight for the present, are touchstones of Pound's whole method and expectation in writing his poem: like the Confucian classics themselves, *The Cantos* are intended to be a new *paideuma*, a storehouse of significant moments among the "ancients," which will serve as both a chronicle and an immediate *"rappel à l'ordre"* (*GK*:95).

It is the Confucian idea of a "gentleman" (a Western equivalent would partake of both the Renaissance man of *virtù* and the eighteenth-century *honnête homme*) that Pound holds up as a true goal. Significantly, it is a goal that can be reached by study and concentration alone: there is no appeal, in Confucius, to any divine redemption or supralogical grace. The single most crucial theme Pound found confirmed in Confucian ethics is its ability to maintain a sense of the sacred, to acknowledge universal forces, without positing a fallen humanity. Confucianism can speak of a heaven without regarding it as mankind's true dwelling-place; instead, man, earth, and heaven *together* form the Confucian trinity. The "Holy City" neither violates nor, as in Dante's *Paradiso*, stands outside Nature. Unlike St. Augustine's *De Civitate Dei*, the Confucian texts insist that a perfect *polis* can be built in one lifetime and on this earth as the completion of a fully humanized world and center of a truly humane worship.

According to H. D. Smith, Chinese thinking "conceived of 'salvation' as the attainment of the status of the 'perfect sage.' This was a state of being which was possible for all men to reach through an enlightened understanding of 'the nature of things,' and on the basis of that understanding to a harmonization of one's own nature with that of the cosmos. There was no need to postulate a personal God. The whole of nature was 'spirit-fraught,' and the spiritual worked through and manifested itself in the processes of nature. There was no need for a Savior or for radical conversion, because the root of goodness was in all men and only needed 'natural' development."[8]

In the end, it is also always to Nature that Pound appeals:

for aid in preserving his sanity in the Pisan cage, "When the mind swings by a grass-blade / an ant's forefoot shall save you" (LXXXIII:533), or in justification of his economic doctrine, "And the lesson is the very basis of solid banking. The CREDIT rests *in ultimate* on the ABUNDANCE OF NATURE, on the growing grass that can nourish the living sheep" (*SP*:270). Indeed, there is a strong sense in which Pound's "gods" are an attempt to infuse the Enlightenment's God-as-Nature with more personal and "imminent" characteristics. W. B. Yeats was the first to notice this desire, and in a letter to Lady Gregory (7 April 1930) compares Pound's Confucius to a dull eighteenth-century moralist.[9] Yeats's observation is undoubtedly malicious, but it does show an instinctive perception that much of Pound's Confucianism really belongs in an eighteenth-century context. This is, perhaps, partially due to the poet's use of Pauthier and De Mailla for his initial access to Confucian thought, but, more significantly, Pound himself seems to have consciously paired Kung and the Enlightenment as two attempts to understand the nature of man, and to define the basis of a sound government and a human ethics, without the religious intolerance or philosophical narrowness of earlier European creeds. As we saw in the previous chapter, even *The Cantos'* economics, in which land is considered the basis of prosperity and culture, corresponds more to the ideas of Mencius or the eighteenth-century physiocrates, and Thomas Jefferson, their heir, than to any modern doctrine including Major Douglas'.

In the cantos written after 1930, Pound regularly drew upon the central beliefs of Confucianism and his Jeffersonian faith in the virtues of an agrarian society to see nature as the true "ground" of all human culture and religious worship.

> Manners are from earth and from water
> They arise out of hills and streams.
> (XCIX:698)

> Ethics are born from agriculture.
> (Chung Yang XX, 5; *C*:149)

But as a student of Confucius, Pound never needed to posit an antagonism between nature and the city, and this realization is one of his most important contributions to modern poetry. He is one of the first English poets since the Augustans for whom the city is more than a gathering-place of human misery and tedium. (Here, for example, T. S. Eliot with his "Falling towers" and Infernal Underground seems much more conventional.) To a large extent, it was in the Confucian wedding of nature and society that Pound was able to find a model combining and reconciling two antagonistic strains in poetry: the classical (and neo-classical) conviction that man's most complete existence was as a citizen of the *polis*, and the Romantic notion that Nature is at once man's comforter and source of his finest instincts.

It is from this synthesis, with its roots in the Confucian doctrine of harmony, of a *positive* interaction between two opposing principles (yin and yang, *polis* and *gea*), that much of Pound's finest writing springs, and it remains among the most important reasons why later "city" poets were able to read *The Cantos* with so much pleasure as both a permanent contemporary and a guide.

Yet even critics sympathetic to Pound's Confucianism have been disturbed by his brutal unfairness to Taoism and Buddhism throughout the Chinese Dynasty Cantos. His contempt is all the more unjust since there are clear Taoist influences in one of his own favorite "Confucian" texts, the *Li Ki* or "Record of Ceremonials." In the poet's defense, it is usually argued that during his years in Rapallo, Pound had to rely almost exclusively upon De Mailla's heavily biased account, and that the cantos composed after Pisa are full of Taoist themes. Hugh Kenner makes the strategic suggestion that only after the political crisis of the Thirties, and the ravages of the war, was Pound at last able to let his real Taoist and mystical instincts emerge into the poem.[10] I think that Kenner's argument contains a good deal of truth, although, as I shall argue in the next chapter, this change in *The Cantos* indicates a radical shift in Pound's intention, and the "mystical" strains increased after Pisa because of a fundamental re-thinking of the poem's rightful audience and temporal horizon. There is also a danger of over-correction implicit in Kenner's "defense." Even in *Rock-Drill* and *Thrones*, whenever Pound wants to unite his religious and historical themes, he relies

heavily upon Confucian ethics and historiography. Throughout *The Cantos*, mystical, or even Taoist and Buddhist, motifs
can appear, but they cannot be granted any systematic status.
Until *Drafts and Fragments*, the mystical themes are acknowledged only as single, disparate perceptions, because what
Pound rejected in Taoism was precisely the same encouragement of a withdrawal from political life, of a seeking for personal salvation and enlightenment independent of society,
that he had already condemned in Christianity. The Taoist
and Buddhist emphasis on the struggle between a higher soul
and a corrupt or "illusory" world would have displeased
Pound *irrespective* of De Mailla's polemics, and even independent of Pound's allegiance to Confucianism.

What distinguishes Kung's teaching from other philosophies is, in R. L. Brown's phrase, "the positive doctrine of
ordo," an *ordo* that is at once an ethical, political, and religious
imperium. If Pound is like Odysseus visiting Tiresias for guidance on his personal *nostos*, he is also like Dante, trying to
learn the principles of a just government for which some of
the Emperors earned their elevation to the Sphere of Jupiter in
Paradiso XVIII. There is nothing in the *Tao Te Ching* to aid
the poet in the second quest, and as long as a political *ordo* remained a paramount concern there was little chance Pound
could ever have been more than half-hearted in his attitude
towards Taoism. In reality, I think it was largely those aspects
of Taoist philosophy which had *already* been integrated successfully into the framework of Confucianism (a historical
progression of which Pound was unaware until his incarcera-
tion at St. Elizabeth's) that he instinctively chose to emphasize
in *Rock-Drill* and *Thrones*, rather than those motifs which
might be regarded as contradicting Kung's thought.

•   •   •

"In the gloom, the gold gathers the light against it."
(XI:51)

"One finds light best in darkness."
Meister Eckhart

If it is true that Pound was attracted primarily to those elements in mysticism which could co-exist with his secular

convictions, then clearly one of the critical tests of such an argument is the use made of neo-Platonism throughout *The Cantos*. Neo-Platonism not only possesses one of the richest traditions of philosophico-mystical writings, but, in the hands of many of its followers, it gradually merged with the same kind of thaumaturgy Pound found so distasteful in its Taoist manifestations. I intend to go into some detail about neo-Platonism in *The Cantos* both because of its significance in understanding the complexity of the poem's religious principles, and because, in spite of its acknowledged importance, this aspect of Pound's thought has been examined much less carefully than the Ovidian or Homeric derivations. Since Pound truly believed that a knowledge of the "mysteries" was an essential element in providing the tribe with patterns of mind and conduct necessary to its well-being, his epic, in order to fulfill its own intentions, must include those "mysteries."

One of the basic differences separating Confucianism from Christianity, Taoism, or Buddhism is, as has been indicated, the absence in Kung's thought of any need for redemption or appeal to an extra-human grace. Character, study, and self-discipline suffice to make a man a sage. Since there are no supra-logical divine truths, no mystical revelation is required, and the Pauline warning that in Christ's sacrifice, "hath not God made foolish the wisdom of the world" (I Cor. 1:20) would have seemed "foolishness" not only "unto the Greeks" (I Cor. 1:23) but unto the Confucians as well. Similarly, neo-Platonism, for all its mystical tendencies and association with magical practices, was at its best never suspicious of the unaided power of the intellect. Like Confucianism, Plotinus' thought placed no emphasis on Divine revelation.[12] In *Enneads* II.9.9, Plotinus explicitly warns his disciples that τὸ δὲ ὑπὲρ νοῦν ἤδη ἐστὶν ἔξω νοῦ πεσεῖν ("To be [to set oneself] above the Intellect is already to have fallen away from it.")[13] In the same section, he also cautions against theological dogmatism in a manner designed to appeal to any reader of Ovid: "It is not by crushing the divine into a unity, but by displaying its exuberance" that men pay proper homage to the creative principle of the world.[14] R. T. Wallis summarizes the gulf between neo-Platonism and Christianity in a paragraph that exactly parallels the Confucian distance from any "revealed" religion: "The differences separating Plotinus from Christian mysticism are . . . fundamental; above all his mysticism lacks any sense of sin or of the need for redemption. In Plotinus, our true self is eternally saved and all that is required is to wake up to this fact, a process requiring self-discipline, but perfectly within the soul's own power."[15]

Not only are Plotinus' writings important to Pound for their own sake, but many of Pound's favorite Medieval philosophers owe an enormous debt to neo-Platonism, both in the details of their argument and in the images through which it is conveyed. One of the central concepts, for example, in Johannes Scotus Erigena (c. 810 to c. 877) is an emphasis on man's innate perfection, a natural state of wholeness which can be brought into conscious awareness by purification of the will alone, without divine intercession. Pound, as we have seen, frequently appeals to Erigena's dictum that authority comes only from reason. But there is another sentence in that philosopher's writings which is equally dear to Pound, and to which he once seems to refer directly. Erigena explains that, "Evil is no more in human nature than it is in the angelic nature. It is not planted in the *nature* of man at all, but is solely in a perverse motion of the will."[16] In "The Teacher's Mission," Pound says, "The evil, like all evil, is in the direction of the will" (*LE*:62).

Ultimately, even the whole theme of Light as the single most significant manifestation of the Divine—*Lux enim per se in omnen partem se ipsum diffundit*—derives from Plotinus and Porphyry. An essential neo-Platonic conviction was translated into Medieval Latin by the aphorism, "bonum diffusivum sui" ("the good diffuses itself") with the Plotinian explanation that, "entities that have achieved perfection of their own being do not keep that perfection to themselves, but spread it abroad by generating an external 'image' of their internal activity" (e.g., the outflow of light from the sun).[17] In this sense, *moral* qualities are also emanations of an inner illumination—"onestade risplende" (XCIII:626; "Honesty shines")—and the many Provençal and Italian verses celebrating the immediate, transparent luminance surrounding the "gentil donna" are seen by Pound as proof of an essential, neo-Platonic strain persisting in the best Medieval poetry.

Beyond a doubt, however, the single most important text of the entire neo-Platonic tradition is Plotinus' *Enneads*, and it is directly from Plotinus that Pound derived his understanding of neo-Platonism. One of the texts which apparently drew Pound's attention to Plotinus was John Shawcross' new edition of Coleridge's *Biographia Literaria*, which was published in 1907. At the end of the third essay, "On the Principle of Genial Criticism" Coleridge offers his famous definition of beauty as " καλόν quasi καλοῦν i.e. *calling* on the soul . . . ,"[19] and then, in support of this interpretation, quotes a lengthy passage from *The Enneads* (I.6). That Pound was familiar with this book is proven by his own quotation from Coleridge in the 1907 poem "In Durance."

> 'Quasi KALOUN.' S.T. says Beauty is most that, a
> 'calling to the soul.'
>
> (*Per*:20)

In *The Spirit of Romance* (1910) Pound again praises "Coleridge's most magical definition of beauty—καλόν quasi καλοῦν" (156). (Coleridge himself throughout the *Biographia* often refers to and quotes Plotinus, and in Chapter XII he pleads for a better edition of the neo-Platonic philosopher in words that readers of *The Cantos* have often applied to Pound's own text: "no writer more wants, better deserves, or is less likely to obtain a new and more correct edition.")[20]

Initially, Pound seems to have used G.R.S. Mead's edition of Thomas Taylor's (1758-1835) translation, *Selected Works of Plotinus* (London, 1895), and the 1908 poem "Plotinus" contains a direct reference to this text: "As one that would draw through the node of things, / Backsweeping to the vortex of the cone, / . . . I was an atom on creation's throne / And knew all nothing my unconquered own."[21] Later, Yeats became a great admirer of Stephen MacKenna's monumental translation of the complete *Enneads* (cf. Yeats's *Letters*, p. 717, 719), and it is likely that he communicated some of his enthusiasm to Pound.[d] At least in *The Cantos* themselves, Pound twice

[d] MacKenna's first version of *The Enneads* was printed in five volumes

juxtaposes Yeats with Plotinian themes in a manner that indicates an intimate association between the two. Yeats's "Nothing affects these people / Except our conversation" (LXXXIII:528) is placed directly after Gemisto Plethon's neo-Platonic argument for the hydrogenesis of the gods: "Gemisto stemmed all from Neptune." In Canto CXIII, Pound again links Yeats and Plotinus, joining the philosopher's idea that "the body is inside the soul. / the lifting and folding brightness" (788:89; cf. *Enneads* IV.3.23) to Yeats's similar observation in the sculptures of Notre Dame, "That Yeats noted the symbol over that portico / (Paris)" (789).[22]

Plotinus also discusses a pictorial convention of writing for which he makes claims that are strikingly similar to Pound's whole argument about the epistemological advantages of the ideogram. Although a direct connection cannot be proved, it is at least plausible that Pound recalled Plotinus' passage during his work on the Chinese characters and developed a view which is, in fact, a combination of the neo-Platonic and "Fenollosan" theories.

> Similarly, . . . the wise of Egypt . . . indicated the truth where, in their effort towards philosophical statement, they left aside the writing-forms that take in the detail of words and sentences—those characters that represent sounds and convey the propositions of reasoning—and drew pictures instead, engraving in the temple-inscriptions a separate image for every separate item: thus they exhibited the absence of discursiveness in the Intellectual Realm.
>
> (*Enneads* V.8.6.)[23]

Plotinus, that is, attributes to pictorial writing a fidelity, not merely to natural forces, but even to the workings of the whole "Intellectual Realm." Philosophically, at least, Pound's epistemological privileging of the ideogrammic method can

---

from 1917-1930 in a *de luxe* edition by the Medici Society. Subsequent editions, revised by B. S. Page and distributed by a commercial publisher, followed within a few years. Today, the third edition, published by Faber & Faber in 1962, is still considered the best translation of Plotinus available to an English reader.

be grounded just as convincingly in Plotinus' theory as in Fenollosa's notes.

Even Pound's use of *The Odyssey* as one of the foundations of his own epic seems to contain neo-Platonic overtones. Without Penelope and Ithaca as the cynosure of his adventures, Odysseus might easily have been tempted to remain with Kalypso or Nausicaa, and Homer's epic become the kind of picaresque novel-in-verse for which it is often misread. Plotinus, in *Enneads* I.6.8, crystallized a tradition of philosophical interpretation of *The Odyssey* by seeing that:

> Odysseus is surely a parable to us when he commands the flight from the sorceries of Circe or Calypso—not content to linger for all the pleasure offered to his eyes and all the delight of sense filling his days.
>
> The Fatherland to us is There whence we have come, and There is The Father.
>
> What then is our course, what the manner of our flight? This is not a journey for the feet; the feet bring us only from land to land; nor need you think of coach or ship to carry you away; . . . you must . . . call instead upon another vision which is to be waked within you, a vision, the birth-right of all, which few turn to use.[24]

The voyage home to a Just Realm is here seen not merely as a physical, but also as an intellectual, ethical, and spiritual journey, a search for truth much like "E.P.'s" in *The Cantos*. Unlike Homer's hero, this Odysseus must go to hell several times: "A second time? Why? man of ill star?" (I:4). The reason for the multiple descents is only in part because Pound's model for Canto I, the Renaissance Latin version of Andreus Divus, contains the line, "Cur *iterum* o infelix linquens lumen Solis / Venisti" (*LE*:262). More importantly, once hell is understood as an intellectual and social condition, there is no single way out, no private exit by "boat or chariot."

Finally, not only does Pound's image of "the great ball of crystal" (CXVI:795) derive from Plotinus (via Medieval Light Philosophy), but there is another term, equally crucial to the poem's conclusion, that has distinct and hitherto unnoticed Plotinian echoes. The last completed Canto ends on a word of hope and encouragement, and it is one that should be examined with care.

> A little light, like a rushlight
>   to lead back to splendour.
>   (CXVI:797)

The great dream of *The Cantos*, a poem which would mirror and encourage the generation actively engaged in building a just kingdom, is dead. The sole hope that remains is "a little light," the clarity of both his own poem, now in its most humble guise, and of the splintered heaven which appears only "in flashes" of "splendour." Clearly, "splendour" is meant to sum up all the images of light, the crystal and jade of Canto XC, and the "almost solid" stream of brightness sanctifying the basilica (Cantos XCIII and XCV) with which the Holy City has become associated. Pound's choice of words is far from arbitrary. Plotinus uses the word ἀγλαΐα ("splendour") in a highly personal way to describe the primary Intellect to which man must rise, the source of all good and goal of all efforts (*Enneads* VI.9.4).

This entire section of *The Enneads* poignantly matches Pound's conviction that there is a primal truth which remains valid, irrespective of our failure to attain, or to describe adequately, its plenitude: "i.e. it coheres all right / even if my notes do not cohere" (CXVI:797). Like Pound in the closing moments of *The Cantos*, Plotinus, at the end of his own text, points to the failure of his discourse to encompass the *splendour* of the One, while still affirming the value of his work as an instigation, an aid on an arduous journey. The necessity for Plotinus, just as for Pound, is to learn how to see correctly: "can you see with eyes of coral or turquoise" (CX:777); "to 'see again,' / the verb is 'see,' not 'walk on' " (CXVI:796). Plotinus calls his words only an aid, a disciplining of vision whose realization is, finally, a matter of individual desire and will.

> "Not to be told; not to be written:" in our writing and telling we are but urging towards it: out of discussion we call to vision: to those desiring to see, we point the path;

our teaching is of the road and the travelling; the seeing must be the very act of one that has made this choice.

There are those that have not attained to see. The soul has not come to know the splendour There; it has not felt and clutched to itself that love-passion of vision known to the lover come to rest where he loves. Or struck perhaps by that authentic light, all the soul lit by the nearness gained, we have gone weighted from beneath; the vision is frustrate; we should go without burden and we go carrying that which can but keep us back; we are not yet made over into unity.[25]

Finally, the ἀγλαΐα is important in another of Pound's sacred texts, since it is one of the standard Homeric epithets appropriate to water, especially when the reference is to a sacred foundation or temple district.

> . . . ὅθεν ῥέεν ἀγλαὸν ὕδωρ
> (. . . "whence did flow splendid water.")
> *(Iliad* II.307)

Thus, in the last words of his poem, Pound pays his deepest tribute to the author of *The Enneads.* "Ἀγλαΐα" directly connects the Homeric, neo-Platonic, and Medieval strains in Pound's mystical imagination. From their union he is granted one final vision: a hope for the "splendour" which can still be reached if only man holds fast to the truths made visible in "the discontinuous gods," and described by the philosophers of both divine and human order. In *The Cantos*, to coin a hybrid aphorism, it is indeed true that "ἀγλαΐα diffusivum sui." For all the poet's earlier "asperities" it is difficult to imagine a less sectarian vision, or, left for his readers, a more generous testament.

•   •   •

"Strive to bring back the god in yourselves to the Divine in the Universe."

—Plotinus[26]

The gods undoubtedly exist in *The Cantos*. Their presence illuminates the text at constant intervals, and adds a richness to Pound's natural descriptions rare in modern poetry. And yet the actual role played by Pound's divinities is fundamentally different from that in traditional epics. Strangely enough, it is perhaps the most important of these differences which has escaped any meaningful attention. The gods are real, but they have no historical influence. They can and do intervene in an individual's life; as the poem progresses, they become ever closer and more vividly present to Pound during his suffering in Pisa and in St. Elizabeth's, but their influence is purely personal. The divinities do not (as they do in Homer, Virgil, or Dante) move with any concern for human history. Human society can make it more or less difficult for individuals to be aware of the gods, but these deities have no power to control the course of events. It is not just that man is free to make a hell or *paradiso terrestre* of his world; the problem is more centrally linked to the absence of any sense of historical development in Pound's world-view. The connections between the moment of vision and the surrounding darkness are elaborated no more clearly in the mythical realm than they are in his chronicle of factual events. A correctly ordered society will replace the statue of Aphrodite, "By Circeo, by Terracina, with the stone eyes / white towards the sea" (XXXIX:195). Conversely, the presence of the gods acts as a harmonizing influence on the social order. Yet, no matter how true such a view is, it remains curiously resistant to any further questions. *Why* the gods have withdrawn from most men's range of vision is not explained any more than is the reason for a decline in social equity, and simply to see the two events as inexorably linked only substitutes an infinite regress for a genuine solution. A strictly theological view of human events (as in the *Commedia* or *Paradise Lost*), or the positing of a group of gods who control events for their own, private ends (as in *The Iliad*), can still be considered "historical," in the sense that the text provides an explanation for man's development through time. In *The Cantos*, however, there is a religious force which the poet deliberately refuses to systematize into an explanatory principle. Like Pound's historiography, his religious beliefs result in brilliant "moments," but the process of their interconnection remains, like

Lao Tzu's *Tao*, strictly inscrutable. No matter in how many manifestations or different eras the gods are shown to appear, the effect is one of historical stasis. The most fundamental meaning of metamorphosis, a change in external form without a corresponding change in the inner essence, is, in itself, static. Diana and Aphrodite may take on the shape of a butterfly or of a barefoot girl, they can even help save Pound from an emotional breakdown, but the extent of their efficacy is always purely personal and does not, as it does in traditional epics, determine the course of public affairs. The human and divine are juxtaposed throughout *The Cantos*, and the result is often a startling insight into single characters, but, of necessity, the emphasis on an essential, metamorphic identity destroys any sense of history as a constituent category of concrete, human existence.

As long as the subject matter is one of primal, unchanging individual emotions (jealousy and revenge, as in Canto IV), Pound's metamorphoses do create a valid bridge between the various individual manifestations of the archetype; but, inevitably, the success of such an approach becomes more circumscribed when the material itself derives its importance from a specific historical nexus. In Canto XCI, for example, Pound links Drake, Actaeon, and Agamemnon in their respective encounters with a powerful woman (queen and goddess, Elizabeth and Artemis) and although poetically the "doubling" is managed at least as skillfully as the Ovidian and Provençal fusions of Canto IV, the significance of the relationships thus established removes the particular complexity, the "local" meaning, which individualizes Elizabeth I as a historical figure.

> Ἐλέναυς That Drake saw the armada
>   & sea caves
> Ra-Set over crystal
>   moving
> in the Queen's eye the reflection
> & sea-wrack—
>   green deep of the sea-cave
> ne quaesaris.

He asked not
nor wavered, seeing, nor had fear of the wood-queen, Artemis
that is Diana
nor had killed save by the hunting rite,

sanctus.

(612)

The opening epithet, "destroyer of ships," applied here to both Drake and his queen—twin heroes of the repulsion of the Spanish Armada—is especially effective. We have already seen how Pound adopted Aeschylus' bitter word-play with Helen of Troy's name, and now he employs it to link Helen, Eleanor of Aquitaine, and Eleanor's spiritual, as well as historical, successor, Queen Elizabeth I. Moreover, just as Pound transfers Aeschylus' list of Helen's attributes to other queens, so in Ra-Set, his own syncretic deity, he has created a fusion of the sun and moon, of male and female principles, a particularly apt "parallel" to the "virgin queen" of England. The last lines of the passage quoted recall the disastrous consequences of offending the goddess: Actaeon turned into a stag for stumbling upon Diana while she was bathing, and Agamemnon compelled to sacrifice his daughter Iphigenia for boasting that he was a better hunter than the "maiden of Delos"— "Agamemnon killed that stag, against hunting rites" (LXXXIX:602). The whole section is a striking, composite series of *exempla* on the power, for both good and evil, of such women, and the care men must exercise in dealing with them. George Dekker interprets the canto as "a resolution of the courtly and pagan ideas of Eros as an instigation, of creative activity on the one hand, and of destructive activity on the other," and in the figure of Elizabeth he sees "an attempt to reconcile Artemis and Aphrodite. . . ."[27] Such a reading seems very close to Pound's intentions, and there is a consummate technical skill apparent in the ease with which the different themes are linked. It is equally important, however, to see that, in effect, he has taken Queen Elizabeth out of any definite context: she is now only one of the many female divinities whom the poet views *sub specie aeternitatis*. Earlier references to her as "Miss Tudor" (in the same canto) or, in LXXXV, as

"Queen Bess" who "translated Ovid," do not make her presence any more concrete; nor does the fragmentary list of legislation passed during her reign, which Pound introduces at the end of *Thrones*, add much genuine historical depth.

Pound's linking of the divine and the human is limited to isolating whatever aspects of a figure partake of some absolute, archetypal *forma*. The links with previous incarnations of that archetype are not in the least historically determined, since from the beginning it was only the timeless characteristics which he could select for inclusion in his metamorphoses. Queen Elizabeth, insofar as she *is* Diana and Aphrodite, stands outside all temporal determinations, and it is solely in this role that Pound is able to incorporate her into the mythic dimension of his poem.

I have chosen this example from Canto XCI deliberately, in order not to simplify my argument too much. Seeing Elizabeth I as an almost mythic figure does, after all, fall into a long literary tradition to which both Spenser and Shakespeare made permanent contributions. Pound's success in his own handling of the trope is a formidable achievement, and it is only the particular limitations of his mythological vision as a means of finding meaning in history which I am questioning. A far more troublesome passage, such as the celebrated opening of *The Pisan Cantos*, can illustrate how arbitrary and unilluminating Pound's collapsing of the historical and the mythical often becomes:

> Manes! Manes was tanned and stuffed,
> Thus Ben and la Clara *a Milano*
>   by the heels at Milano
> That maggots shd/ eat the dead bullock
> DIGONOS, Δίγονος, but the twice crucified
>   where in history will you find it?
>   (LXXIV:425)

This moving elegy—like a troubadour's pledge of allegiance to his fallen lord, as Richard Freudenheim has remarked—compares Mussolini's death to the crucifixion of the Persian sage, Manes, brutally killed for his beliefs.[28] Pound mourns because Il Duce, unlike Dionysus ("the twice-born," Δίγονος—i.e., conceived once in Semele's womb and then, after her death, carried in his father, Zeus's, thigh) will not be resurrected, and, as in any pastoral elegy, the entire landscape is made to reflect the poet's grief with images of a violent rupture in the ritual order of the agricultural calendar. Poetically, these lines are as brilliantly executed as any in the poem, but, unlike the Elizabeth-Artemis-Ra-Set juxtaposition, it is hard to see a reason for, or justice in, the mythological connections. But because the text has not established any specific code by which the divine and the historical are measured against one another, the reader can make no appeal against, or demand an explanation for, Pound's "visions" without departing from the terms of the poem itself. (In the *Commedia*, for example, where the Divine Laws are firmly established and systematically ordered, the reader is *expected* to be shocked that the first person Dante encounters in Purgatory is the pagan suicide Cato, and the poem is careful to indicate how such a seeming violation fits into the higher pattern of God's justice.) In Pound's text, the temporal appearance and vanishing of the divine archetypes, as well as the ethical basis for the various "doublings" of specific mortals and deities, remain unexplained. Neither the metamorphoses, nor the *ordo* of the mythical realm, are controlled (as they are in Yeats's cyclical recurrences) by an externally imposed scheme, and this is one of the most liberating aspects of *The Cantos'* use of mystical insights. At the same time, however, that very freedom prohibits Pound's juxtapositions of human and eternal to come to grips with a historical event in its real complexity. The glimpses of unexpected parallels function, in principle, in the same way as the ideogrammic method, and, although they do create many of the most luminous moments in *The Cantos*, they cannot, as has been claimed for them, offer a meaningful basis for understanding a particular individual, let alone an entire culture. Nor can they, as do Joyce's scrupulous and ironic correspondences between the *Odyssey* and *Ulysses*, offer a major structure to the poem.

The letter Pound wrote to his father in 1927 explaining the

"plot" of his epic clearly shows the particular function of the mythic elements in *The Cantos*.

> 1. Rather like, or unlike subject and response
> and counter subject in fugue.
> A.A. Live man goes down into world of Dead
> C.B. The "repeat in history"
> B.C. The "magic moment" or moment of metamor-
> phosis, bust thru from quotidien into "divine or
> permanent world." Gods, etc.
>
> (*L*:210)

Surprisingly, this brief sketch is closer to the core of the poem than many of Pound's later pronouncements. More specifically, it already contains the germ of his whole attempt to fuse the personal and artistic (A.A.) with the historical (C.B.) and religious (B.C.) aspects of his world-view. Already, in this fairly early letter, though, it is apparent that the *process* which could link the "repeats" throughout history, and which could account for the manifestation of the "divine world," has no place in the schema. The three themes are, of course, interrelated, but only in the minds of the poet and reader, never in the events themselves. It is the phrase "magic moments" which contains, in miniature, the essence of much of Pound's religious thinking. Moreover, it is precisely in his belief in "magic moments" that Pound most resembles his literary contemporaries.

In his study of Hermann Hesse, Theodore Ziolkowski has drawn attention to the attempt in modern literature to overcome what German writers felt was a *Zerfall der Werte*, an omnipresent breakdown of traditional values in the face of new scientific and psychological discoveries.[29] The urge to find a new unity which could transcend the disintegration of established bourgeois norms finds one expression in what Hesse called *magisches Denken*, a vision of a realm of true simultaneity where all human expression is grasped as somehow unified, as part of a harmonized, unchanging order. With very different techniques, and based upon different epistemologies, Proust's *moments privilégiés* and Joyce's "epiphanies" can also be seen as partaking of the same striving. Yet, unlike Proust or Hesse, Pound's magical moments are expressly intended to be used as "co-ordinates for social reform." The historical conditions that lead many other writers to withdraw into their own aesthetic, inner realm, only encouraged Pound all the more to transform *society* until it should be in harmony with his desires and intuitions. But the insight into magic moments for all its didactic and polemical force, cannot, as we have seen in two specific cases, adequately engage historical reality on its own terms.

Since so many critics have seen the two codes—historical and mythological—as complementary, this criticism is bound to raise strong objections. Yet, I think it is even insufficient to point out that there is no *mediation* between the two codes; it would be more accurate to say that, as explanatory systems, the two are not merely separate but, all too often, mutually exclusive.

Because Pound intended his poem as a historical and moral "instigation," not only for his contemporaries, but also for future generations of readers, and because he was, in any event, profoundly dissatisfied with most of the interpretative schemas proposed by orthodox historians, a metamorphic presentation of his themes seemed particularly apt. For him, an awareness of metamorphoses is a specific kind of mythological thinking, and as such represents an intuitive, essentialist insight which is at once universal, indirect, and open-ended. A mythic tale (the metamorphic element being the re-emergence of the structurally same thematic configurations in different settings) does not pretend to an analytically exhaustive "reading" of its constituent parts. It remains permanently over-determined, available to successive "decodings" by new readers, the terms of each "decoding" being affected as much by the needs, habits, and expectations of those readers as by the internal logic of the myth itself. In crediting myths with such a strong synthetic and totalizing power, Pound was not only anticipating the conclusions of modern theoreticians like Lévi-Strauss, he was also very much in harmony with the attitudes of his own generation. Sir James Frazer's *The Golden Bough* (1890), for example, seemed to many of its early readers to prove the enactment of a few, primal rites (myths) in a broad variety of settings and communities (metamorphoses). Not only did T. S. Eliot draw upon Frazer for *The Waste Land*, but, as John B. Vickery has shown in *The Literary Impact of The Golden Bough* (Princeton, 1973), Frazer's arguments exercised a profound fascination upon numerous artists in the first decades of this century. At the same time, intuitionalist philosophers tried to provide a new, theoretical foundation for traditional subjectivist claims that intuitively grasped images embody a fundamental level of truth unavailable to rationalist formulations. They argued against the absolute priority of logical systems or syllogistic reasoning, and, much like Pound's dictum in *Guide to Kulchur* (127), claimed that only a language of metaphors and images can express the intuitions which grasp the essence of things. Since an image makes no claim to a full representation, it alone preserves the integrity and essential mystery of the intuited truth. From whatever sources Pound ultimately derived his faith in the unique authority of mythic imagery as a vehicle for universal truths (and his favorite neo–Platonic writers are certainly plausible candidates), there is no doubt that technically, as a means of establishing recurrent thematic motifs in such a long poem, it was a highly welcome creed. The fact that this principle utterly violates every form of inductive procedure did not worry Pound, largely, as I suggested, because scientific induction was never a crucial element of his thinking. However, there is a strong sense in which his reliance upon myth and metamorphoses does undermine the entire theoretical horizon of the poem. Essentialist intuitions, especially in the form they take throughout *The Cantos*, eliminate the very historical imperatives the poem seeks to formulate. Specific textual examples of this gap, the absence of any concrete links between "magic moments," have already been discussed, and form the basis for my disagreement with the type of holistic reading proposed most notably by Daniel Pearlman. Mythological presentation is ostensibly employed to clarify and to expand the significance of specific events, but instead it radically displaces them, shifting their significance out of *any* historical context. The fundamental principle of a literary myth is, in Roland Barthes' phrase, to "transform history into nature."[30] The authority of a mythic interpretation only serves to give "an historical intention a natural justification,"[31] by making what is contingent and subject to man's *praxis* appear eternal and immutably ordered. The very degree to which the poem's narrative development is dependent upon the recurring, metamorphic appearances of the same fixed constellation of archetypal events marks the limits of its success as a *modern* verse epic. It is here, in this irreconcilable contradiction between the text's disparate intentions, that the language becomes confused; the verse must simultaneously engage two different recuperative systems, one diachronic and contingent, the other synchronic and necessary, and even for a poem with the absorptive capacity of *The Cantos*, the resulting burden is simply too great.

Ultimately, the reliance upon mythology threatens to displace the very freedom of action *The Cantos* intend to celebrate, and it is only because Pound refused to provide a single, coherent theory of recurrences and magic moments that the specific options available to men acting in a historical context can figure in the poem at all. Here, as so often in *The Cantos*, it is the *discontinuities*, the gaps between the text's rival codes, which allows meaning to emerge. The contradictions I have described only limit the poem's hopes of "making it all cohere," of finding a formula able to encompass cosmos and polis, pattern and accident, within one "ideogram."

Of course, "Art very possibly *ought* to be the supreme achievement, the 'accomplished;' but there is the other satisfactory effect, that of a man hurling himself at an indomitable chaos, and yanking and hauling as much of it as possible into some sort of order (or beauty), aware of it both as chaos and as potential" (*LE*:396). Pound *tried* to write that perhaps impossible work, a modern verse epic. Certainly he succeeded in including more diverse components of the tribe's lore, recapturing in the process more domains for the province of verse, than any other modern poet in English. Yet there are moments when one can be grateful for his failure to achieve the kind of unity, the perfect integration of different themes and techniques, which his admirers so often insist on finding. The mythological and historical axes of *The Cantos* do not succeed in either negating one another, or becoming reduced to a single, unified but frozen pattern, only because they interact more sporadically than consistently, because we can respond to each in turn without always having the synthesis Pound himself clearly longed for forcing itself upon us. To bemoan the work's incoherence or to "prove" its total internal consistency, seem to me two equally pernicious critical responses, neither of which will permit an adequate experience of the poem.

It is in the realm of human temporality that the tension between the mythical and the historical forces in *The Cantos* becomes most apparent. In the working out of that tension, the poem as a unified epic crumbles, and, paradoxically, many of the most assured triumphs of the entire text can be found. Historical causality and mythic insights clash, if anywhere, in the dimension of time, and it is to that clash our investigation is now ready to turn:

> No man can see his own end.
> (CXIII:787)

CHAPTER THREE

. . .

THUS WAS IT IN TIME

"But to hitch sensibility to efficiency?"
(CXIII:788)

"Die wirkliche Genesis ist nicht am
Anfang, sondern am Ende. . . ."
—Ernst Bloch,
Das Prinzip Hoffnung[1]

"It may suit some of my friends to go about with their noses pointing skyward, decrying the age and comparing us unfavourably to the dead men of Hellas or of Hesperian Italy. . . . But I, for one, have no intention of decreasing my enjoyment of this vale of tears by under-estimating my own generation."[2] These lines, so characteristic of Pound's exuberance at its finest, record both the energy he derived from collaborating "with the most intelligent men of the period" (*GK*:217), the "lordly companions" with whom he had struggled to modernize the arts of his day, and his long-standing conviction that with suitable encouragement "you will begin for America an age of awakening which will overshadow the quattrocento" (*LE*:224). We are so used to this aspect of Pound's character that it no longer produces any wonder. Yet, if one considers his hierarchy of values, the intensity of his commitment to earlier poetic traditions, and his veneration for the gods and rituals of antiquity, it is astonishing that he so rarely indulged in sterile nostalgia and so successfully resisted the melancholy role of *laudator temporis acti*.

Underlying Pound's openness to new ideas, his willingness to consider his own age the potential equivalent of any previous era, is a twofold conviction whose terms were analyzed in the previous chapters. First, since a god "is an eternal state of mind" (*SP*:47), it follows that the gods are still alive, "they have never left us" (CXIII:787) and can be brought back into the communal awareness at any time. Second, since a socially just state can be instituted at any time through sheer human will—"The problem that faces us . . . is no longer that of understanding either the problem or its solution, it is a problem of educating the public" (*SC*:14)—there is a clear impetus to remain at once vigilant and optimistic. As one of the principal educators of the new *polis*, the poet must have "pity, yes, for the infected," but precisely because it is the welfare of the whole tribe that is constantly at stake, he must also "maintain antisepsis" (XCIV:635) and keep the image of a rightful order before our eyes. The ideal religious, political, and aesthetic synthesis, that is, does not belong exclusively to any one era or sensibility, but can be brought "into action" whenever human determination is intensely enough engaged. Thus, unlike T. S. Eliot in poems like "A Cooking Egg," Pound will not use the glorious past merely as a mirror to hold in the face of an irremediable modern squalor, nor, as Eliot does in "Sweeney Among the Nightingales," will he suggest that our present degradation has become virulent enough to stain even the heraldic tradition. The famous aphorism from Canto LIII, "Day by day make it new" (265) implies, after all, that there is indeed an "it," a constellation of virtues that can be adapted to every (and any) moment of man's endeavor without passively awaiting propitious historical circumstances or divine grace.

Pound affirmed that the American mind "will undertake nothing in its art for which it will not be in person responsible" (*PM*:63), and that "responsibility" in turn can never be divorced from its ethical, political, and cultural application. To lament the past without attempting a transformation of the present would mean a total abdication of responsibility, just as the desire to ignore the political realities of his time by longing for a general "return to Christianity" seemed to Pound a distressing part of "the postwar . . . gran' rifiuto and, . . . [a sign] of fatigue" (*SP*:53). Similarly, one of his most fruitful insights, an insight which writers like Louis Zukofsky, William Carlos Williams, and Charles Olson echoed in their own artistic credos, was that the old antithesis between the "writer" and "the bourgeois" was passé. At a time when figures like Thomas Mann and Hermann Hesse had made the tensions between the "aesthete" and the "man-in-the-world" the theme of their major novels, Pound had already abandoned as useless such a simplistic antithesis: "Our community is no longer divided into 'bohème' and 'bourgeois.' We have our segregation amid the men who invent and create, whether it be a discovery of unknown rivers, a solution of engineering, a composition in form, or what you will" (*GB*:122). Creativity is a permanent human gift, restricted neither by time nor particular occupation, and should be celebrated in all its manifestations. Pound's instinctive optimism could turn to blind anger and frustration when thwarted, but it also gave him an almost unique ability to champion the achievements of his own epoch without ever undervaluing the tribe's cultural heritage.

I have brought these various statements together to provide a framework for discussing time in *The Cantos*, a theme which, in spite of its obvious significance, has received surprisingly little rigorous attention. Daniel Pearlman's *The Barb of Time* remains by far the most influential study of temporality in Pound's epic, but, for all its acute local perceptions, its essential argument seems to me fundamentally misleading, and its explanation of *The Cantos*' temporal horizon seriously awry.[3] Fundamenally, *The Barb of Time* proposes to understand the poem as "a kind of Hegelian progression"[4] in which the "mechanical clock-tick" of conventional history is initially contrasted with and then vanquished by an ahistorical, "organic" perception of "spirit and time-as-nature" joined in "the reconciling synthesis of love."[5] Such a structure, however, would be only a metaphysical morality play, thinly disguised as a dialectic. There is no dialectic in Pearlman's schema because there is no synthesis, no emergence of a genuinely *new* category out of the initial oppositions, and there is no synthesis because Pearlman has not indicated any way in which the two kinds of temporality—the sequential time of an unfolding history versus the achronological time-as-nature—could ever form a higher unity. Instead, what is required is that "the spirit" learn, through the power of love, how to choose between two types of mutually exclusive relationships to time. Since *The Barb of Time* is committed to seeing one kind of time perception as entirely good, and the other as entirely evil—"historical time is the fundamental enemy of the Self or spirit"[6]—it is hard to imagine why a dialectic would be at all desirable. Yet the misappropriation of Hegelian terminology does not arise from mere carelessness. Rather, Pearlman's critical vocabulary is itself part of a strategy designed to convince us of two interdependent premises: (1) *The Cantos* are a fully coherent, unified text; and (2) it is both necessary and legitimate to dehistoricize the poem in order to grasp the terms within which its essential unity is attained. The logical consequence of these premises—that the specific content of Pound's political, economic, or historical judgments are irrelevant to the poem's deeper structure—is undoubtedly intended to "save" the work from its own moments of blindness, but only at the cost of unintentionally belittling the seriousness of *The Cantos'* concerns.

Because mythological, atemporal perceptions constitute an essential part of the full range of values articulated in the epic, and because often even the strictly historical material is not presented in a chronologically determined sequence, readers eager to dehistoricize the entire poem can point to Pound's avoidance of a linear, sequential narrative as proof of their interpretation. The result of such a view is, in Pearlman's phrase, that "if we regard the Western conception of history as . . . a chronologically ordered, causally linked *chain of events,* we must then define Pound's mind as fundamentally *ahistorical.* He shares the cyclical time-consciousness of archaic man, of primitive, traditional societies. . . ."[7] I think this reading confuses the poem's narrative *techniques* with its intellectual *argument.* Mircea Eliade, to whom so many Poundians turn seeking analogues for *The Cantos,* writes about "prehistoric" societies in a way that should, instead, make the *differences* particularly clear. "Pre-historic," in Eliade, does not refer to the period in which a people live, but rather to the absence of a "sense of history," a sense of change and development, in the various explanations of tribal circumstances. The intention of pre-historic myths and legends, according to Eliade, is to confirm that no change is possible, that the conditions established at the creation of the culture itself are the fixed categories of group survival, with only a dreadful descent into chaos as an alternative.[8] Surely Pound's praise for "practical men like Lenin and Mussolini [who] differ from inefficients . . . in that they have a sense of time,"[9] as well as his repeated insistence upon a radical transformation in the society of his own day, indicates how far he was, at least in the realm of politics, from the immutably fixed, ahistorical consciousness of "archaic man."

Throughout his writings, Pound is often concerned to trace precisely the kind of "chronologically ordered, causally linked chain of events" which Pearlman would have him transcend. *The Cantos'* view of World War I, for example, echoes the analysis proposed by virtually every radical economist of the day, attributing a large share of the blame for the eventual holocaust to the long Anglo-German rivalry for foreign markets and investment capital, and to the fantastic profits available to munitions manufacturers. In the domain of aesthetics, as well, Pound displayed an admirably generous and wide-ranging sense of chronological indebtedness, a sure knowledge of the way in which individuals could advance their respective arts only by building upon the discoveries of their predecessors (something which does not, of course, imply that art "improves" with time, but rather that its very resources are the result of a diachronic accumulation of techniques): "I am constantly contending that if it took two centuries of Provence and one of Tuscany to develop the media of Dante's masterwork, that it took the latinists of the Renaissance, and the Pléiade, and his own age of painted speech to prepare Shakespeare his tools" (*LE*:9-10). Politics, history, and even literature itself thus unite to show that, whenever Pound is most precise, temporality with its concomitant "Western" sense of sequential causality, played a crucial role in his thinking.

I have devoted this space to detailing my disagreements with the structure and terminology proposed in *The Barb of Time* because Pearlman's theory offers the most explicit and programmatic formulation of intuitions common, if less consistently deployed, among many Pound critics. But I have been motivated as well by the sense that Pearlman has seen something crucial in *The Cantos*: a fundamental tension between two different temporal perspectives, the mythic and the historical. In order to save the poem's "unity" and establish its internal coherence, he has been forced to impose a reductively affirmative structure, privileging one perspective and condemning the other until the text's final triumph is the radical abolition of time-as-history within the private realm of one man's consciousness. As the cantos written after Pisa make clear, the tension between historical and mythical time is recognized as both the poem's and the world's tragedy. This is the principal turning point in *The Cantos*, one to which I shall return later in this chapter, but first it is necessary to describe more precisely the conflicts in the interaction of Pound's different temporal perspectives, the way in which "time material" is *unwittingly* used to negate itself. In the process of that negation I am unable to discern any triumph of good over evil, of organic over mechanical time, but only the deep-seated contradictions upon which the poet's own hopes for a fruitful synthesis run aground. There *should* have been a marriage of historical and mythical time, a new unity partaking of the best aspects of both, but neither world nor poem ever provided one. Paradoxically, I think it is more generous, as well as accurate, to recognize that Pound resisted claiming a synthesis he never attained than to decide one of his initial terms represents, in the end, a grand solution. Pound, in the face of strong pressure to "complete" his poem, refused to give it a spurious formal or thematic unity, one which his own materials clearly had not achieved. Without attempting to minimize the contradictions in the poem's own historical frameworks and temporal horizons, one can, I think recognize that Pound's sense of responsibility to each aspect of a contradictory vision, his reluctance to acquiesce in the abolition of either history or myth, timelessness or linear causality, resulted in some of the finest writing in *The Cantos*, and endowed the poem with an authenticity any arbitrary unity would only have compromised. The critical framework I propose does not consist in demonstrating any better or more rigorous dialectic than earlier attempts, but rather in continuing to explore the discontinuities, the oppositions, *The Cantos* neither can, nor given their intentions should, "transcend." *The Cantos* are an epic poem including history. In Chapter One I discussed *how* the process of that "inclusion" takes place. The next question is equally complex: *whose* history is really being told?

•   •   •

"Intelligent understanding of past history is to some extent a lever for moving the present into a certain kind of future . . . In using what has come to them as an inheritance from the past [men] are compelled to modify it to meet their own needs, and this process creates a new present in which the process continues. History cannot escape its own process. It will, therefore, always be rewritten."

—John Dewey, *Logic: The Theory of Inquiry* [10]

In spite of the numerous methodological objections provoked by such a viewpoint,[11] Pound, like Dewey, was concerned with finding "a usable past," with locating in the tribe's history a fund of useful *exempla* with which to instigate present changes. Such a view does not, for either Dewey or Pound, imply that the information thus selected is not also objectively true (that is, as accurate as any purely contingent and humanistic study can hope to be), only that all historical knowledge is selected and then presented according to the criteria, consciously acknowledged or not, of the historian's own polemical intentions. This is also, as we have seen, the explicitly acknowledged framework of Confucian historiography, and the range of examples Pound chose to include in *The Cantos* should not blind us to the fact that it is always *our* history which is being told, that the material is presented primarily to instruct the present.

We do NOT know the past in chronological sequence. It may be convenient to lay it out anesthetized on the table with dates pasted on here and there, but what we know we know by ripples and spirals eddying out from us and from our own time.

> . . . A man does not know his own ADDRESS (in time) until he knows where his time and milieu stand in relation to other times and conditions.
>
> (*GK*:60; 93)

Neither of these statements, although they have often been so taken, argues for a cyclical time or an atemporal history. Quite the contrary: Pound specifies the necessity of comparing the present to the past, thus implying both difference and relationship. He limits only the *way* we become aware of the past. The sequence in which historical knowledge enters our awareness need not be chronologically determined since it is obviously possible to think in succession about events occurring in 1968, 1453, and 1848 (although the process of thinking itself does seem sequential—i.e., has its own internal, linear temporality). We may *select* the historical objects of our attention in an achronological fashion, but that in no way acts as a judgment about the temporal horizon in which those events initially occurred. Pound offers an opinion about our epistemology, not about the nature of historical time *per se*. The "ripples and spirals" eddy out from *our* time, from the particular constellation of interests and needs that made us look for assistance to history in the first place. As with any text which "includes history," there are at least three distinct times superimposed in our experience of *The Cantos*: (1) the time in which the events narrated originally occurred; (2) the time Pound selected these events for inclusion in the poem; and (3) the time of any particular reading and interpretation of the poem. Pound's focus of interest and polemical intention (time 2) may violate *our* conception (time 3) of the poem's fidelity to its own sources (time 1), but in principle at least, there is no necessary antagonism between the three "nows." The desire to create a modern verse epic does not, any more than does the writing of a historical study spanning several epochs, necessitate an arbitrary or atemporal set of hermeneutic principles. In the actual unfolding of *The Cantos*, however, Pound's particular axes of interpretation and narrative strategies do impose serious limitations upon the poem's capacity to engage time-as-history in a meaningful way.

In terms of the poem's temporal frameworks, these limitations can be best understood by recalling how Pound is intermittently willing to introduce chronological causality in his account of a specific series of events (e.g., the origins of World War I, the history of the American Revolution, the battle of Jackson and Van Buren against a National Bank, etc.), but then often removes all traces of historical sequence, causality, or even relationship, *between* eras. The extensive use of documentation vividly testifies to his desire to locate his narration of particular moments with full historical and temporal specificity, but that same specificity is almost immediately drained out of the text when two such moments are brought together, and when the criteria for judging different periods are made explicit.

The whole issue of temporality in *The Cantos* is extremely complex because Pound had several quite distinct grounds for his refusal to respect principles of sequence or chronology in his narrative. The first is that only the poet's consciousness of his "now," his perception of the needs of his age, determines which episodes from the tribe's history should be "made new" and held up to the immediate audience. In this case, the question becomes purely one of how sensitive is Pound's analysis of our needs, and how appropriate to them are the historical *exempla* upon which he draws, but there is no question of a timeless or ahistorical view of existence itself. Charles Olson described this aspect of Pound's structure in one of the *Mayan Letters*:

> Ez's epic solves problem: his single emotion breaks all down to his equals or inferiors. . . . Which assumption that there are intelligent men whom he can outtalk is beautiful because it destroys historical time, and thus creates methodology of the Cantos, viz., a space-field where, by inversion, though the material is all time material, he has driven through it so sharply by the beak of his ego that, he has turned time into what we must now have, space & its live air.[12a]

[a] In this regard it is pertinent to notice that all writing already to some extent spatializes time, i.e., shows sequence and succession through a spatial

The discussion of *The Maximus Poems* will return to consider in more detail what Olson means by "space." At present, it is sufficient to see that Olson attributes *The Cantos'* freedom from chronological narration to my first category, to Pound's conviction that his own perceptions of what the present requires is fully justified. Olson is right in saying that the narrative of *The Cantos* "destroys historical time," but he does not attribute this "destruction" to an "archaic . . . or cyclical time-consciousness." Instead, he regards Pound's "now" as the only time "present" in *The Cantos*. Pound's self-confidence in determining which historical *exempla* are of use locates all events as psychologically contemporaneous, as if they occupied a homogeneous field uniformly open to the poet's gaze. Yet, in the same letter Olson also points out the potential hazards of such a methodology, viz., that there is no assurance the poet's criteria of selection are not largely arbitrary and irrelevant. He accuses Pound of "Bohemianism" and says the perceptions of our condition offered in *The Cantos* are "much too late," are only "the 19th Century stance" of artists who "never speak . . . for anyone but themselves."[13] Olson accepts Pound's technical stance, his solution to the narrative problem of including history in a poem. What he criticizes are Pound's specific judgments, and indeed it is hard to see how any one man's selection of historical *exempla* and recommendations could command general agreement if the choice is determined purely by the interests of his own profession and private "ego."

Yet it is also true that Olson's analysis is unfair to Pound's actual procedure because, as we have seen, Pound did try to "ground" his arguments in what he felt were historically objective and verifiable laws. This is the second of the cruces upon which temporality in *The Cantos* depends, and in many ways it is the most troubling of all. Pound's two principal and

---

configuration of marks on a page. Pound himself always stressed that "the verb locates in time" (*LE*:174), and praised poetry, especially when informed by an ideogrammic sensibility, because of its "superiority . . . in . . . getting back to the fundamental reality of time" (*CWC*:9). In fact, none of Pound's statements, on either verse or on the ideogram, show any desire to "destroy time" or convert chronology into a kind of idealistic geography.

interrelated axes for judging any era (and thus for permitting the juxtaposition of *all* periods)—the absolute authority of the "factive" ruler to determine the welfare of his people, and the degree of interest rate tolerated as the key to economic justice—are radically ahistorical and timeless. They effectively abolish contingent, time-determined causality, and as a result the historical texture of *The Cantos* seems curiously frozen into brilliant but historically unconnected set-pieces. Pound's own explanatory principles reduce history to a series of vivid friezes, full of activity within each panel, but immobile in their interrelationship. Yet this rigidity was far from their intended effect. Instead, he regarded both of his principles of judgment as inductively verified throughout time, and argued that their authority derived precisely from the ability to be applied to a "chronologically ordered, causally linked chain of events" *without* violating or transcending that chain. Pound's explanations of historical causality do effectively destroy diachronic history, but this is an exact inversion of their intended function. Indeed, the contradictions created by applying ahistorical and timeless criteria as if they could answer historical and time-bound questions—all the while convinced those criteria satisfied the demands of a rational and historical argument—came close to making the poem's historical texture either incoherent or trivial. The obvious solution is to see Pound's technique as transforming the poem's historical discourse into a purely aesthetic one, a catalogue of private "jewels of conversation." Probably it is in these terms that most readers ultimately come to terms with *The Cantos*, but such a result violates Pound's notion of what an epic must be as surely as any failure of intellectual coherence and is the exact antithesis of the reading for which he spent so many years contending.

The third and final displacement of temporality comes from Pound's mythological and religious convictions, which, as we have seen, are capable only of isolating the timeless and archetypal aspects of an event, of creating homologues between situations by tearing them from the temporal context which holds the key to their very significance. In effect, the mythical dimension of the poem operates in the same way as Pound's purely historical principles, but the metamorphic code was, from the beginning, explicitly acknowledged as standing outside any time determinants. Its function should have been to complement and enrich the historical code, not merely to recapitulate an already atemporal history by different means. For Pound, a religious awareness of eternal forces and a contingent, temporal knowledge of historical causality must combine in a truly humane *praxis*, but, logically, to make a *combination* necessary the two cannot be identical at the outset, and the authority of their explanations cannot be extended in the same manner to identical material. Pound's historical and fiscal laws, that is, are too often displaced versions of his mythological visions, and whenever this identity becomes apparent, the poem sacrifices its temporal dimension, and his own arguments for human choice and historical freedom are implicitly subverted.

It is ironic that the very domain of man's freedom, the efficacy of human will, so often emphasized by the poet, should be most undermined by *The Cantos'* self-cancelling temporal systems. Temporal development, as Kant has shown, is a necessary constituent of individuality and human freedom, and Pound's narration of history becomes, in Pearlman's sense, "archaic" precisely when it rejoins the conception of an inflexible, static universe in which men can be only the passive victims of their destiny.

Nonetheless, there is a vital distinction that must be kept clear: Pound's narrative strategy, his treatment of all times and epochs as sources of wisdom available to the needs of the poet's "now," is not what threatens the text's temporal dimension or the freedom of choice it can attribute to human development. The techniques he developed in writing *The Cantos*, can be used by other poets to sustain a very different historical perspective and ideological stance. Charles Olson, as we shall see, adopted Pound's solution of turning "time-material" into a "space-field." Yet, by also establishing a genuinely historical sense of causality, by finding a sequential development linking the events of his text, Olson sought to remind his readers of their freedom to remake their own society. *The Maximus Poems* try to demonstrate that a synchronic presentation of chronologically scattered facts is not, as often happens in *The Cantos*, the equivalent of removing temporal causality from the domain of historical endeavor. Pound's tactical decision to choose his *exempla* from the entire domain of human culture, his ability to develop a technique flexible enough to encompass prose documents and lyric refrains, his refusal to accept any material as being beyond the absorptive capacity of his poem, is among his most significant contributions to modern poetics, and remains uncompromised by the specific arguments of his epic.

"How is it far, if you think of it?" (LXXVII:465), the poet asks. In the "now" of our need, guidance from any source is welcome. There is no *a priori* reason that such guidance cannot be selected according to the exigencies of a particular moment and still be understood as initially belonging to a specific temporal nexus. Time-as-contingent-history and time-as-ideal-incarnation: it is these two perceptions that should have fashioned a new synthesis, a present that was both immediate and historical while still partaking of the *forma* of a timeless harmony. Myth and history could have been joined only in a socially just commonwealth whose "temple is holy because it is not for sale" (XCVII:676), a new *polis* that incarnates an ideal order and yet remains a concrete, temporal creation. It was to this goal that *The Cantos* were dedicated for numerous years, and it was the shattering of this dream that burst the poem asunder in its wake. *The Cantos* were intended to mirror, in verse, the contemporary political and ethical fulfillment of history's deepest hopes—not the abolition of time as historical development. Instead, the poem was left to reflect the fragmentation of its world, written not in the accents of an instructor to the entire tribe, but with the sorrow of a fellow victim, "a man on whom the sun has gone down / . . . of no fortune and with a name to come" (LXXIV:430; 439).[14] History, time, and his epic poem had finally been condemned to remain a series of "drafts and fragments." To claim any higher unity would only have been another version of the *"gran' rifiuto"* already rejected long before.

· · ·

The "world [is growing] ahistorical in a sinister sense. . . . All specifically modern art can be regarded as an attempt to keep the dynamic of history alive. . . ."
—Theodor Adorno[15]

"But the beauty is not the madness
Tho' my errors and wrecks lie about me
And I am not a demigod,
I cannot make it cohere."
(CXVI:796)

As Donald Davie has justly observed, Pound's repeated confessions of failure, expressed both in interviews and in numerous passages of *The Cantos* themselves, have satisfied no one. "On the contrary one gets the clear impression that for Pound to confess his faults is almost worse than having committed them. For the lines of battle are drawn: one is 'for' modernism, or else against it; and for Pound . . . to waver in his place . . . is profoundly demoralizing for ally and adversary alike."[16] Poundians have offered, in explanation for the anguished self-reproaches of the poet's last years, his old age, the psychological depression following his release from St. Elizabeth's, and even domestic tensions among the members of his immediate family. Although such tactics are obviously inadequate, Davie's point about *The Cantos* as a canonic text of modernism regularly attacked or defended *en bloc*, though true, also does not bring us any closer to an understanding of the work's own, internal disintegration.

Indeed, all of these statements about the poem's "errors and wrecks," including Pound's own, are only partial truths—*The Cantos* were not "completed" for reasons that lie at the heart of the whole project, and which have rarely been adequately or even reasonably explained. The relative "failure" of *The Cantos* is dependent upon the very objectives with which he embarked upon his poem. This statement by no means lends support to trite objections that no single man could know enough to write an epic such as Pound envisioned, that if only he had studied St. Thomas, Karl Marx, or some other suitable authority, he might have found an intellectual scaffolding sufficiently rigorous to guarantee the poem's coherence. *The Cantos'* disintegration has little to do with how much or how little Pound actually *knew* about history or economics or religion. Rather, he was from the beginning caught in an irreconcilable dilemma. He wanted *The Cantos*, as was said at the beginning of this study, to be true to two spheres: in the subjective, inner dimensions of his own mind and poem, and also in the objective, public world around him. The extent of Pound's artistic ambition was at once more fiercely arrogant and more modest than has been recognized, since to him *The Cantos'* "resolution" required, indeed demanded, confirmation in the realm of external, communal events. His poem was to push the Romantic theory of "organic growth" to its limits by taking as its model not a single plant but the very history of his age. An "ending" in one sphere (the Poem) without a parallel resolution in the other (the Tribe's *praxis*) would have underminded the correspondence between word and world on which *The Cantos* as an epic poem were themselves built. Such an ending, that is, would have removed even the "now" of *The Cantos'* own time from the realm of lived, historical experience. For all Pound's freedom with linear time, the historicity of his own present remained *the* inviolable *donné* of his epic, one he was unwilling to sacrifice for the formal autonomy of *poésie pure*. This is the principal reason Pound had, so misguidedly, to insist a single generation could establish a just commonwealth. If the Holy City were attained only in his mind, that triumph could never, by itself, fulfill the original demands of his poem.

Even Pound's initial hesitations in embarking upon a modern verse epic testify to the strain he already sensed between two visions, an aesthetic versus a social ideal of harmony: "But the man who tries to express his age instead of expressing himself, is doomed to destruction" (*GB*:102). Although we may consider his choice of Mussolini's Italy singularly wrong-headed, *The Cantos* required some actual dispensation, some visible public order, to synthesize the two visions. Walter Benjamin said that Fascism tends to aestheticize politics, while Communism politicizes aesthetics. In this sense, Pound was neither a Fascist nor a Communist since *The Cantos* consistently try to do both things at once. They seek, that is, to derive a direct political and economic instigation from works of art and religious rituals, while, at the same time, treating contingent historical determinants as if these were aesthetic absolutes.

However, the truly dreadful thing about Pound's aesthetic "invention" of Mussolini (and it was clearly always an impossible, almost feudal idealization, maintained long after most Italians had abandoned Il Duce) is that we can*not* call it just that, cannot hide behind the notion that Mussolini's New Order is a "fiction" the poem had to create in order to assure its own coherence. This refuge is denied us because the Fascist state's "virtues," by the poem's own exigencies, had to be politically and socially verifiable, had to be an objectively demonstrable proof that Pound's instincts were not wrong, that politics and aesthetics could be harmonized to the disadvantage of neither. Pound is thus "responsible" for his praise of Mussolini in a way fundamentally different from, say, Pindar's encomia on Hieron, tyrant of Syracuse, or Louis Aragon's odes to Stalin. Mussolini's presence in *The Cantos* is intended to satisfy a need that is at once aesthetic and political, and it is no good to label Pound as simply another misguided and socially naïve artist. There are times, I think, when it is less demeaning to give a man "credit" for his worst errors than to remove from him the capacity to err. Pound had indeed "hitched his sensibility to efficiency," the efficiency of a despotism whose severity was mitigated primarily by incompetence, and the poem, as well as the man, should be permitted the responsibility of its own misjudgments.

From the beginning of *The Cantos* to the end of World War II, Pound was determined to believe that the world could be rectified in one generation, that the Holy City could be constructed during his own life-span. Logos and Mythos, temporal achievements and timeless patterns of order, were to find their synthesis not by authorial fiat (the solution open to a lyric poet) but by the actual practices of the Italian Fascist and corporate state. The instant when, in the stockade at Pisa, Pound finally admitted that this hope had been destroyed, that he was left, "As a lone ant from the broken ant-hill / from the wreckage of Europe, ego scriptor" (LXXVI:458), the poem he had hoped to write was doomed.[b]

The many ingenious and devoted attempts to show that the poem *is* unified, that the separate narrative and thematic codes do finally merge, are not only blatantly untrue to the actual statements of the text, they also misunderstand the essential nature of Pound's project, and for the epic tale of the tribe unwittingly substitute the type of self-sufficient lyric he expressly did *not* wish to write. *The Pisan Cantos* are more tragic than we have usually recognized, not because they relate Ezra Pound's personal suffering, but because, amid the ruin of his social world, he is forced to acknowledge that for now the just kingdom exists *only* in the mind—*dove sta memoria*. All the outcries of an unbowed faith: "I surrender neither the empire nor the temples / plural / nor the constitution nor yet the city of Dioce" (LXXIV:434); "What thou lov'st well shall not be reft from thee / What thou lov'st well is thy true heritage" (LXXXI:521), which have become the touchstones of Poundian admirers, are cries of defeat as well as affirmations of human potential. The poet is left not to inhabit, but only to "*dream* the [ideal] Republic" (LXXVIII:478, emphasis mine). None of these statements are paradisial insights achieved through love; they are an attempt to preserve whatever can be salvaged from the wreckage of the poet's hopes. When Eugene Paul Nassar, for example, says that Pound was never arguing for one specific city of Dioce or a particular *paradiso*

---

[b] If such a claim seems extravagant, it can be illuminating to consider the analogous reactions of many Soviet poets in the period 1917-1928. Men such as Blok and Mayakovsky who had hailed the Russian Revolution wrote their long poems in the full conviction that their generation would see the establishment of a universal and ideal communistic state. With the introduction of the New Economic Policy and the gradual increase in Stalinist tyranny, these poets lost their first enthusiasm and, for the most part, emigrated or committed suicide. Pound, instead, held on to whatever parts of his original vision could survive the breakdown of Europe, and wrote some of his finest lines from the tensions of affirmation-in-defeat.

terrestre, that he was aware of transience and accepted it as inevitable, the critic is confusing the aesthetic and political strands of Pound's vision.[17] Like most commentators, Nassar takes the circumscribed, agonized affirmations of Pisa as the fulfillment of *The Cantos'* initial hopes, when they are, instead, the very abandonment of those goals. Pound, as we have seen, felt that any decline from a good government is not due to inherent limitations in the just society, but solely to human deviation from a theoretically stable system (cf. the Chinese Dynasty Cantos). In *The Pisan Cantos*, permanence has been achieved solely in the realm of myth (Artemis, Kuanon) or art (Pound's memories of Ford, Joyce, Yeats, and all the other "companions" of his youth); the world whose renovation the poem was intended to celebrate has been surrendered to those who

> . . . conquer with armies
> and whose only right is their power
> (LXXVI:463)

In such a world, even the noblest triumphs of the imagination must be tinged with a bitter awareness of defeat.

As the poem continues, the worlds of Mythos and History split ever further asunder. After Pisa, the link between the marvellously granted insights into a realm of calm and fruitfulness and the realities of contemporary history becomes ever more problematic until, by the time of *Drafts and Fragments*, the severing is almost total. *The Cantos*, of course, do not "abandon" history. Indeed, to do so would mean abandoning the poem's own character as an epic, and *Rock-Drill* and *Thrones* continue the historical discourse with as much determination as before. But now, at a point when, according to conventional expectations, Pound should be drawing his different thematic strands together, he refuses to show history moving towards any resolution, and he multiplies *exempla* and arguments as if the poem were still *in mediis rebus*. Pound does not, as in many epic conclusions, use even the most assured paradisial visions as a catapult from which to transcend history, nor as a higher synthesis within which to unify the diverse strands of his own poem. Indeed, as I have said, logically speaking, the experience of a mythic realm could never form such a "synthesis" since it was already posited as one of the two initial categories and must therefore itself *participate in*, not *constitute* the new, and never attained, higher stage. Ironically, Pound had anticipated his own predicament many years earlier when, in *The Spirit of Romance*, he had recognized that "an epic cannot be written against the grain of its time: the prophet or satirist may hold himself aloof from his time, or run counter to it, but the writer of epos must voice the general heart" (228). But only after 1945 was Pound finally compelled to realize that his interpretation of human history could never hope to "voice the general heart" of his contemporaries. The poet now explicitly acknowledges the wreckage caused by entertaining incompatible ambitions:

> That I lost my center
> > fighting the world.
> The dreams clash
> > and are shattered—
> and that I tried to make a paradiso
> > > terrestre.
> > > (CXVIII:802)

It is Pound's most cherished dream of all, the historical reinstatement of an earthly paradise that is here labeled the seed of all his errors. *The Cantos* disintegrate because Pound's different dreams cannot combine; they "clash," and in the process suffer a mutual "shattering." Critical attention has largely focused on the paradisial images of *Drafts and Fragments*, on the wonderful integration of the Na-Khi landscapes into the geographic code of the poem, but the tragic nature of much of these descriptions has, in the process, often been passed over. The emotional thrust of many specific images in these last pages is deeply sorrowful, even when the details seem to commemorate monuments of great beauty. Pound himself is acutely conscious of this shift in tone and calls the section "Θρῆνος this is a dying" (CXIII:786), a threnody or funereal dirge. Thus, he refers again to the great churches he has spent a lifetime admiring, but the ones he now mentions are not, like St. Hilaire or Santa Maria dei Miracoli, still in daily use; instead, they are tombs such as the Empress Galla Placidia's (d. A.D. 405) Byzantine mausoleum in Ravenna, or the deserted Venetian island of Torcello, whose cathedral is today used largely as a museum.

Artemisia now becomes the crucial figure of the poem's closing. First, she shares her name with a plant used for purification in the Na-Khi ceremonies, a plant which also carries tragic Biblical echoes of pain and grief—the genus artemisia includes wormwood and gall. Second, she is linked in sound to the lonely moon-goddess Artemis, whose lover, Endymion, lies in perpetual sleep: "Neath this altar now Endymion lies" (CX:779). And, finally, as Queen Artemisia, the widow of Mausolus of Halicarnassus (d. 353 B.C.), she erected the lavish tomb from which we inherit the word mausoleum.[c] In a sense, the Artemisia-Artemis-Mausolus triad crystallizes the dominant imagery of this section: the moon shining on a widow who mourns her dead lover now forever lost to her, frozen within his massive tomb, as Pound's own dreams of a just state remain unfulfilled within the pages of his epic.

Even the splendid Na-Khi rites, supposedly invoked for their paradisial authority, are often anything but optimistic in tone.[18] [2]Har-[2]la-[1]llü-[3]ko, the first of the ceremonies to figure in *Drafts and Fragments,* is a propitiation of the Demons of Suicide. An earlier reference, in the middle of *Thrones*—"His horse's mane flowing / His body and soul are at peace" (CI:727)—draws upon imagery from [1]D'a [3]Nu, the Na-Khi funeral ceremony, and contains a prayer that the weary spirit finally be granted rest among his ancestors. Even the Confucian echoes now harmonize with the melancholy strain in all these rituals. Pound no longer looks towards Confucian historiography, with its promise of a stable government, for guidance; instead, he turns to "Li Sao, Li Sao, for sorrow"

---

[c] Pound had long been familiar with the story of Queen Artemisia and Mausolus, and drew upon it in his *Homage to Sextus Propertius*: "Nor the monumental effigies of Mausolus, / are a complete elucidation of death" (*Per*:209). Yeats was also fascinated by the statues of Mausolus and Artemisia at the British Museum, and perhaps it was from him that Pound first learned of the royal couple. Cf. Yeats's "The Trembling of the Veil," in his *Autobiography*, New York, 1967, p. 101.

(CXIII:788), an epic by Ch'u Yuan (4th century B.C.), which narrates a search for consolation and knowledge among the Queens of Heaven. The epic poet, himself a Confucian administrator, was driven to suicide by court intrigues, and much of *Drafts and Fragments* reads like a desperate attempt to ward off the demons of self-destruction by holding fast to some tokens of beauty.[19] Critics have often made much of the more "positive" formulation Pound gave Eliot's famous lines from *The Waste Land* in Canto VIII: "These fragments you have shelved (shored)" (28). Although I have always found such arguments hard to understand—"shelving" seems to me more like an affectionate joke at Eliot's excessive "bookishness" than an optimistic transformation of his image—in Canto CX Pound appropriates Eliot's verse without any "hopeful" alteration: "From time's wreckage shored, / these fragments shored against ruin" (781). Pound's situation in *Drafts and Fragments* is, if anything, more despairing than that of the narrative voice in *The Waste Land* because the sense of old age, impending death, and personal failure all refer to situations the poem has itself already chronicled and partially created, and to which the previous one hundred and nine cantos give an incomparable resonance.

> The purifications
> > are snow, rain, artemisia,
> > also dew, oak and the juniper.
> > > > (CX:778)

It is "purification" Pound now seeks, not instigations, and the very term is inexorably linked with an offence that must be cleansed. Thus, when Pound again refers to Hell, he does not do so in the *persona* of Odysseus, godlike in his intellect and curiosity. Instead, he sees himself with "the mind as Ixion, unstill, ever turning" (CXIII:790). Ixion was bound on an endlessly spinning wheel as punishment for his arrogance and presumption, and in this switch from the Homeric hero to the justly punished culprit, Pound has, in characteristically indirect fashion, uttered one of his most severe self-criticisms.

Throughout *Drafts and Fragments* there is a sense that Pound realizes, almost with astonishment, how distant much of what he holds dear really is. Instead of asking "How is it far, if you think of it (LXXVII:465), he simply states:

> Felix nupsit,
>   an end.
> In love with Khaty
>   now dead for 5000 years.
>   (CX:779)

This time there is no more question of "making it new." In the last completed canto, Pound again quotes the opening of one of Dante's greatest short poems (cf. V:20), but now that the reference is to the events of his own personal and artistic existence, the effect is shattering:

> al poco giorno
>   ed al gran cerchio d'ombra
>   (CXVI:797)

Dante's sestina begins "al poco giorno e al gran cerchio d'ombra / son giunto, lasso!" Pound does not add the "I have come, alas!" to his borrowed image of a short day and a great arc of shadow, but his reticence only makes the reader all the more aware of the poet's infirmity. Even the seemingly triumphant image of "Crystal waves weaving together towards the gt/ healing" (XCI:611) becomes, in *Drafts and Fragments*, far less assured than before.

The crystal, the dazzling white light of paradise which contains all other colors within itself, represents Plotinus' Divine Unity, the emanation of the Holy City, and the visual equivalent of a Redemptive Love. But it is also the poem itself, and when Pound writes

> I have brought the great ball of crystal
>   who can lift it?
> Can you enter the great acorn of light?
>   (CXVI:795)

he is despairing not only of his own generation, but even of his hopes for future readers. He is no longer confident that they will be able to establish a just kingdom, or that the materials he has assembled in *The Cantos* can aid them in the endeavor. The fear that his own "palimpsest" (CXVI:795) is fatally marred by the "error of chaos" (CXIII:788), that it is only a tangle of unfinished words, is in many ways the most grievous self-reproach of all.

The last words of the entire epic are a gentle, almost muted, prayer for forgiveness. Only nature, the sound of the wind over the earth, can "speak" in the accents of the paradise Pound had hoped to celebrate. It is a startling ending, and a deeply moving one, but to see it as a "synthesis" seems like a mockery of the very anguish the lines so clearly contain:

> I have tried to write Paradise
>
> Do not move
> Let the wind speak
> that is paradise.
>
> Let the Gods forgive what I
> have made
> Let those I love try to forgive
> what I have made.
> (CXX:803)

Pound's choice of words in this final plea is painfully precise. His sins are so grave, and the consequences of his acts ("what I have made") so destructive, that although he can ask the Gods for absolution, all he feels justified in requesting from those he loves is that they *try* to pardon him. There is a terrible loneliness in this image of a man who fears that he has caused too much suffering to be forgiven by any human being, even by those dearest to him.

I have so far emphasized only the tragic aspects of Pound's final cantos, primarily as a corrective to other, more positive, readings, and to show that Pound's initial presuppositions about what an epic poem must be enforced the inconclusiveness and fragmentary nature of the "concluding" sections. Once history had failed Pound, *The Cantos*, because of purely internal, structural exigencies, would have demonstrated the splitting apart of myth and world, the inability to find any valid synthesis, irrespective of the poet's health or age. In ef-

fect, his refusal to provide a coherent ending demonstrates
how closely his conception of a modern verse epic adheres to
the criteria described in the Introduction. A less demanding
objective would have enabled Pound to unite his poem along
purely aesthetic and religious lines, and the last sections could
have demonstrated the joyful triumph of mythos over history
instead of the threnody of loss that the text so fully reveals.

Long before, in the prison-cage at Pisa, Pound had written
"I don't know how humanity stands it / with a painted
paradise at the end of it / without a painted paradise at the end
of it" (LXXIV:436). To me, these lines indicate the ambivalence Pound felt towards any purely religious transcendence.
Humanity cannot survive without the hope of some divine
and eternal principle at the end of its path, but it also cannot
endure the prospect that this truth exists solely at the *end* of its
journey. Mankind can only really live, can only fulfill itself, if
the paradise is created *in its midst*, if paradise becomes, not the
terminus of existence, but its daily condition. Yet *Drafts and
Fragments* are still full of affirmative visions of an uncorrupted
nature. Pound does find, as he wryly puts it, "a nice quiet
paradise / over the shambles" (CXVI:796), but surely the language here indicates considerable irony towards his own earlier and much grander hopes. Even at the end, the poem contains an assurance that "it coheres all right / even if my notes
do not cohere" (CXVI:797). Many years earlier in his *Guide to
Kulchur*, Pound had insisted that "Truth is not untrue'd by
reason of our failing to fix it on paper" (295), and now he
again affirms the presence of a divine pattern of order even
though his own text has failed to reflect it adequately. Perhaps
it is also permissible to find in these lines the hope that his
"dream"—the creation of a *paradiso terrestre* as a concrete,
human possibility—does cohere as well, in spite of the fact
that neither his age nor his poem could bear witness to such
an achievement. In any event, it is significant that this passage
occurs just before the vision of "A little light, like a rush light
/ to lead back to splendour" (CXVI:797), which I have
analyzed in connection with Plotinus' ἀγλαΐα. The text of
The Enneads also concludes with an affirmation of the truth of
the Divine Intellect, even while confessing the inadequacy of

the philosophical treatises in which that Intellect was cele-brated. At the end, amid all his sorrow, Pound has found a *caritas* catholic enough to call upon a "God of all men, none excluded" (CXIII:788), a sense of humility strong enough to pardon all his old antagonists. He charges himself "do not surrender perception" (CXIII:790). As indeed he never did. Unlike Hercules, the demi-god of *The Women of Trachis*, Pound could not make it all "cohere," but, unlike his admir-ers, he retained far too much "perception" to claim he had done so. "Time is the pure element of Pound's success."[20] So ran the judgment of William Carlos Williams, one of the first of Pound's "lordly companions," and among the last to die, leaving the poet ever more alone. The "now" in which the eternal and the temporal, logos and mythos, were to have been fused had turned dark, a "present" in which only "the dead walked / and the living were made of cardboard" (CXV:794). It was indeed "time" for *The Cantos* to end.

CHAPTER FOUR

• • •

THE LANGUAGE OF
THE TRIBE

"A program . . . is a core about which/not
a box inside which every item."
　　　　—Ezra Pound to Robert Creeley[1]

"Das Ganze ist das Unwahre."
　　　　—Theodor Adorno[2]

"The narrative is . . . to be regarded not as an end in itself but
as a vehicle for transmitting the material of the tribal encyclopedia which is . . . dispersed into a thousand narrative contexts."[3] Thus Eric Havelock describes the Homeric epics.
Pound, too, was attempting to write a tribal encyclopedia,
one adequate to the the needs of his own day, and thus, of
necessity, incorporating far more, and often quite different
kinds of, material than sufficed for the Homeric age. Pound
had far too sure a grasp of language to think any poem could
literally be a "mapping" of the real world, could offer any
one-to-one correspondence between the totality of the world
and the words of his poem. The Agassiz/Fenollosa method of
the "luminous detail" was explicitly designed to guarantee
that his selection of a few characteristic *exempla* from the
tribe's entire heritage was a "scientifically" valid technique
for isolating the necessary elements of a new cultural "program." Such an ambition requires, however, not only a very
definite notion of what constitutes the required historical and
ethical information, but also a view of language that assumes
the communicability in verse of that knowledge. In this chapter I want to explore Pound's sense of language itself, not so
much his specific poetic techniques, which have attracted extensive analysis, but the linguistic "ground" upon which the

entire project is based. Such an analysis will raise general aesthetic and linguistic issues ranging considerably beyond the procedure of *The Cantos*, but these excursions are required both to examine the poem's understanding of language, and to obtain a clearer view of the theoretical foundations of any modern verse epic. And, since the last chapter concluded with an analysis of *The Cantos'* gradual thematic fragmentation, it is with the same topic, the aesthetics of an ending, that the present investigation can most profitably begin.

Although Pound's theory of language is intimately connected to *The Cantos'* failure to achieve any final synthesis, the two concerns can, at the level of theory, initially be kept distinct. Accordingly, for the sake of clarity, I first want to raise the question of "endings" strictly on its own terms, to establish a framework in which the notion of a conclusion can be regarded as a valid aesthetic *problem*, and not merely as an axiomatic necessity. Once this has been achieved, the relationship between *The Cantos'* thematic structures and their linguistic grounding can more readily be demonstrated. Moreover, from such a foundation it is possible to derive an understanding of the poem's intentions at a level that is still more basic than its explicitly developed thematic concerns. But precisely because *The Cantos'* assumptions about the nature of language govern all of its procedures without ever receiving a programmatic articulation, the discussion will, at least at the beginning, need to look in a number of different directions for guidance. The purpose of such an exploration is not the imposition of a unique critical model, but rather the opening of a field of aesthetic *choices,* one too often blocked by the imposition of unexamined criteria, and irrelevant *a priori* demands.

Hitherto, in this study, a number of seemingly contradictory claims have been allowed to emerge. It is obvious that, unlike many Poundians, I regard his poem as incoherent and fragmentary, even, in some of its governing assumptions, as self-contradictory. Yet, I am not persuaded that the first of these conclusions is, in any sense, synonymous with an *en bloc* condemnation of *The Cantos.* There are grievous flaws in the work, lapses of taste as well as of judgment, but the absence of any grand resolution, of a convincing synthesis of its constituent elements, is not among them. Yet this "defense" of *The Cantos* is quite dissimilar from Donald Davie's wariness about the whole topic of "ideas" in the poem, and from his comparison of the epic to "a sea" of which it makes no sense to demand a "structure" or a "finish."[4a] Rather, it is Pound's ideas about what constitutes a valid historical explanation that are responsible for some of the poem's major contradictions, and it is also Pound's ideas about what an epic poem must be that assured *The Cantos'* inconclusiveness.

Before we venture any judgment about the aesthetic effects of the poem's final configuration, the question of "endings" needs to be posed with more care than it is usually granted. Paradoxically, Pound's refusal (or inability) to "finish" his poem may well constitute one of *The Cantos'* greatest strengths and itself represent a significant contribution to modern poetics.

I have taken up Davie's word "finish" with particular pleasure, because, in a different medium, it has already acted as the polemical focus for two competing aesthetics. Much of the history of modern painting, from the middle of the nineteenth century until the late 1950s, was seriously preoccupied with the question of "finish," with the *fini*, or polished and homogeneous surface that served as the trademark of an accomplished painting. "The *fini* is . . . a smooth and glossy painting, with shadings, transitional gradations between colors, and unbroken modeling of forms. This *fini* is associated

---

[a] Davie draws mainly upon Allen Upward and Yvor Winters in discussing "Ideas in the Cantos," but his distrust of Pound's success in presenting coherent intellectual arguments leads him to a defense of the poem that comes perilously close to Kant's famous definition in *The Critique of Judgment:* "by an aesthetic idea I mean that representation of the imagination which induces much thought, yet without the possibility of any definite thought whatever, i.e., *concept*, being adequate to it" (Oxford, 1952, pp. 175-176). However, since Pound intended *The Cantos* to have "ideas" in the sense of verifiable propositions directly relevant to the nature of government, art, religion, and history, these must be confronted—and criticized—on their own terms. One cannot adequately engage Pound's genuine realizations or justify his "errors and wrecks" by refining out of existence *The Cantos'* polemical and paedagogic dimension simply because it is articulated in a work of art.

with the qualities of probity, assiduity, professional conscience—and also discretion."[5] The purpose of "finishing" a
painting was to assure the critic and the purchaser that the artist knew his trade, that he had indeed labored to earn his pay.[b]
Yet, in a manner remarkably similar to much "new critical"
thinking about the seamless unity of a poem's language, the
fini "proves" the artist's labor by removing all of its actual
traces: "It cleans up, rubs out the traces of the real work,
erases the evidence of the brush strokes, glosses over the
rough edges of the forms, fills in the broken lines, hides the
fact that the picture is a real object made out of paint."[6] Paint
is deliberately idealized, its gross materiality and physical resistance disguised as much as the artist's technique can assure.
The subject matter of such art, even though it might, in a
crudely literal sense, have its origin in the world (e.g., Ingres'
portraits) was equally idealized, a harmonious *stasis* intentionally antithetical to the unstable domain of quotidian reality.

A profound revolution was inaugurated when painters like
Courbet refused to "finish" their works, when the physical
presence of paint and brush was openly acknowledged. Painting itself became defined not as the fixing of an ideal, but as
another human activity which is never complete, as a series of
attempts ("drafts and fragments") whose significance has little connection to surface unity or to formal completeness.
Curiously enough, the "roughness" of such art was retained
in the service of the artist's subject as much as in homage to
his medium. The visible evidence of the painter's struggle, of
his labor with the materials of his craft, "increases the impression of reality given by what is represented. By emphasizing
the painting as representation, the artist confirms the existence of what is behind the representation."[7]

Yet, as Clement Greenberg observed, "the paradox in the
evolution of French painting from Courbet to Cézanne is
how it was brought to the verge of abstraction in and by its

---

[b] The whole issue of a painting's "finish," and of the need for a work of art
to demonstrate a coherent resolution of its elements, was central to the
Whistler-Ruskin controversy: Pound's sympathetic understanding of Whis-
tler's "searches" and "uncertainties" is evident in his 1912 poem, "To Whis-
tler, American" (*Per:*235).

very effort to transcribe visual experiences with ever greater fidelity."[8] By the 1940s, American Abstract Expressionists like Pollock, de Kooning, and Kline, pushed the revolt against every kind of finish to its limit while, at the same time, rejecting any appeal to an external, represented subject. Their emphasis on the *process* of painting, on recording its failures as well as its triumphs, led to a complete discarding of all the conventional art-studio techniques by which a piece had traditionally been recognized as completed. The "act" of creating (hence "action painting") itself became the center of interest, a kind of drama established in large part by revealing the hesitations, the tensions, of actually producing a painting (different layers of paint, sudden changes of form, fragments from earlier versions, etc., were all retained as part of the final, "incomplete" picture). A "finished" work was considered not too difficult, but, paradoxically, too easy. It was regarded as an undesirable claim for closure, an unearned synthesis of the artist, his materials, and the world, at a time when both canvas and painter were supposed to demonstrate their openness towards the infinity of other possible decisions and choices any "closed" work systematically excludes.

Later in this chapter it will become apparent that Pound employed many techniques analogous to the open, inconclusive form of Abstract Expressionist painters, but that he did so from a significantly different and far more conventional aesthetic intention. Indeed, one of the major difficulties with *The Cantos* is that they rely upon specific modernist techniques for which an adequate aesthetic analysis exists, but do so on behalf of intentions that require an entirely opposed critical framework, one which was elaborated to deal with very different works. Pound's dilemma is that he unites aesthetic principles which most of modern art has kept rigorously distinct, and hence, in the absence of a sufficiently flexible critical methodology, his poem has rarely received the kind of theoretical investigation which its historical importance, as well as its intrinsic merit, should have ensured.

Before we take up this theme as the foundation for a discussion of *The Cantos'* language, however, it is useful to conclude our questioning of "endings" with a glance at some of the

other models proposed. The examples selected include painting, music, prose fiction, and even philosophical discourses,
and I am aware of the risks involved in proposing any very
precise analogy between the formal practices of one art and
those of a quite different one. Nonetheless, it is an explanatory strategy Pound himself often employed, and in a discussion of "endings" a series of comparisons seems the clearest
means of bringing certain critical assumptions into a sharper
focus. Pound often compares *The Cantos* to a fugue, and it is
interesting to notice that structurally a fugue need not end with
a resolution of themes such as characterizes a classical sonata
or symphony. As R. Murray Schafer, a Canadian composer
and musicologist who has edited Pound's musical criticism,
points out, "if one understands the nature of the fugue one
will realize that . . . the *Cantos* though numerically incomplete
have, nevertheless, always been structurally complete. Ideally
a fugue has no point of termination. It could continue its con-
trapuntal involutions without ever coming to a logical point
of rest . . . what brings a fugue to end is no long chain of
cadencing fireworks but a simple device which can be executed within as short a space as half a bar—the pedal point."[9]
   Even from the vantage point of more traditional literary
criticism, the notion of a "well-rounded" work, of a piece
that must always provide a satisfying "ending," has by no
means gone unchallenged. Throughout the second half of the
eighteenth century there was considerable interest in deliberately incomplete texts, in poems or paintings where the audience's imagination was left free to speculate on elements
never formally "closed" by the artist. David Hume's celebrated treatise "Of Tragedy" (1757) argued for the inherently
greater emotional power of an unfinished work and drew
upon the Elder Pliny (*Natural History*, 35) for classical support. Exactly a century later, George Eliot in a letter to her
publisher, John Blackwood, also stressed her fear that what is
finished is, of necessity, dead (1 May 1857): "Conclusions are
the weak point of most authors but some of the fault lies in
the very nature of a conclusion which is at best a negation."[10]
In recent times Theodor Adorno has shifted the grounds of
the argument from a purely aesthetic to a political and ethical

level, and his much-quoted aphorism, "the whole is what is untrue" from the *Minima Moralia*, emphasizes that in an age of societal fragmentation a genuine work of art must itself mirror that fragmentation and refuse the consolations of a tranquilizing synthesis. Adorno's defense of the seeming incoherence and fragmentary nature of much modern art is grounded upon the politico-moral assumption that "a successful work . . . is not one which resolves objective contradictions in a spurious harmony, but one which expresses the idea of harmony negatively, by embodying the contradictions, pure and uncompromised, in its innermost structure."[11] This is remarkably close to the Pound of *Drafts and Fragments,* a Pound who rejected any transcendence of the contradictions in his world through a purely aesthetic gesture, and who allowed the tensions of his own themes (time and eternity, history and myth, self and society) to remain manifest even at the cost of sacrificing *The Cantos'* formal unity.

Finally, one of the clearest statements of the whole modernist position was already clearly articulated in 1886 by Friedrich Nietzsche in *Beyond Good and Evil.* Nietzsche saw that far from being the paramount virtue usually claimed, "completeness" was itself a mystification, that the boast of having included everything necessary to the validity of even a single work was the most presumptuous claim of all:

> —Bad enough! The same old story! When one has finished building one's house, one suddenly realizes that in the process one has learned something that one really needed to know in the worst way—before one began. The eternal distasteful "too late!"
> The melancholy of everything *finished!*[12]

I have ventured upon this "digression concerning endings" in part because the topic itself is of such importance in modern aesthetics, and in part because of its very immediate relevance to all of the works with which this study is concerned. Any judgment on the coherence of *The Cantos, Paterson,* or *The Maximus Poems* will have to confront the same issues, and such a judgment should make explicit the foundations of its own critical assumptions. To situate the problem in a historical context does not determine the result of any particular inquiry, but it does provide a basis for seeing more clearly the questions at stake. Either critical judgment—the demand for a work's total coherence, or the acceptance of its heterogeneity—seems to me plausible and intellectually honest, but only if the underlying premises are understood.

Formalist critics (and those who insist on seeing *The Cantos* as unified are reluctant formalists, justifying his text by criteria Pound regularly subverted) feel that a poem really only exists *qua* poem if all its motifs do resolve, if the work exhibits an internal autonomy in which the strains of its various constituent elements (metrics, images, themes, etc.) form a new synthesis, a formal perfection exactly defining the privileged domain and character of art. In R. P. Blackmur's wonderful formulation, "Poetry is life at the remove of form and meaning."[13] And yet there exists a strong aesthetic and philosophical tradition which permanently strains against the barrier of that "remove," which insists upon a closer correspondence between word and world than modern formalism thinks desirable.[c] In any case, strictly speaking, neither linguistics nor philosophy, and certainly not literary criticism, has ever provided a definition of "unity" that a new set of texts has left unchallenged. The question of "what are the formal, linguistic conditions which will account for our sense that a poem or an essay is a unified structure of meanings and not merely a set of random sentences"[14] is still far more open than any hitherto proposed models will admit. Pound, as we saw in the Introduction, rejected the linguistic autonomy of *poésie pure*. By the time of the Post-Pisan cantos, his principles had also brought him to a rejection of the "laws" of unity and coherence. Or, more precisely, he was compelled to leave unresolved a set of antithetical narrative codes that he had always hoped to see unified.

---

[c] It is also true that Blackmur's *dictum* unconsciously reveals a specific, modern and Western, conception of "Life." At other times in history, or under different philosophico-political dispensations, life itself already manifests "form and meaning," and the function of art is only to be adequate to that stable and ordered reality. The notion of life as a chaotic, random flow which art can transcend or correct is itself an ideological interpretation disguised as a universal truth.

Undoubtedly, as Herbert Schneidau has argued, the examples of Ovid and Chaucer encouraged Pound from the beginning to reject the kind of straightforward, linear narrative that would greatly have facilitated the creation of a unifying conclusion: "Ovid's Metamorphoses are a compendium. . . . Chaucer's Canterbury Tales are a compendium. . . . The Tales have lasted through centuries while the long-winded mediaeval narratives went into museums" (*ABC of R*:92).[15] Yet this analogy cannot be given too much authority, since the inconclusiveness of *The Cantos*, as opposed to the poem's digressive, often anecdotal narrative, is fundamentally different from that already formally implicit in any compendium of tales. The fragmentation of *The Cantos* was not part of its initial premises; it only became inevitable due to Pound's continued insistence upon the explicit interpenetration of public events and poetic structure, even after the chance for a satisfactory political *imperium* was lost. A closer analogy seems to exist in the tradition of modern art itself, a tradition in which *The Cantos* already figure alongside novels like *Der Mann Ohne Eigenschaften* and *Naked Lunch*, operas like *Lulu* and *Moses und Aaron*, and paintings like de Kooning's "Gotham News" and Picasso's "Algerian Women" series, works to each of which the conventional criteria of a coherent surface and a satisfactory resolution of parts seems curiously irrelevant. *The Cantos*, like so many of these accomplishments, fail to realize any all-embracing synthesis, but this "failure" may well have salvaged the poem's own troubled authority. The history Pound's intellectual criteria so nearly drained out of the poem was reintroduced by its open, inconclusive structure, and, in spite of the potential textual rigidity threatened by its author's own (mis-)judgments, *The Cantos*, in the very act of "failing," ultimately did remain very much "a poem including history."[d]

· · ·

"Throughout all history and despite all academies, living language has been inclusive and not exclusive."

(L:347)

[d] I realize that this description seems to heroicize the tragic despair Pound felt about the fragmentation of his epic, about the failure of myth and history

If we now return to the earlier discussion of the *fini* in painting, an interesting analogy between the desire for a "closed"
and even-textured painting, and the linguistic attitudes of
formalist criticism, becomes apparent. For Ingres, as I indicated, the smoothness of surface and harmonization of parts
accomplished by the *fini* was directly linked to the idealization
of both his medium and subject. Ingres himself wrote, "The
brushstroke, as accomplished as it may be, should not be visible: otherwise it prevents the illusion, . . . it calls attention to
the process: *instead of thought, it betrays the hand.*"[16] Initially,
painters like Courbet wanted to abolish the *fini* and acknowledge the physical properties of their medium out of a desire to
emphasize the external reality of the objects painted. In other
words, the revolt against the *fini* combined a representational
aesthetic with a self-conscious emphasis on the artificiality of
the means of representation.

Today, this seems a curious strategy, because in most modern art the works which draw explicit attention to their status
as paintings, which record the struggle of an artist with his
medium, avoid any notion of representation. Paintings by
Pollock, Rothko, or Kline strive for a kind of *peinture pure*
whose "subject matter," like the "themes" of *poésie pure*, is
the autonomous process of its own unfolding. Such a historical perspective is particularly relevant to Pound, because *The
Cantos* are written in a language whose intentions and modes
of presentation occupy antithetical positions in modern aesthetics. On the one hand, Pound remained firmly committed
to a referential view of language. He repeatedly insists upon
the direct connection between the discourse of poetry and that
of the social world. In place of the "negative discourse" of

---

to cohere in a new dispensation. To see *The Cantos* entirely as a heroic
achievement would distort the work as much as any claim for its unity. But
there is an important distinction between recognizing the courage in Pound's
refusal to settle for an inauthentic resolution, and using that recognition—
contra Pound—to ignore the very real "failure" which *The Cantos* record. As
an epic, that is, *The Cantos* rightly express their ultimate inability to fashion a
new synthesis for the tribe as a bitter defeat. However, if one considers *The
Cantos* as one man's *attempt* to write a modern verse epic, it is perfectly
legitimate to applaud Pound's fidelity to the imperatives of his initial project,
and to acknowledge that only the poem's "incoherence" saved the integrity
of its historical foundation.

Mallarmé, which "attempts to isolate the act of signification from its results, that is, from the formation of a signified,"[17] Pound sought a "positive speech" whose signifieds were validated in the public realm of mankind's entire history. Yet he did not conclude that such a view entails, as it did in the traditional aesthetics of representation, a language "so constructed as to dissolve its signifiers in the very process of forming a signified."[18] Far from treating language as a transparent medium, present merely to convey a privileged signified, *The Cantos* constantly assert their own literariness, their status as a poem. Pound's preoccupation with the materials of his craft, with the power of language, is, in this sense, analogous to Courbet's or Cézanne's rejection of the *fini*, not to the Abstract Expressionist abolition of an external subject matter: it is intended to assure a more scrupulous fidelity to the world the language is re-presenting in the domain of art.

Critics have often marvelled that a writer as committed to the social efficacy of verse as Pound, someone who stressed the need for maintaining a direct link between poetry and living speech, could have produced a poem so manifestly "difficult," so full of seemingly autonomous signifiers as *The Cantos*. Yet this apparent contradiction stems directly from a stance that combined a very modern technique with a determinedly conservative aesthetics. Unless we are able to follow Pound's linguistic intentions, especially when these violate the cherished assumptions of *both* formalist and realist theoreticians (by uniting their presumably mutually exclusive positions), we risk seriously misunderstanding the entire foundation of *The Cantos*.

Pound joins the "modernist" preoccupation of a struggle with language, of a textual surface whose signifiers appear to exist in an absolute and undecodable privacy, with a far older, representational, notion of literary discourse. Essentially, he can unite the linguistic features of *poésie pure* with a rejection of any *fini*, can incorporate a plethora of seemingly autonomous lexical, rhythmic, and even "painterly" signifiers into a text that insists on the referential nature of its discourse because of his astonishingly comprehensive sense of the world to which that language refers. Because the world itself, both in its purely natural aspect and as a historical realm of human

achievement, is seen as inherently significant, because the interaction of men, earth, and gods can assure the presence of a
wholly sufficient beauty, Pound's language need not transcend the world in order to attain a higher perfection. The
reaction against the "priority of the signified" of classical aesthetics was based in part on a conviction of the poverty of the
phenomenal world when compared to the infinite possibilities
of linguistic creation, and in part on the necessary vulgarity
(or political cooptation) of any discourse that affirmed its link
to the polluted speech of the public realm. Pound, however,
understood that the options available to literature were not restricted to a choice between the poetic absolutism of a "negative discourse" or the banalities of journalism and social(ist)
realism. The goal remained "to purify the language of the
tribe," but unlike Mallarmé's, this purification would give
back to the tribe a language worthy of its own possibilities
and adequate to its real needs—it was not intended to ground
a poetics purified of all social complicity. Pound's signifiers
could be so dense, allusive, and intricate because the domains
which they represent are equally so, are capable of providing a
signified for the most complex linguistic manifestation.

   As an illustration, one can examine two of Pound's characteristic pronouncements about language, pronouncements
that articulate the aesthetics so often regarded as mutually
exclusive:

A. I believe in an ultimate and absolute rhythm as I believe
   in an absolute symbol or metaphor. The perception of
   the intellect is given in the word, that of the emotions in
   the cadence. It is only, then, in perfect rhythm joined to
   the perfect word that the two-fold vision can be recorded.

   (Trans:23)

B.

in

discourse

what matters is

to get it across e poi basta

(LXXIX:486)

Pound's comments, in the Introduction to his translation of Guido Cavalcanti, certainly seem to belong to the realm of *poésie pure*, to conventional affirmations of an absolute poetic discourse far removed from all questions of communal speech. One could argue that in a preface to the work of a thirteenth-century lyric poet, Pound chose to emphasize only one part of his entire aesthetics, but such a solution, although in part justified, also seems facile, since the entire passage obviously expresses one of his most sincerely held beliefs. However, if the comments are examined more closely, what emerges is not a defense of linguistic autonomy but a very rich and personal notion of representation. The word as a purely *written* signifier fixes and communicates an intellectual perception, a signified whose content belongs to the realm of verifiable ideas and intuitions. The *sound* of the word and the combination/juxtaposition of different acoustic units (phonemes, syllables, whole words or lines, etc.) "gives" a mood or feeling, an emotion which the rhythm "creates" only in so far as it is adequate to an already posited human state. Notice, as well, that in life the two psychological manifestations—intellectual perception and emotional reaction—arise together and form a single manifold. Yet language may with perfect success convey *one* of these and still fail to "give" the other, whereas if the perceptions were themselves linguistic in origin, there could be no question of a partial communication. Poetry can make permanent, it allows the communication of human ideas and feelings, but it is not a closed, self-reflexive system. The terms "absolute and ultimate" do not, as they would for Mallarmé, designate the poetic *autonomy* of the symbol and cadence, but rather their optimal *correspondence* to a human condition, their degree of fidelity to an intellectual-emotional complex, which itself is not necessarily a linguistic phenomenon. Thus, in 1919, writing in *The New Age*, Pound declares that ". . . the poverty of modern art movements lies in the paucity of the mental reference of the artists,"[19] and, in Canto XCVIII, Pound condemns an excessively mechanical rhythm, not, as we might expect, for its melodic dullness, but because it results in a distortion of the poem's intellectual precision: "and as for those who deform *thought* with iambics"

(687; emphasis mine). Language, that is, remains mimetic, even if its subject is a single moment of intense consciousness, and its form a highly wrought literary *ballata*.

The lines from the midst of *The Pisan Cantos*, my second example, are especially surprising since their immediate context is one of the most highly allusive, personal, and even, in the conventional sense, "lyrical," of the entire poem. Yet they seem to propose a thoroughly utilitarian conception of language, a privileging of the signified as total as that in any realistic tract. However, a few lines earlier, Pound had playfully begun to notice how the appearance of birds on a wire "writes" a musical score—"4 birds on 3 wires, one bird on one / . . . 5 of 'em now on 2; / on 3; 7 on 4" (LXXIX:485-6)—and then compared the creation of poetic form to the art of incising a figure in stone, or of casting a statue: "the imprint of the intaglio depends / in part on what is pressed under it / the mould must hold what is poured into it" (486). Thus, one can immediately situate his comments about "getting it across" in discourse within a context of aesthetic speculations that describe how the actual materials of an art and its formal subject matter must cooperate, how the artist must learn to respect both his medium and his themes. Yet, it is also clear that Pound means his exclamation about "what matters in discourse" quite seriously. The crucial word in his phrase, however, is "it," the subject which the discourse must somehow transfer to the hearer/reader. In the comments from the Cavalcanti Introduction, that "it" was a complex intellectual-emotional perception, one requiring a "perfect rhythm joined to the perfect word" simply in order to "get it across." By the time of *The Cantos*, that content has become far more intricate, its subject matter (the tale of the tribe) so richly layered, so various and multiple, that even the most transparent and purely functional language will, in its final articulation, be at least as complex as any Mallarméan lyric, intent only upon its own *via negativa*.

In both passages, then, Pound maintains that writing demands a supreme craftsmanship, that language must be cared for as a sculptor cares for the stone he has quarried and the tools with which he cuts, but he avoids any onesided empha-

sis on either the signifier or the signified to the exclusion of
the other. In this double focus, Pound's understanding of language rejoins the description of his ambitions for a modern
verse epic proposed in the Introduction. An epic is addressed
to the entire tribe as a collective and draws upon the audience's collective heritage. Pound thus felt at liberty to narrate
whatever might persuade his readers to apply the possibilities
latent within that heritage to their own lives. There is an underlying assumption, moral rather than anthropological, in
presenting so many different cultural situations: the hope that
seeing certain human experiences and institutions expressed
in a wide variety of contexts will make us more open to the
possibility for change and reform in our own sphere. Apollonius of Tyana, John Adams, or I Yin are not included in the
poem for picturesqueness, but in order to persuade the audience of the foolishness inherent in treating contemporary
values and practices as the only ones conceivable.

Similarly, since Pound believed that "the gods" did, in fact,
exist, that the tribe's religious and mythical symbols were
manifestations of universal truths, *The Cantos* could draw
upon the most traditional literary archetypes without severing the bond connecting word and world. The "myth-kitty,"
about whose bankruptcy Philip Larkin spoke in the 1950s,
remained very much full and available for Pound, and his language could refer to "Bright gods and Tuscan, back before
dew was shed" (III:11), because he was sure a sufficiently
acute perception of the world would find something real to
which these words exactly correspond. The language of myth
and belief, just as much as that of historical discourse, is designed to "get across" truths whose objective status is assured
irrespective of the poem's success in achieving the best formulation.

Pound is willing to use all the devices of post-Mallarméan
lyric verse, from a complex typographical deployment of the
poem's spacing, to a total freedom from normal syntactic and
grammatical sequence, but he does so on behalf of a highly
complex notion of *mimesis*. In his theory, there exist a number
of permanent truths, capable of widely various manifestations
and metamorphoses; equally important, there is a series of

contingent, time-bound, and historically verifiable "facts." Language is the medium in which both of these subjects must find a memorable form, must be communicated to the tribe, but subject and expression do not constitute an identity. There is reference in *The Cantos* but no illusion of presence, no idea that the language of poetry is a kind of divine performative utterance creating *ex nihilo* what it names. Presence and generation are placed in the world of nature and social activity (in which language plays a role, but as one *among* a series of forces), not in the confines of a literary text. As a result, the poet constantly confronts the limitations of his own technique and knowledge, his need to learn more about what the tribe requires, and how best to narrate that information (hence the title *A Draft of XXX Cantos*, with its suggestion of openness towards future revisions and alterations). But he need never despair of the potential narratability of the tribal heritage *per se*.

The Cantos are a poem which struggles to achieve, not a distance from the world, but an adequacy to that world's inherent complexity. Pound's ambition is not the purification of language from the corruption of public reference, but the purification of those public referents themselves. The epic is intended as the rediscovery and celebration, in an appropriate discourse, of certain purified social, aesthetic, and religious practices directly available for communal appropriation, and as a critical *exposé* of their impure existing counterparts. Thus, the self-conscious theme of the work's own creation, of the artist's struggle with his medium, is one aspect of the epic, but it does not, as in so much modern lyric verse, become the text's sole or even dominant concern. Language itself cannot be an epic's primary theme, any more than the poet can be an epic's central hero. The "anxieties" surrounding both were, as we shall see in the next chapter, far from negligible, but their significance was constantly linked to other, and in Pound's eyes more pressing, crises.

•   •   •

"Basil Bunting told me that the *Cantos* refer, but they do not present."

—Ezra Pound to Allen Ginsberg[20]

"The world doesn't spend all its time reading books, and we all assumed that they do. We have far too many references . . . that will weigh against us as the century goes on."

—Basil Bunting to Jonathan Williams[21]

There is one aspect of Pound's poetics towards which I have constantly gestured throughout this chapter, but which has not yet been confronted directly. That aspect is, of course, the "difficulty" of *The Cantos*, the fact that many sections simply do not mean very much, even to the most sympathetic reader, without extensive annotations. Moreover, for other, more immediately accessible cantos, a knowledge of Pound's sources is still of great help in enriching both our aesthetic appreciation of the poem's technique, and our ability to follow its argument. This is an ungrateful topic for analysis, because every reader's situation (i.e., the amount of extra-textual information he requires) is so different, and every reaction so personal (i.e., how much of an irritant or stimulus will the necessity to consult reference works constitute?) that any general statements seem particularly hazardous. One fact, however, is clear: the argument by some of Pound's admirers—that the text can be understood in any significant sense without external aid—is a pure fiction. It seems to me dishonest to pretend this is not the case, and little can be gained defending Pound on untenable grounds.

However, once this truth is admitted, a number of qualifications are possible. The first is that Pound tends to repeat his favorite *exempla* throughout the poem, often in new contexts and with a meaning that is made richer by a cumulative accretion of specific instances. Thus, one may not know much about King Deioce's seven-walled city, nor about Mont Ségur, Excideuil, and the Abbaie de Chasse Dieu, let alone about the various Chinese and Japanese "holy places," but, simply by following their textual appearance, we find that the single theme of a constantly endangered sacred temple-city as the locus for a civilized society comes into sharp focus. The second qualification is that today almost any text with references to the literary tradition requires a heavily footnoted edition, if not an annotated index. Yet neither of these qualifications, although true, is very powerful. If the meaning of the temple-city, and even of some of the Chinese characters, does emerge with a patient and recollective reading, this is just not the case with Pound's transcriptions from *The Eparch's Book* and Paul the Deacon's *History of the Lombards*, nor with his extensive reliance on Couvreur's edition of the *Chou King*, etc. Pound virtually admits as much, when, in the midst of his incorporation of *The Eparch's Book*, he suddenly breaks the surface of the text with an assertion whose very presence indicates considerable unease: "If we never write anything save what is already understood, the field of understanding will never be extended. One demands the right, now and again, to write for a few people with special interests and whose curiosity reaches into greater detail" (XCVI:659).[e] Without massive external aid one can read large parts of *The Cantos* only by the Romantic technique of a *recherche des beautés*, a searching for individual poetic "gems" with a happy disregard of the awkward pages separating the discrete magic moments. Similarly, the argument that numerous other works also require factual explanation is only of limited value, since the sheer mass of annotations necessary to understand *The Cantos* is vastly in excess of that needed for most major literary achievements. There comes a point when a sufficient difference in quantity becomes a difference in kind, and this, I believe, is true of *The Cantos*' dependence upon its readers' familiarity with arcane, secondary sources.

The effect, however, of such a procedure remains an open question. Many readers, myself among them, have found a great deal of pleasure in following the suggestions of *The Cantos*, in going to their sources not merely to see how Pound used them, but for knowledge interesting in its own right.

---

[e] In this passage from Canto XCVI and indeed at numerous points throughout *Rock-Drill* and *Thrones*, Pound has clearly abandoned the hope of reaching any audience except for the most devoted students of *The Cantos*. The tribe whose collective heritage was to be the poem's principal concern has been reduced to "a few people with special interests." This narrowing of the poem's intended readership is perhaps the clearest sign of Pound's own recognition that, after Pisa, *The Cantos* could no longer aspire to be more than a partial, unresolved series of "drafts and fragments," a step toward the new tale of the tribe, rather than that epic itself.

Still, such a reaction, although obviously not unusual, is just as obviously far from universal. People who are quite willing to devote considerable effort to "difficult" poetry (the texts of Mallarmé or John Ashbery, for example) still balk at the prospect of a work whose understanding cannot be derived from even an extended number of long and patient readings. It is hard to criticize such a decision, one based upon perfectly justifiable aesthetic criteria. On the contrary, it is Pound's poem that constitutes the exception, and, like all exceptions, it must establish its own, and perhaps even idiosyncratic, claims. *The Cantos* require *students*, something quite different from the scrupulous and attentive *readers* demanded by even the most intricate texts (although Pound's poem certainly needs the latter as well). In many ways, this is not a requirement that should be encouraged among those a writer can reasonably expect from his audience, and readers who regard it as a violation of the contract governing the mutual demands that poet and public may place upon one another have strong grounds for their complaint. Nonetheless, although I think that *The Cantos* do, at least for long stretches, justify this exceptional demand by the force of their aesthetic and intellectual interest, a strictly formal justification already exists in their singular ambition to narrate the tale of the tribe, a justification based upon the very linguistic principles I have been describing.

It is a truism that a "tribal encyclopedia" cannot possibly present in sufficient detail even a scattering of the information required to generate a renewed political, ethical, and cultural awareness. This is especially so with an author who, like Pound, attempted to incorporate wisdom from a multitude of cultures, who sought, long before the notion became fashionable, to break with the long tradition of Occidental ethnocentrism. As the poem progressed, Pound drew upon ever more and various types of cultures, championing, if not a "global village," then certainly a global perception. But, as the *exempla* began to multiply, and the types of details selected became more intricate, he had little choice but to *refer* to subjects *The Cantos* consider essential but could not *present* in any extended way. The "method of luminous detail" gradually became less a means of summarizing the central aspects of a given period or sensibility than a way to whet the reader's appetite to learn more about a particular topic.

This is a serious change, and it points to a distinction often ignored by critics. When, for example, Pound quotes a single phrase by St. Ambrose, "Hoggers of harvest" (LXXXVIII:581), he certainly does not expect us to read all of the Saint's writings. Rather, this "luminous detail" is intended as a kind of synecdoche, a striking formulation standing for the whole Medieval Church's view of fiscal honesty and for its condemnation of usury. But, when Pound opens Canto XCVII with the lines, "Melik & Edward struck coins-with-a-sword, / 'Emir el Moumenin' (Systems p. 134) / six and ½ to one, or the sword of the Prophet" (688) this "luminous detail" has quite another purpose.[22] It is intended to send us to Alexander Del Mar's *History of Monetary Systems* to see how a nation's political self-determination must coincide with control over its own currency.[f] Scholars who, like Max Nänny, see *The Cantos* as trying to gather all the "nuggets of wisdom" from the past, and record them in a memorable form in order to assure their survival, are quite correct about lines likes "Hoggers of harvest," but miss the very different purpose of the second type of "luminous detail."[23] Basil Bunting's fear that he and poets such as Eliot and Pound had relied too much on books seems more appropriate in describing this aspect of Pound's technique, and in *Rock-Drill* and *Thrones* references of the "Melik & Edward" type

[f] The citation is from Chapter IX, "Moslem Moneys," of Del Mar's book. In the 1895 London edition, the relevant passage reads, "In A.H. 67 (A.D. 686) Abd-el-Melik, being at that period involved in civil war with the Mardaites, bought peace of Justinian II, . . . by the payment of a tribute of 1,000 gold solidi or dinars per annum for ten years. Down to this time these coins were struck by Abd-el-Melik, with Roman emblems and legends upon them. Six years later the Arabian caliph, . . . determined to assert his independence of Rome, and by a token understood of all the world. He struck gold coins with his own effigy, holding a drawn sword, as afterwards did Edward III, when he renounced the same dread authority. . . . The monetary system of Abd-el-Melik consisted of coins of purely Arabian type and legend. The ratio between silver and gold was that oriental valuation of 6½ to 1, which marked for several centuries the line of separation between the Moslem and Christian States of Europe" (pp. 171-172).

begin to appear with increasing frequency, and at disturbingly short intervals.

An epic, as Havelock stressed, is (although far from exclusively) a kind of history book, and Pound's model, like that of the Enlightenment *philosophes*, was a "universal history" which can never be fully presented in a single text, but must constantly refer its readers to more detailed "local" studies. *The Cantos* are expressly (although again, far from exclusively) didactic in intent, but here the author himself is among those being educated, and the startling introduction of new topics at a time when the poem should be drawing its concerns together is meant both to show that an education is never over, and to communicate the enthusiasm attendant upon any fresh discovery. Pound's openness to new information, his willingness to sacrifice the formal coherence of a conventional poem for the sake of its shape as an "education," acts as a significant freeing of *The Cantos* from the static character of his actual historical beliefs, and returns a sense of motion and energy to a text that often threatened to become a series of frozen tableaux.

Moreover, Pound's language was, from the beginning, referential. The words of the poem were intended to direct readers to events and forces active in the world outside the text, and his increasing reliance upon the other *books* in which those events are narrated in greater detail, while undeniably often an irritating practice, is logically quite consistent. Pound's habit of pointing the reader to other writings, to books which themselves constitute one of the tribe's most enduring accomplishments—cf. Douglas' "increment of association"—reveals, not the arrogance of which the poet is so often accused, but a chastened sense of how limited is the knowledge any single work can encompass. Pound is equally convinced that, "with one day's reading a man may have the key in his hand" (LXXIV:427), and that "there is no substitute for a lifetime" (XCVIII:691). I believe the first statement applies to the universal truths, the general principles of ethics, government, and belief, which a man may grasp in a moment of intellectual/emotional illumination, and which can be fully *presented* through a single "luminous detail." The second declaration indicates the specific, factual context in which those principles have been manifested, their success or failure in the actual testing-ground of human history. For this type of knowledge even a lifetime is insufficient, and the aid of other studies to which *The Cantos* can *refer* is indispensable. Perhaps the proportion between the two kinds of perception should have been drastically altered. Certainly, in *Rock-Drill* and *Thrones* the number of passages written in a purely referential shorthand, incomprehensible without a knowledge of Pound's sources, increases alarmingly. Yet such a shift, it must be recognized, represents a change in degree only; the technique was present from the beginning and is a perfectly consistent outcome of his poetics. The real problem with Pound's procedure is less the specific difficulty of his references than the potential contradiction between this aspect of his narrative technique and the intentions of *The Cantos* as an epic *for* as well as *about* the tribe. *The Cantos*, after all, were committed not only to recording their audience's heritage, but also to having that record somehow influence the tribe as a whole. Yet Pound never expected his poem to be read by a wide audience. He did hope, though, at least for a considerable time, to reach those in a position to affect the course of public policy and communal behavior (cf., "History is a school-book for princes" LIV:280). For Pound, the proper audience of an epic need not include the entire tribe directly, nor even a particularly large percentage of its citizens, but it must speak to readers capable of putting the values it asserts "into action" for the general public good. Theoretically, it is at least possible that "luminous details" like "Hoggers of harvest" could serve as a reminder of an ethical and fiscal rectitude as necessary today as in St. Ambrose's Italy. Lines like "Melik & Edward," on the other hand, can never do more than provide material for academic exegesis and are really addressed only to the "tribe" of Poundian scholars. The ratio between the two narrative conventions maintained at different points in *The Cantos* seems to me an excellent index of Pound's own confidence in his poem as an epic capable of articulating values recognized as essential for the entire community. As that confidence wavered, the balance became increasingly weighted towards the presentation of his private arcana. Yet it is only just to acknowledge that even this hermetic lore seemed to Pound to contain indispensable wisdom from which society as a whole might profit. No matter how esoteric the subject matter, or how peripheral it seems to *our* sense of the community's needs, it is never presented as an example of the poem's self-sufficiency. Irrespective of the practical obstacles to an immediate comprehension of its discourse, and even independent of Pound's changing attitudes towards his audience, *The Cantos'* language always remained, in principle, committed to a signifying world and a communicable *praxis*.

·   ·   ·

"I believe in technique as the test of a man's sincerity"

(*LE*:9)

"But the one thing you shd. not do is to suppose that when something is wrong with the arts, it is wrong with the arts ONLY."

(*GK*:60)

Because Pound was firmly convinced that "it is the business of the artist to make humanity aware of itself" (*LE*:297), stylistic precision becomes a political as well as an aesthetic imperative. Artistic excellence is a moral and social category, since good writing remains the essential source from which an adequate language is made available for everyone's use. Thus Pound unhesitatingly speaks of "the immorality of bad art" (*LE*:43) and compares the technical carelessness of the negligent writer to the "falsification" of a physician which may result in the patient's death (*LE*:43-4). It is obvious that in these statements Pound is concerned with technique as a necessary attribute, not of poetry's autonomous perfection, but of its social function. But he never insists that an author's conscious intention need be didactic. Rather, the communal nature and social use of language will, in itself, assure that a scrupulous technique is of public utility:

It does not matter whether the author desire the good of the race or acts merely from personal vanity. . . . In pro-

portion as his work is exact, i.e., true to human consciousness and to the nature of man, . . . so it is durable
and so it is "useful"; I mean it maintains the precision and
clarity of thought . . . in non-literary existence, in general
individual and communal life.

(*LE*:22)

In a sense Pound is here redefining and generalizing the
concept of "propaganda." Great literature need not argue for
any specific social policy or party program, it need not even
seem to engage the political arguments of its day, but in its
very attention to the state of language—a state Pound rightly
understands as historical and changing—it safeguards the
essential medium through which men order their world.
Pound's general attitude towards the relationship between
politics and language has, largely because of the abysmally
wrong-headed direction of his specific allegiances, often been
misunderstood. Yet in this sphere, as in so many others, his
convictions were closer to classical doctrines of the relationship between ethics and the state than to any modern ones.
According to Jürgen Habermas, for example, Aristotelian
"politics was understood to be the doctrine of the good and
just life; it was the continuation of ethics. . . . In the final instance, politics was always directed toward the formation and
cultivation of character; it proceeded pedagogically and not
technically."[24] Political leaders, in this conception, should be
educators, not administrators, and Pound's typically personal
variation on the theme is to entrust to the creative writer the
task of guarding the medium of that education, of, in effect,
being the linguistic conscience of political discourse.

It is from this foundation that Pound was able to argue for
an essential identity between the seemingly contradictory
roles of artistic craftsman and social critic. The identity was
not grounded upon an idealization of verse, but constituted
by the very function of language itself. The accurate use of
words is a necessary pre-condition of correct political and ethical, as well as aesthetic, activity.

The *mot juste* is of public utility. I can't help it. I am not
offering this fact as a sop to aesthetes who want all au-

thors to be fundamentally useless. We are governed by words, the laws are graven in words, and literature is the sole means of keeping these words living and accurate.

(LE:409)

Pound saw in the *mot juste* a crucial guardian of communal survival, and, long before Orwell made a similar insight the basis of some of his most brilliant essays, Pound warned about the concrete, social dangers of a bureaucratized "news-peak" divorced from the reality of human needs. He recognized that "if the terminology be not exact" the government itself will be unable to "conduct business properly" (GK:16), and was convinced that the corruption of language was the first step in a loss of civic responsibility and freedom.

> & of brain-wash
> 1st/ the symbol/
> corruption of Symbol
> (CVII:760)[g]

Pound was probably one of the few men for whom Flaubert's aphorism, "If they had read my 'Education Sentimentale' these things [i.e., the Franco-Prussian War] would not have happened" (SP:189), contains a literal truth. Confucian historiography is full of analogous comments about the social peril of ignoring the insights of purely "literary" texts. Achilles Fang, for example, says that the *Odes* even served as a kind of "straw poll" to test the *mores* of the Empire and are a characteristic example of the Chinese fusion of politics and poetry.[25] Pound's own instinctive reverence for the authority of the great writer was nourished by a singular combination

---

[g] In this regard, Pound's infatuation with Mussolini becomes all the more astonishing. The political and economic misjudgments that led Pound to champion Italian Fascism are, if pernicious, at least consistent with his general attitudes, but how he could not have been disgusted by the utter vulgarity and brutal chauvinism of the Duce's language is genuinely inexplicable. Even German writers like Heidegger and Gottfried Benn who went through a period of allegiance to the Nazi Party, were ultimately revolted by the regime's savagery and petit bourgeois philistinism. Pound, however, did not even seriously question his estimation of Mussolini until well after his 1958 release from St. Elizabeth's.

of Confucian doctrine with the nineteenth-century resurrection of the artist-as-seer.[h]

For Pound, there is no radical separation between his text and the world, between the language of poetry and society's public discourse, except when one or the other suffers a "falsification" and becomes diseased. Thus, in a revealing choice of words, he speaks of "Monetary *literacy*, sans which a loss of freedom is consequent" (CIII:732; emphasis mine). The basic principles necessary to establish an economically just society have already been described in various crucial texts. The failure to apply those principles is, therefore, a kind of illiteracy, a refusal to read the necessary documents, or an ignorant misreading of their content. In either case, Pound's own description stays within the discourse of textuality, of reading and interpretation. That is, he recognized in money a sign-system, a semiological code, whose signifiers could either correspond to the real signifieds of human activity (industrial production, trade, etc.) and natural bounty (the increase in domestic animals and crops), or be perverted into an arbitrary language whose referents are manipulated at will for the private gain of the usocracy and to the inestimable harm of its innocent users. The accusation of abandoning literature for economics makes little sense when applied to Pound, since money, like politics, was to him already a linguistic category, just as literature, in turn, had an essential role in the governing of the state.

In 1910, Allen Upward, anticipating by over 15 years the research of the Frankfurt School, and by more than 40 years the theoretical investigations of the *Tel Quel* group, wrote

[h] The great Austrian satirist Karl Kraus also linked a concern for language with political and moral honesty, and, like Pound, often quoted Confucius on the relationship between the accurate use of words and the possibility of attaining social justice. In his *magnum opus, Die Letzen Tage Der Menschheit*, Kraus showed his disgust for the attitudes that had led to and sustained World War I by narrating at least one third of his "drama" through direct quotations from contemporary newspapers, government pronouncements, war reports, etc. Kraus lets the society condemn itself simply by quoting back its own language. The shock in reading this book is that certain utterances—their form as well as their content—were even possible in an Austria that still prided itself on its "Kultur."

that "Words are, like money, a medium of exchange."[26] What happens when the economic exchange is thwarted, Pound witnessed in the Great War and subsequent Depression. Yet not until Pisa did he become convinced that his own solutions were condemned to political silence, that his social language, whether right or wrong, could no longer be "exchanged" against any public confirmation. By the time of his arrest, in other words, the necessary circulation between the words of the state and those of his poem had become irrevocably blocked.

·　·　·

"I shall have to learn a little greek
to keep up with this
but so will you, drratt you."
(CV:750)

"I would like to invent some kind of typographical dodge which would force the reader to stop and reflect for five minutes (or five hours), to get back to the facts mentioned and think over their significance for himself, and draw his own conclusions."
—Ezra Pound, *Money Pamphlet*, No. 6[27]

I have argued that language itself cannot be the dominant theme of an epic, and from the time of *A Draft of XXX Cantos* until *Cantos LII-LXXI* this is true of Pound's poem as well. Yet as *The Cantos* continue after Pisa, increasingly more space is devoted to the subject of a "just language," and the link between a healthy society and a care for words often becomes the text's explicit and primary concern. The analysis of legal documents like *The Eparch's Book* and moral-philosophical codes like *The Sacred Edict* in *Thrones*, and even the great increase in the number of ideograms presented throughout *Rock-Drill*, are part of Pound's attempt to demonstrate the authority and sources of an exact language. Hugh Kenner rightly says, "the governing science of *Rock-Drill* is natural growth. . . . The governing science of the next sequence, *Thrones*, is philology: luminous words and their meanings, seeds of mental growth."[28] Kenner's description already links both sections through the theme of "growth," but I think the relationship can be stated still more explicitly in terms of language and it indicates the changed emphasis in Pound's entire project.

After Pisa, Pound realized his epic could never be "finished" through the celebration of an existing just society. However, rather than abandon history entirely, he was intermittently still able to think *The Cantos* might serve as a sourcebook for future generations who would once more have a chance to inaugurate a decent political order. Hence the praise of embattled heroes fighting a corrupt environment; hence also Pound's effort to leave a record of full linguistic "sincerity" for the future to use. The language of the poem and the institutions of society should have participated in a common purification, but in the face of the failure of one side of the equation, the other became all the more important. Language can still be saved from the smashed ant-heap of contemporary history, and with it the record of the historical past can also be preserved from destruction. Indeed, amid the wreckage of his immediate political goals, the preservation of "the record" has become the only gift Pound can still offer to the tribe. It is precisely in terms of an offering that he begins to speak of the *mot juste* in *The Pisan Cantos*:

perfect 誠   the word is made

better gift can no man make to a nation.

(LXXVI:454)[1]

It is not that language has been divorced from politics; rather, the temporal horizon of its social efficacy has been radically deflected. Instead of being directed at the present audience, *The Cantos'* public discourse is now addressed primarily to the future. The work's actual present, on the other hand, is increasingly concerned with the private realm of the poet's own consciousness, since this domain and its artistic expres-

[1] The ideogram (ch'êng³) stands for "sincerity," which Pound glosses as "The precise definition of the word, pictorially the sun's lance coming to rest on the precise spot verbally. The righthand half of this compound means: to perfect, bring to focus" (C:20).

sion are the only areas he is still capable of immediately affecting. A linguistic record of sincerity *can* be compiled by one
author's solitary labor, but its application in the communal
sphere must await another age and a new set of opportunities.

Pound begins to regard his language less as a means of immediate instigation than as a testament, a monument of what
was possible even under the most inauspicious conditions.
The sense of encouraging achievements is still present, but the
immediate polemical urgency has been greatly diminished.
The prose passage in Canto XCVI, justifying lengthy incur-
sions into new domains, indicates that Pound now realized
political wisdom, not just aesthetic excellence—Binyon's
"Slowness is beauty" (LXXXVII:572)—can come into focus
only slowly and with much labor. Thus, Pound's science of
"luminous words" in *Thrones* is not, as one might have expected, based upon primarily aesthetic masterpieces. More
frequently the "seeds of growth" are planted in public documents such as Leo's edict specifying the trade and monetary
regulations governing Constantinople, or Sir Edward Coke's
Institutes of the Laws of England, which themselves reveal how
a few "luminous words," those of the Magna Carta, can unfold a pattern of justice rich enough to guide a nation for centuries. John Peck's suggestion, that Pound rhymes *lex, lexis*,
and λόγος, is an apt summary of the guiding associations in
Thrones.[29] The words of a just legal and economic order are
themselves a kind of poetry. Pound is so concerned with
Leo's or Coke's choice of words, with the fiscal and political
precision of their texts, because their care in speech parallels
his sole remaining power: the artist's private perfection of his
technique, which, by the public nature of language itself,
maintains a connection to the tribe's social *praxis* now closed
to Pound the individual.[j] Texts like these are linguistic/

---

[j] Earlier in this chapter, I discussed the modernist "critique of perfection,"
the hostility of many artists towards the ideal of a "finished" work. My praise
of Pound's "perfection of his technique" is not meant as a corrective to the
previous argument. The reaction against the *fini* certainly did not argue for
technical carelessness; instead, it rejected the idealization of the artist's
medium, the removal of the traces testifying to his struggles with his materials. Throughout *The Cantos* Pound sought the most effective and aes-

political "seeds of mental growth," but they survive today purely as words, signs waiting to be "made new"—like *The Cantos* themselves.

Yet if Pound is compelled to postpone the communal realization of his dreams, and to devote himself exclusively to the testamentary offering of a perfect word, he does not always do so with the paradisial equanimity usually read into the later cantos. There are frequent outbursts of frustration and impatience in the post-Pisan sections that are quite different in origin from those uttered before.

Earlier, Pound had been driven to rage by the refusal of the world to apply the insights of reformers such as Pietro Leopoldo and Major Douglas: "per forza, dam blast your intellex" (XXXVIII:190). It was always the very *simplicity* of the solutions, the possibility of their instant incorporation into a nation's legal framework, that provoked his anger at the delays, not any private crisis or sense of neglect. Now lines like "so will you, drratt you," although partially playful, also strain against a narrowing of his horizons; they betray his personal isolation, his restricted (quite literally and legally) access to the world. Pound's solitude is now that of a dishonored (not merely ignored) prophet, one who can no longer, even in his most confident moments, hope to "voice the general heart" (*SR*:228) of his own time. He now often defends his past actions, and protests that he was "not arrogant from habit, but furious from perception" (XC:606).[k] For all the marvellous clarities of imagery in *Rock-Drill* and *Thrones*, there is also a querulous impatience with his readers, a sense that since only the future will be able to recognize the justice of his cause, the immediate audience, except for "a few people with special interests" (XCVI:659), no longer represents a fit

---

thetically "perfect" technique possible, but he never tried to erase the evidence of his labor, and the poem amply records his continual changes of focus, self-corrections, etc. Even the most desperate and single-minded search for artistic perfection can co-exist with an almost violent rejection of the *fini*, as the example of Cézanne clearly demonstrates.

[k] Later, in Canto CIV, Pound even applies the same "defense" to Hitler ("Adolf furious from perception," 741), and it is impossible to see these outrageous lines as anything but a cry of willful defiance, an attempt to wound opponents who had become his judges and captors.

readership. I think much of the obscurity in these parts of *The Cantos*, their increasing reliance upon foreign languages (no longer, as before, accompanied at some point by an English equivalent), is part of that same alienation, a visible, textual shrug of "gran dispitto" from a poet incarcerated by his own country in a hospital for the criminally insane.[30]

The poem's public discourse, as opposed to Pound's recording of his inner, paradisial insights, strains under the intolerable pressure of no longer having any expectations of the immediate audience for whom it was, as an epic, initially destined. Future recognition, the compensatory hope of a mistreated lyric poet, offers much less consolation to the writer of an epic, and Pound's fragmented historical discourse, the multiplications and almost impenetrable condensations of his sources, is an indication that he often no longer knew for whom the text was being written. The political and economic language had, in a sense, finally become "autonomous," but it was an autonomy of defeat, enforced by his uncertainty about the future, combined with his sure awareness of present ruin.

I have chosen to emphasize the growing tensions in Pound's linguistic practice throughout *Rock-Drill* and *Thrones*, not from an ignorance of the many instances of poetic clarity, but because it is those instances alone upon which commentators have regularly seized. Paradoxically, however, one of the greatest sources of obscurity in the later cantos—the multiplication of unglossed ideograms—has a double function, only one of which betrays Pound's new distrust of and distance from his readers. The ideograms are also the linguistic link to the world of nature which Kenner calls the "center of gravity" in *Rock-Drill*, and they correspond perfectly to the philological excursions of *Thrones*. To Pound, the ideogram represents the one form of written language which has been used to build a society, but which is also based directly upon natural forces. Ideograms thus have a kind of double focus, pointing to both the world of human activity and to the unchanging patterns of natural energy and fruition.[1] Because Pound was convinced that signs granted by na-

---

[1] The Chinese character for writing itself, *wen*, already links nature and culture, social courtesy and the pattern of the stars. "The word *wen* signifies a

ture itself are infinitely richer than any conventionalized notation—"and from nature the sign" (CII:730)—the ideogram assumed a privileged, almost sacred, value in his eyes. By its joining of cosmic order and human observation, the ideogram, like a religious icon, can induce calmness and meditation.[31] It forces the reader "to stop and reflect," but it also compels the *poet* to go slowly, to draw each character with a care and patience that makes anger or bitterness impossible. The ideogram is a tangible sign of order in the cosmos, and its tracing is possible only when the hand holding the brush moves, for a few moments, in unbroken sympathy with that larger harmony. Pound had always longed for order, in politics, art, and even in his own sometimes unstable temperament—"or, 'Perché' said the Boss / 'vuol mettere le sue idee in ordine?' / 'Pel mio poema.' " (XCIII:626); "OR-DER / tò kalón" (*JIM:*128)—and the ideogram offered him both a graphic, visual representation of his desire, and a self-disciplining technique necessary to attain it.

As Christine Brooke-Rose and Suzanne Juhasz have observed, the ideogram is also a lexical equivalent of Pound's more conventional metaphors, built as these are out of compounds ("nymphs white-gathered," "shadow-wet," "glare-purple") that juxtapose natural elements without explicitly designating the connective terms.[32] The problem of sequence and connectives in language has been a major dilemma, at least since the eighteenth-century theoreticians, Condillac and Destutt de Tracy. As Foucault says, "If the mind had the power to express ideas 'as it perceives them,' there is no doubt that 'it would express them all at the same time.' But that is precisely what is not possible, for, though 'thought is a simple operation,' 'its expression is a successive operation.' "[33] The

---

conglomeration of marks, the simple symbol in writing. It applies to the veins in stones and wood, to constellations, represented by the strokes connecting the stars, to the tracks of birds and quadrupeds on the ground (Chinese tradition would have it that the observation of these tracks suggested the invention of writing). . . . The term *wen* has designated, by extension, literature and social courtesy." Quoted in: Jacques Derrida, *Of Grammatology*, Baltimore, 1976, p. 123.

ideogram is the one form of writing that seems to permit the notation of simultaneity: it makes possible the transcription of holistic experiences as opposed to the syntagmatic, linear notation of Western languages.

Von Humboldt, one of the heroes of science and language in the later cantos, and a direct intellectual ancestor of Frobenius, described the twin aspects of speech as *energeia* (creative process) and *ergon* (the object created, a kind of linguistic homologue of Spinoza's *natura naturans* and *natura naturata*). Fredric Jameson shows how these two principles have been taken up in modern linguistics as a distinction between *énonciation* (the act of enunciation) and *énoncé* (the completed utterance).[34] In this context, the ideogram is a kind of *ergon* or *énoncé* in which the history of its making, the creative *energeia-énonciation* is still fully visible and decodable.[m] This conception of the innate order and creativity of the ideogram, of its mediation between the co-equal realms of nature and culture, ensured its authority, making it seem to embody the very type of consciousness Pound thought crucial for a new civilization.

However, there is one difficulty in understanding Pound's veneration for the ideogram, a problem seldom raised by his explicators, but which obviously limits the accuracy of studies that see the poet as resurrecting the tradition of the *oral* epic. In his initial understanding of Chinese writing, an understanding he was not seriously to revise for many years, the ideogram has little sound value. Thus, its use in poetry would remove all the acoustic elements, the "perfect rhythm" which he had so often praised, and the "melopoeia" for which he had waged so many critical battles: cf. "[Poetry] is an art of pure sound bound in through an art of arbitrary and conven-

---

[m] Throughout this discussion, my description is, of course, based on Pound's own understanding of the Chinese written character. It is more important to understand the function of the ideograms in *The Cantos* than to criticize Pound for his imperfect knowledge of Chinese. In fact, however, as Joseph Needham says, "Of the 49,000 characters given in the great dictionary Khang-Hsi Tzu Tuen of +1716 not more than five percent are pictographs and symbols." (*Science and Civilization in China*, Cambridge, 1954, Vol. I, p. 32.)

tional symbols" (*SP*:33).[n] Leibnitz, one of the first Europeans to be deeply interested in the ideogram as a possible "universal language," had praised it expressly because it was easily learned by *deaf mutes*, hardly an encouraging recommendation for a poet with one of the finest metrical gifts in English verse. Paradoxically, however, this absence of sound, this stillness in which the eye alone must concentrate and sharpen its clarities, also gives the ideogram its unique role, as *one* element among the poem's various languages. The ideogram is uniquely suited as a "focus" for meditation because of the very priority it assigns to sight. The divine brightness of Plotinus and Erigena, the sunlight pouring down like rain in the Provençal troubadours and the *dolce stil nuovo* poets, finds its best graphic representation in a word that is also a picture, an image that must, like the phenomenon it records, be seen in order to convey its meaning. And, as the poem had already proved itself capable of absorbing prose, there is a sense in which the presence of such purely visual, mantric symbols, reveals that Pound's epic can also incorporate drawing, the science of sight.

The gigantism of Pound's ambition often seems akin to the nineteenth-century hope for a *Gesamtkunstwerk*, Wagner's term for a new form that would synthesize the essential elements of every separate art into a single masterpiece. The decisive aspect of this endeavor, however, is that Pound was able to conceive of his new art form as a linguistic creation, as a new kind of epic *poem*. At a time when the distrust of language has become endemic, when both philosophers and poets write about language as if it were an inhuman force, to be venerated for its self-sufficiency, or deplored as the major obstacle between mankind and an accurate perception of self and world, Pound was able to maintain his faith that a series of linguistic practices could be fashioned which together would reveal, not betray, the rhythms of nature, the patterns

[n] That Pound was extremely concerned about this possible loss of musicality is made clear in a letter he sent Katue Kitasono in 1940. He writes, "I *need* ideogram . . . but I also need sound and phonetics," and even suggests that the Japanese adopt "the Latin alphabet" to convey the tones of the ideogram (*L*:347).

of human consciousness, and the ethical bases for a humanized society. Only from such a faith could a tale of the tribe be conceivable, and Pound's whole project is grounded upon this astonishingly comprehensive belief in the possibilities of language. All of the poem's words are an implicit celebration of those possibilities, and all of *The Cantos'* different narrative codes, fragmented and even mutually contradictory though they remain at the thematic level, represent a consistent unfolding of a unified, deep structure of linguistic certitude.

Pound's confidence in language is logically prior to, and unrestricted by, the actual historical, fiscal, or religious doctrines championed in *The Cantos*. Pound was able to celebrate language without attributing to it a transcendent, superhuman authority; he could believe in the interpenetration of words and actions without debasing the first, or undervaluing the second term. The history of subsequent American poetry suggests that his sense of language as a human possibility, his attempt to free language from both a mystifying aestheticism and an equally mystifying pseudo-realism, may well constitute his single most significant achievement. As he himself well-knew:

> better gift can no man make to a nation

> Here error is all in the not done,
> all in the diffidence that faltered
> (LXXVI:454; LXXXI:522)

CHAPTER FIVE

·   ·   ·

IDENTIFICATION AND ITS VICISSITUDES

"Geschichtlichkeit (historicality) is not
worship of the past, but the recognition of
the temporality of human experience."
—Wilhelm Dilthey

"The names we stole don't remove us."
—John Ashbery, "Grand Galop"[1]

Ashbery, of course, is right: the burden of responsibility for
our own words and gestures is not lessened by the appropriation of another's name or the accents of a distancing idiom.
Yet how often in modern literature has the very necessity of
naming, the knowledge that we acquire speech only through
the words of others been experienced as a radical im-
poverishment of the writer's own identity, a "removal" of his
right to exist as an *author*? We still use the term *persona* as
though it offered an explanation, not a problem, as if the right
relationship between poet and mask, between the writer's
presence in his text and that of the different characters
through whom his voice also emerges, presents no more than
a series of technical stratagems, impersonations easily recuperated and enjoyable largely for the brilliance of the per-
formance. We admire a man who can "do the police in different voices" without worrying what kind of warrant he holds
that must constantly shift its center of articulation and mode
of discourse. To say that the artist's voice takes form as the
cumulative total of all his local strategies is by now an in-
grained habit, but one singularly unhelpful when confronting
the dilemma of his self-representation within his work. In an
epic poem that deliberately seeks models of exemplary con-

duct for the entire tribe, that looks for clearly articulated *values* as well as experiences, the difficulty of determining the most fruitful relationship between its narrator(s) and its heroic *exempla* becomes particularly acute. For Pound, that difficulty resulted in a major crisis, necessitating his drastic revision of the first published *Cantos*. Indeed, the struggle to attain a satisfactory response continued throughout the entire poem and itself constitutes one of the primary strands of the final text.

Throughout this chapter, my discussion will center on the question of Pound's self-representation in *The Cantos*. Yet that question in turn is directly linked to the larger issues of the poem's narrative structures and their success in generating a framework within which the values and judgments he intends to affirm can be inscribed. My concern, in other words, will no longer be with the specific content of those judgments, nor with the intellectual theories upon which Pound drew to "ground" his intuitions, but, rather, with how the text's formal discourse(s) enable us to derive *any* continuous interpretation from the mass of incidents, characters, and details making up the poem. It is important to realize that, in this context, the question of "coherence" is directed to a different and more fundamental domain than that of theme. The issue now is how the poem's words can be linked together as a sequential flow, to what voice(s) we can attribute the work's heterogeneous material, so that a particular intentional utterance is recognizable rather than a series of unconnected, random phrases. Paul Alpers, confronting a related problem in *The Faerie Queene*, says "It would seem axiomatic that for any narration there must be a narrator"[2] and then proceeds to demonstrate just how elusive and problematic such an "axiom" can be when applied to Spenser's poem. Since *The Cantos* are to be more than Pound's private aesthetic-religious vision, the issue of determining the poem's "actual or putative source," of establishing a coherent relationship between its narrator(s) and narrative that is also consistent with the work's epic ambitions, is even more complex, and yet upon its successful resolution depends the very existence of *The Cantos* as a single, decipherable text. Had Pound faltered here, in this first and most essential crisis of narration and coherence, we would not continue even today to be so concerned with any other, subsequent limitations in the work.

That the three *Cantos* Pound published in *Poetry* (Chicago) in 1917 all bear the mark of a desperate uncertainty, about both the general possibility of finding any coherent structure for a modern epic and the poet's personal capacity to make sense of his world through verse, is by now a critical commonplace. The dilemma of how to use historical figures, how to give speech to others, or, rather, to take on others' voices without thereby losing one's own, is omnipresent, forming the dominant concern of all three fragments. The matter of Pound's revision of these early drafts has been much discussed, and I do not intend to engage that topic directly here. Instead, I want to look at a moment of displaced self-revelation, an instant when Pound's text directly narrates the results of excessive identification with something both dearly and wrongly loved. If I treat the passage as an implicit commentary upon Pound's struggle with the process of assuming another's character, of discovering the necessary limits of identification and distancing, my reading arises not from any methodological eccentricity, but out of a conviction that many of the text's thematic strands can be seen as diverse aspects of a central intention: a quest for the proper relationship to the objects of one's own desire. Whether the dilemma is posed in terms of aesthetics, economics, social policy, or sexuality (and much of the force of *The Cantos* comes from seeing these as interrelated concerns), the long search for patterns of order that generates the poem's momentum is essentially the need to learn what constitutes the content and mode of a productive (individually and socially) love. *The Cantos* are, in every sense, "an education," for their creator as well as his readers, and, different though Pound's beliefs are from St. Augustine's Christian orthodoxy, the purification of the will to love—*ordinata dilectio*—lies at the core of both their writings.[a] Even justice, the most clearly social and legislative re-

---

[a] Pound's presence as a character in his own text, his sense that an epic can

sponsibility of a well-ordered state, is linked by Pound to an individual, volitional psychology. In Canto LXXXVIII, Pound calls justice a proper direction of the will, *directio voluntatis* (576), a phrase he had used earlier to summarize Dante's great epic: "The whole of the *Divina Commedia* is a study of the 'directio voluntatis'" (*J/M*:17). To set love in order is, I believe, the poem's dominant categorical imperative, uniting (without ever displacing) all the particular instances. How natural, then, that the text's first struggles should center on Pound's own disordered love, that the specific artistic dilemma he confronted in determining the very structure of his poem should recapitulate, in a personal, almost confessional mode, the larger thematic concerns of *The Cantos*.

To fashion a poetic voice adequate to the multiple demands of so ambitious a poem is, in large part, a question of narrative technique and aesthetic judgment; to learn, in pain, how "to care and not to care" seems, intuitively, to come from an entirely different realm of human experience. Yet it is an index of both the seriousness and the enormous risk inherent in *The Cantos* that much of this difference is denied, that the "technical struggle" of acquiring speech is morally and psychologi-

---

include the poet among the members of the tribe receiving instruction, distinguishes *The Cantos* from classical epics. A similar strategy was adopted by both Williams and Olson and has its ancestry in Whitman's personal involvement with the historical subject-matter of his poem, his struggle to unite a subjective narrator's voice with a chronicle of the decisive events of his time (the American Civil War, Lincoln's assassination, etc.). In a sense, Whitman is among the first poets to have realized and made use of the insight subsequently formulated by Wilhelm Dilthey: "The first condition for the possibility of the study of history is that I myself am a historical being." And, as is evident from the example of Pound, Williams, and Olson, it is with the far-reaching implications of Dilthey's insight that the modern poets who sought to make human history the center of their work inevitably had to come to terms.

Solely at the level of one man's "education," the issue of *The Cantos'* coherence does not arise, since all the material is tautologically unified as the perceptions of a single consciousness. However, Pound was not attempting to write a modern *Prelude* (although *The Cantos* include the verse autobiography as *one* of their constituent elements), and the poem's historical, political, and mythical codes required quite different (and never fully attained) principles of coherence.

cally linked to the thematic content of the ensuing discourse. "To measure is all we know" wrote William Carlos Williams.[3] In the Ur-Cantos, Pound learned just how painful it can be to acquire even the rudiments of a just "measuring."

•   •   •

"De la vaporisation et de la centralisation du *Moi*. Tout est là."

—Charles Baudelaire, "Journaux Intimes"[4]

And Ignez?
        Was a queen's tire-woman,
Court sinecure, the court of Portugal;
And the young prince loved her—Pedro,
Later called the cruel. And other courtiers were jealous.
Two of them stabbed her with the king's connivance,
And he, the prince, kept quiet a space of years—
        Uncommon the quiet.
And he came to reign, and had his will upon the dagger-
   players.
And held his court, a wedding ceremonial—
He and her dug-up corpse in cerements
Crowned with the crown and splendor of Portugal.
A quiet evening and a decorous procession;
Who winked at murder kisses the dead hand,
Does leal homage,
"Que depois de ser morta foy Rainha."
Dig up Camoens, hear out his resonant bombast:
                  (Ur-Canto Two:186)[5]

For the moment, I do not want to insist upon the curious homologue between Pedro's setting the dead Ignez upon his throne and Pound's anxious question about his own poem's manner of "resurrecting" the illustrious dead:

. . . what were the use
Of setting figures up and breathing life upon them
            (Ur-Canto One:115)

But it is impossible not to sense that Pound's insecure relationship to the beloved figures of his imagination forms the principal crisis of the Ur-Cantos. Throughout these drafts, his introduction of historical and literary characters appears so frantic because he does not begin with any definable identity of his own for which he is then able to find analogues or "conversational partners" in the past. Yet he is equally unable to grant these figures an autonomous discourse, to let each one speak independently of Pound-as-narrator. Instead, an initial process of identification is seen as absolutely necessary for the creation of Pound's own poetry. The question "What's left for me to do? / Whom shall I conjure up; who's my Sordello" (Ur-Canto One:117) is both crucial and dangerous for the entire poetic project. On one level, Pound is merely echoing, albeit with desperation, the conventional poetic plea for a suitable subject matter, a "high theme" appropriate to his ambition. Yet there is a distinctly unsettling implication in the formula's precise articulation. The poet does not, as is customary, assume the independent status of his own powers which only lack an adequate occasion for speech—rather, he does not yet exist *qua* poet until not merely a *theme* is found, but *another voice* emerges through whom he can learn to speak. Who and where is the character in whom Pound must alienate himself in order to write his own poem? Who must he become, in other words, in order to be, at the end, himself?

Throughout the Ur-Cantos, Pound's stance remains essentially passive and frustrated. He summons up subjects, settings, and poets from the past only to regard them with the longing of a fascinated inferiority: "I have but smelt this life, a whiff of it—" (Ur-Canto One:120). He refers everything in the poem back to his need for an appropriate *persona* so that, paradoxically, the very intensity of his desire prohibits him from giving to any speaker a convincingly realized discourse. Pound's constant intrusions, his compulsion to annotate, give sources and indicate connections, his anxiety immediately to test whatever possible relationship the historical material has to his present artistic crisis, only emphasizes the temporal gulf separating him—and his readers—from the very subjects of the poem. Nietzsche once warned that it was dangerous to know more of a thing than we can creatively live up to. Pound's efforts in the Ur-Cantos testify how anguishing the separation can be when knowledge exceeds the capacity for any corresponding (and thus genuinely responsive) action, and like the farmer's son described at the end of Ur-Canto Two, Pound is emotionally trapped, "Back once again, in middle Indiana, / . . . Adoring Puvis, giving his family back / What they had spent for him, talking Italian cities, / Local excellence at Perugia, / dreaming his renaissance" (Ur-Canto Two:188).

In this context, the description of Pound's consciousness as "fundamentally ahistorical" and "archaic," which I criticized in Chapter Three, becomes genuinely revealing. Pearlman's analysis, that is, fits the troubled Pound of the Ur-Cantos far better than the strong poet of the later, revised epic. The degree to which Pound was initially capable of presenting only a movement of repetitive substitutions and thwarted identifications traces the extent to which he was himself trapped in an Imaginary and alienated relationship to the objects of his desire. As Leo Bersani suggests, "perhaps all relations . . . dominated by the order of the Imaginary are condemned to a nonproductive time, that is, to the time of exact repetition. The enterprise of constituting the self in the other and of transforming the other into an *alter ego* means that . . . all relations are perceived as relations between identical terms."[6] Thus, instead of authenticating a poetic voice, the Ur-Cantos demonstrate the terrible emptiness of a consciousness that experiences itself only negatively, that knows itself primarily by all that it lacks. Since it is, in principle, never possible for Pound to attain a complete union with the other voices quoted, all that his own sensibility can do is emptily state itself by stating the objects of its desire: "What have I of this life, / or even of Guido? / Sweet lie!—Was I there truly? / Did I know Or San Michele?" (Ur-Canto One:120). Instead of a poem, what results is, as Pound ruefully confesses, a series of fetishes, "a catalogue, his jewels of conversation" (Ur-Canto Three:249). King Pedro and the Indiana farm-boy depict two models of fetishization, and yet each does no more than enact, *in extremis*, the situation of a poet who still clings (to an identificatory, dependent relationship with the figures of his desire) when, in order to establish his own authority as a writer, he knows the time has come for leaving.[b]

•   •   •

"Thus the shadow of the object fell upon the ego."
—Sigmund Freud, *Mourning and Melancholia*[7]

For Pound, the shadow of all that had been lost did not permanently block the creation of his own voice. The tone of melancholia that haunts the Ur-Cantos gave way, as has often been noticed, to an astonishingly confident deployment of different historical and mythic character, different modes of discourse, and numerous fully realized dialogues. The brilliant decision to adopt the structural *role* (not merely, or even primarily, the *persona*) of Odysseus questioning the illustrious dead in an effort to learn both how to "return home" and what actually constitutes man's proper home (the Dantean theme seen as a moral and political, not an anagogical, quest) has been much admired and closely studied. Less often remarked is that by mythologizing the narrator's relationship to those he interviews, Pound has broken through the web of excessive identification. He explicitly established an initial distinction, introducing through the framework of a conversation a kind of detachment from what he sees and an obligation to let the various figures speak for themselves. From the ambiguous and constantly shifting space of the interlocutor's role (where is Pound-Odysseus standing in the first 71 Cantos, from what locus is the poet's voice actually heard?) Pound has found a means of introducing historical figures without having their presence overwhelm his own self-representation. Conversation implies a certain equality

[b] In Chapter One, I discussed the importance of *ordo* in Confucian thinking. I believe, however, that the entire theme of stability and order contains a clear psychological, as well as political and aesthetic, meaning for Pound. His longing for precise demarcations, for clear hierarchies and "gradations," was perhaps in part a reaction to the temptation to lose his own identity in the work and voice of others. *Abulcia* or random, aimless drifting, is what Pound, at a certain stage, seemed to fear most (cf.: *Hugh Selwyn Mauberley*, Canto VII, etc.).

among the speakers, and the poem's judgments can now appear, not as anxious intrusions into the text, but through the
silent arrangement, juxtaposition, and selection of the historical *exempla*. Pound's own voice as a character in the poem is
only intermittently heard offering direct judgments. The rest
of the time, it remains implicit, advancing the epic's argument
through the speech he now gives over to others. The full
thematic meaning of a particular canto (or, for that matter, of
The Cantos as a whole), does not reside in any of the specific
episodes it presents, nor even in the strictly additive, sequential total of those episodes, but rather in the unspoken links
between them, in the internal logic that connects seemingly
disparate narrations. In discovering what the terms of that
logic are, what framework of argumentation could connect
the text's diverse moments and *exempla*, we collaborate with
Pound and (re-)create the poem's meaning as we are reading
it, rather than merely repeating or paraphrasing a meaning already expressed in the words of the poem. Pound's authorial
"voice," I think, is often implicitly and theoretically definable
as that unspoken "marginal presence" which silently articulates (makes sense out of) the gaps in the printed text, a voice
we only really discover in the process of "speaking it" ourselves.

The whole theme of the poet and Pound's different heroes
acting as specific embodiments of the archetypal figure,
"Odysseus the voyager," seems to me much over-valued as
the text's main integrating principle. Surely it is impossible to
experience, for example, either the Adams/Jefferson sequence
or the Chinese History Cantos primarily as the chronicle of
two civilizations Pound-Odysseus encounters on his *nostos*.
Large sections of the poem simply do not fit such a paradigm
or belong within so fixed a scaffolding. There is little gain in
reading *The Cantos* as if they were structured like a *Ulysses* in
verse, and critics desperate to find "major form" in the poem
usually apply schema of coherence that are manifestly inadequate to the work.[e] Obviously, Pound as historical and

---

[e] T. S. Eliot's famous footnote to *The Waste Land*, in which he claims:
"Tiresias, although a mere spectator and not indeed a 'character' is yet the
most important personage in the poem, uniting all the rest. . . . What Tiresias

mental traveller dominates certain cantos, and Forrest Read and Hugh Kenner, among others, have made excellent use of this motif in their analyses, but far more sections of the poem are simply given, generated with no locatable or definable narrative source. Roland Barthes' notion that "le discours, et non tel ou tel de ses personnages, est le seul héros positif de l'histoire"[8] seems a more satisfactory realization. I would add that although the historical attitudes governing the poem, the problems it presents and the terms of their resolution, obviously originate in the attitudes of a definite historical author, within *The Cantos* themselves only the tribal heritage as an entirety can be posited as the synthetic, all-seeing consciousness capable of integrating the disparate moments of the narrative. Nor is this a simple tautology, equally true of every literary work. In a first-person narrative, for example, a character is established to whose perceptions and consciousness the entire text can be attributed: the words of the tale are his, even when he overhears and then records the speech of others. (Hence the question of his "reliability" as a faithful or honest chronicler; precisely because we only really hear one character, can the author undermine our confidence in his perceptions, and allow the reader the gratification of an insight denied to the actual "source" of the narrative.)

Pound, however, wished to create quite a different "fiction," one uniquely appropriate to an epic poem. He wanted the text to give the impression of the tribe's own heritage narrating itself, of the different historical voices addressing us as if without the mediation of one unique narrator or controlling author. It is almost as though the texture of *The Cantos* were designed to illustrate Karl Popper's idea of an "epistemology without a knowing subject," of information objectively exist-

---

sees, in fact, is the substance of the poem" (*The Complete Poems and Plays*, New York, 1962, p. 52), is a curious example of an author himself providing a cripplingly reductive explication of his text's narrative structure. I think that Tiresias serves as little more than a name, a sign around which the coherence of the poem is to be recuperated and by which its textual unity can be assured. Eliot's note, if my interpretation is correct, represents an attempt to forestall conventional accusations of incoherence by insisting upon his poem's closure within an implicit unifying consciousness even though such a recuperation is fundamentally untrue to *The Waste Land* itself.

ing and available for communal use without necessarily being fully realized in any single individual's competence. Ideally, within the fiction of the poem, the question of "reliability" does not arise, since there is no one "character," no "knowing subject," or even omniscient author, through whom the narrative is being communicated. In the most literal sense it is only the poem in its prolonged unfolding which undertakes the quest announced in Canto I. Or, to put the matter somewhat differently, Odysseus is only one particular, although the most frequently presented, configuration of the narrative discourse: it is *The Cantos* which "sings" him and not the other way around.

> "Flaubert . . . en maniant une ironie frappée d'incertitude, opère un malaise salutaire de l'écriture: il n'arrête pas le jeu des codes (ou l'arrêt mal), en sorte que (c'est là sans doute la *preuve* de l'écriture) *on ne sait jamais s'il est responsable de ce qu'il écrit* (s'il y a un sujet *derrière* son langage. . . ."9

Although Barthes is describing the decisive rupture in the narrative strategy of conventional novels inaugurated by Gustave Flaubert, many of the same critical terms apply to the way historical *exempla* are presented in Pound's text, and in the face of so radical an aesthetic it seems merely trivializing to read the poem as a looser, more episodic, version of traditional verse narratives. It is precisely in those sections deprived of any easy recuperation through a definable narrator or point of view that the poem most fully asserts itself as an epic, that the writing reaches a structural independence from what Pound himself had called the "medievalism" of Joyce's Homeric parallels (*LE*:406). Tactically, Pound's refusal to indicate a specific narrator enables him to create the illusion that it is History itself, not any one particular author, that is presenting the factual details of the poem, and it is fascinating to see a technique which in Flaubert is used to *undermine* the reader's confidence in any stable values, being applied in *The Cantos* with the contrary intention, that is, to *increase* the authority of the poem's positive judgments. In practical terms, the immediate results of Pound's willingness to allow the separate sections of his poem to exist without any locatable narrator is a decisive change in the presentation of historical *exempla*. Now, far from simply identifying with figures from the past, Pound is able to uncover through their presentation a set of putatively objective principles governing history. Independent and verifiable laws of culture, history, and language have been inscribed in place of a dependent, imaginary identification, and in the revised opening of *The Cantos* Pound removes both the story of Ignez da Castro and the painter trapped in Indiana. Their lesson, it would seem, is already exhausted.

●　　●　　●

> Time is the evil. Evil.
> 　　　　　A day, and a day
> Walked the young Pedro baffled,
> 　　　　　a day and a day
> After Ignez was murdered.
> Came the Lords of Lisboa
> 　　　　　a day and a day
> In homage. Seated there
> 　　　　　dead eyes,
> Dead hair under the crown,
> The King still young there beside her.
> 　　　　　　(XXX:147-8)

Midway through Canto XXX, the crucial summary to the whole first section of *The Cantos*, the story of Ignez reappears, breaking the surface of a text that had seemed to leave such anxieties behind eleven years earlier. Now there is no elaborate annotation, no mention of "Camoens' resonant bombast," only an image starkly simple in its portrayal of Time and loss experienced as sheer horror.[d] What Pedro is doing,

---

[d] Although this type of echo is impossible to prove, I am struck by a curious parallel between the description of the dead Ignez "Seated there / dead eyes, / Dead hair under the crown" and the lament for Henri Gaudier-Brzeska in *Hugh Selwyn Mauberley*, "Charm, smiling at the good mouth, / Quick eyes gone under earth's lid" (*Per*:191). Notice, however, that while Pound mourns Gaudier's death, he does not seek to deny its reality. The senselessness of the war's carnage appalls him, but what Pound wants to preserve is Gaudier's

however, is pathetically and cruelly attempting to defy the irreversible pressure of time, to refuse his acquiesence in the
decay of the beauty he cherished most. Pedro is not just dam-
aged in his love and self-esteem. His anger is turned outwards
against the court he now rules and the grotesque ceremony
the poem describes is itself an act of pure frustration and rage.
In one of the aphorisms from *Also Sprach Zarathustra*,
Nietzsche describes just this other, savage, side of melancholia, and his analysis offers a perfect commentary on Pedro's act. "This, yes, this alone is *revenge itself*: the will's an-
tipathy towards time and time's 'It was.' "[10]

"Time is the evil. Evil." This judgment, absent from the
1917 narration of Ignez's violation, links Pound's new perception to Nietzsche's insight: the narcissistic ego, unable to accept its own temporality (and the death of the beloved if accepted must inevitably lead to an understanding of one's own
mortality), turns against both itself and the world in a
paroxysm of vengefulness. The problem of accepting the
temporal limits of one's potential achievements and that of
excessive identification with the "magic moments" of beauty
are thus revealed as fundamentally one. But Pound no longer
identifies with Pedro, no longer fears the King's gesture as the
symbolic analogue of his own poetic stance. The phrase
"Time is the evil. Evil" arises neither from Pedro's self-
understanding nor from Pound's anxious concurrence; only
incidentally is it even an index of Pound's more confident acceptance of the role of commentator since it is in this part of
the canto (as opposed to the earlier "Compleynt") that no authorial presence, no "I," is posited *within the text,* from whose
point of view the actions are narrated. Instead, the realization
originates in the autonomous, objective realm in which all of
the text's judgments are securely inscribed. The initial predicament in the Ur-Cantos has become objectified into a condemnation of a culture that hypostatizes its treasures while
refusing to "make them new," that sentimentalizes art and
desire without wanting to give them a living (and therefore

sculpture and his memory, not the artist's corpse. The difference between
Pound and King Pedro is that between a generous *mourning* and a pathologi-
cal *melancholia.*

also a perpetually different) form. Later in *The Cantos* Pound himself establishes this parallel between Pedro's action and the values of a decadent society by ending the famous Usura Canto with the lines, "Corpses are set to banquet / at behest of usura" (XLV:230). The necrophiliac "setting up" of Ignez is itself a kind of psychological hoarding, a refusal to place one's desire in harmony with the natural rhythms of life and death ("Thy day is between a door and a door," XLVII:237), just as, in Pound's eyes, usury is the economic mis-use of time's inherent capacity to bring forth increase. Pedro's mad repetition is the compulsive, reifying side of recreation, and the principle of metamorphosis, the freedom to transform and rearrange the heraldic *exempla* of the cultural past, which Pound has employed throughout the first thirty cantos is here implicitly validated as the proper antidote to Pedro's sterility.[e]

And yet where does Pound himself stand in relationship to the charges he has levelled at a culture of regressive repetitions? He has, it is true, through the role of Odysseus the voyager-interlocutor found a structuring device that permits the establishment of three basically distinct sets of voices: (a) the "marginal enunciation" that is, in theory, always deducible, connecting the different episodes; (b) the scattered metamorphic versions of "E.P.-Odysseus," each of whom is capable at times of assuming the grammatical and structural function of the subject of a narrative sequence; and, (c) the

[e] Many years earlier, in *The Spirit of Romance* (1910), Pound wrote, echoing Aristotle's comments on *Oedipus Tyrannos* (*Poetics* 14), "the great poem, 'Ignez da Castro,' was written in deeds by King Pedro. No poem can have such force as has the simplest narration of the events themselves" (230). Critics often quote this passage as a kind of commentary upon Canto XXX, but I think that in the intervening years Pound had grown to realize that Pedro's deed is quite clearly a bad poem, is the model of all bad (i.e., sterile) relationships to the objects of desire. Had Pound wished to present Pedro's love for Ignez in a positive light, he would undoubtedly have mentioned the magnificent tombs erected at Alcobaça by the King's orders, twin memorials on which the life of Ignez was depicted in marble sculptures. The inclusion of this information would have altered the whole emotional tone of the passage, establishing a structural parallel between Pedro and Ignez and couples like Mausolus and Artemisia or Sigismundo and Isotta. The fact that Pound selected only the most eccentric—and historically disputed—episode from all the available details, makes a "sympathetic" reading even less convincing.

figures present largely as historical *exempla*, the characters encountered along the Odyssean *periploi* who counsel "E.P.-Odysseus," or, more often, who exist quite independent of any Odyssean framework, notable representatives from the tribal heritage speaking within the text's structurally autonomous narrative. *Within* his own poem, however, it is possible for Pound to ground his speech only through a prior act of self-mythologization (voice "b"), through the assumption of a role which, as we have seen, can only be concretely realized in relatively few sections of the text. At the poem's core, the presence of Pound's personal voice, his ability to speak *in propria persona* (and the conventional Latin expression is, in this context, singularly revealing) remains an unresolved dilemma.

Pound frequently intends, as I have said, to create the fiction of a "work that is not a fiction," to have us accept the poem's discourse as the objective speech of the entire tribal heritage and not merely of Ezra Pound, the individual. Such a strategy is designed to deflect our habit of treating any poem as a purely subjective, aesthetic vision, but, since the text can never be co-extensive with the world to which it refers, the problem of selection (or rather, the problem of *who* is determining the selection) still remains. The difficulty is that while Pound has not established any authoritative voice *within* the poem whose principles of selection and judgment we are ready to accept, he has also refused to let us see the text's diverse enunciations as originating in a single, omniscient author standing outside the narrative. The "marginal voice" I have mentioned, for example, is, of course, not History as an hypostatized allegorical figure summoning characters and drawing moralistic conclusions. Nor does it bear more than a distant family resemblance to Robert Durling's "imaginatively constructed source" of speech.[11] The "marginal voice" which we "hear" (by speaking it ourselves) in the gaps between the poem's words is a purely formal and logical discourse: it is the theoretically discoverable articulation of the arguments uniting diverse *exempla* and separate incidents, but it cannot choose among different political and historical options or decide which incidents merit inclusion in *The Cantos*.

The "marginal voice" only comes into existence once at least two different episodes are present together in the poem—it is the *consequence* of the text's juxtapositions, not their *source*. The reason this entire strategy is so dangerous for Pound's whole endeavor is that, unlike Flaubert, he wants his work to be more than either a pure triumph of the aesthetic will or a demoralizing diagnosis of society's incurable stupidity. Instead, one of the poem's governing intentions is to argue for certain specific values, and in such a project the absence of an assured narrative voice, the impossibility of assigning speech to a single responsible source, risks undermining the whole ethical and polemical dimension. [12]

The first thirty cantos are an astonishing poetic *tour de force*, but often they give the impression of a series of set-pieces, a pageant of isolated, momentary encounters. The terms that could connect the diverse episodes are wanting since there is not yet established a consciousness authoritative enough to guarantee the validity of the work's startling juxtapositions.[f] When the reader is baffled, incapable either of determining the logic connecting different episodes or of finding that logic more than trivial, a violent break in the text's coherence takes place, and even the "marginal voice" seems temporarily silenced. What is interesting though, is that the problem has nothing to do with the "difficulty" of specific passages. Rather, it seems that in order to be fully effective, to guarantee the values which the poem is celebrating, even the marginal voice must, at some point, surrender its autonomy and establish its presence directly in the words of the poem itself.

Critics sympathetic to Pound have felt compelled to over-emphasize the Odysseus motif because only if we keep the theme of a *nostos* constantly in mind can the poem's events be consistently located. The instant we focus on an individual

---

[f] The analogy with the ideogram is, as I argued in the previous chapter, of little value here. Since Pound's juxtapositions, unlike those of the Chinese written character, are not certified by an entire culture, are not validated by the *community* of written speech users throughout the tribe's linguistic history, there is no voice but his own to give them authority. The patterns he discerns may be right or wrong but the responsibility for their fashioning must still be assumed somewhere in the text where they are first articulated.

part we lose our bearing. As is true of some collages, the parts assert their autonomy; they become a subject in their own right and undermine any sense of a larger, synthetic subject. The lack of focus arises because Pound's own voice, withdrawn to the interstices of the various dialogues, still has not attained a satisfactory self-representation. Although the resulting ambiguity of narration often acts as a positive force, freeing Pound from the posture of an intrusive and appropriating commentator, and implicitly asserting that the historical or mythical material is meaningful in its own right, the formula will not hold when an experience of total loss sweeps over the man himself, when a crisis is registered not only through cultural and aesthetic terms but, in the deepest sense, as ontological. When, in other words, Odysseus becomes No-Man and Ezra Pound reaches Pisa. "Time is the evil. Evil" was introduced in 1928 to generalize the psychopathology underlying Pedro's act. The next time we hear the phrase is almost twenty years later. Then, however, the words are only those of a single man, a prisoner with his mind at the breaking point, his political and mythic dreams shattered into irretrievable fragments. Ironically, in Ezra Pound's discourse, in fragments begins responsibility.

· · ·

> Time is not, Time is the evil, beloved
> Beloved the hours βροδοδάκτυλος ['rosy-fingered']
> as against the half-light of the window
> with the sea beyond making horizon
> (LXXIV:444)

"Time is not, Time is the evil, beloved / Beloved the hours." Or, in the words of a different metaphysic, only through Time is Time redeemed. But, in Pound's anguished meditation, there is no question of "redemption," only an affirmation that, irrespective of historical vicissitudes, love and memory endure in the privileged space of a purely individual consciousness. In prison Pound discovered a new kind of love, one purged both of narcissistic identification and of the compulsion to represent its desires as objective certitudes.

Paradoxically, it is the freedom to assent to loss, to admit the difference between his individual longing and the structure of history, that succeeds in negating Time's destructiveness, that grounds the articulation of desire in the one locus where Time is undeniably permeable to the contingencies of the present. "Beloved the hours" inaugurates an emotional flooding that will sweep over Pound's whole past. In Pisa the source of the images is freely stated—we know both who is speaking and from where—and the ambiguities of a dispersed enunciation have been replaced by the specificity of a personal outcry. Only the poet's own memory, the love whose traces have formed his consciousness, can create a new rose out of the steel debris and accidents of history.[13]

The voices of the past do not speak to Pound, it is he who speaks them, "murmuring name upon name" from a place that, as he had intuited long before, is only, "Dove sta memoria—where memory liveth." The realm of the *symbolique* to which Pound had turned in an effort to escape the dead-end of the Ur-Cantos, has been merged anew with the maternal *imaginaire* until

> nothing matters but the quality
> of the affection—
> in the end—that has carved the trace in the mind
> dove sta memoria
> (LXXVI:457)

The greater humility and emotional directness which every reader of *The Pisan Cantos* has noticed may well be due, outside the text, to the circumstances of Pound's actual situation. Within the poem, however, what has happened is that the author has found a new relationship to the objects of his admiration, has found a technique that allows for a full self-representation in the role of the lover who gives rather than borrows names. The much-admired new note of penitence, the thematic confessions of error, result, paradoxically, in a far more assertive *poetic* stance, a far stronger demonstration of independent authorial existence. Pound's voice throughout the Pisa sequence (and, again, still more movingly, in *Drafts and Fragments*) does not exist through any "alter-narrators";

rather, it is they who have been returned to the foundation from which all acts of attention begin, the rag-and-bone shop of a single, nominating voice.

The answer to King Pedro's fixation is not, or at best is only partially, realized in the counter-model of Odysseus at Erebus. Another, equally essential, part of the solution is implicit in the wisdom of Cavalcanti's great canzone, "Donna Mi Prega," in a love that insists upon speaking (in) its own name. The initial surprise is that it took Pound, the individual, so long and required such a terrible ordeal for him to realize his own freedom to speak without masks. The second and far greater wonder is that, as I have tried to show, when that moment did occur, the poem's structure was already flexible enough to incorporate so prolonged and personal an outcry, that when one reads the earlier sections a second time in the light of *The Pisan Cantos* it seems that Pound already knew both what his text required and when to introduce his own voice all along.

·   ·   ·

At first glance it might appear as if many of my arguments are meant to assign a privileged role to those sections of Pound's text whose structure most resembles a conventional lyric or verse meditation. Yet it is equally true that the foregrounding of his private situation is attained only at the cost of compromising *The Cantos'* epic ambitions. In *The Pisan Cantos*, the poem openly records the experiences of an individual's unique sensibility—it no longer pretends to function as a spokesman for values acknowledged as part of the entire community's heritage. I suppose that what distinguishes a *modern* verse epic from its classical predecessors is the necessity, in a society no longer unified by a single, generally accepted code of values, of justifying its argument by the direct appeal of the author's own experiences and emotions. By the time of *Paterson* and *The Maximus Poems*, as we shall see, the pressures of the poet's particular situation had become one of the acknowledged conventions of the new verse epic. But if, as I have claimed in this chapter, the fiction of an impersonal narrative "telling itself" can no longer fully sustain the values for which the poem is contending, it is also true that the issue remains one of degree and proportion. If the *dominant* voice narrating the poem is acknowledged as expressing only the vicissitudes of a single consciousness, the work will be a lyric or a verse meditation in which the historical material serves largely as evidence of a particular author's "jewels of conversation." Thus, even if *at some point* in the text, the poet himself must indicate his personal relationship to the heroic *exempla* held up for our admiration and instruction, the fiction of a strictly autonomous discourse—the voice of the community's heritage telling itself—is still necessary to the existence of an epic and must carry the preponderance of the narrative. Because this obligation is so central to the entire project, I do not believe sequences like *The Pisan Cantos* or *Drafts and Fragments* constitute the poem's major, let alone sole, success. Quite the contrary, I think Pound was profoundly right to withdraw the direct articulation of his own voice after *The Pisan Cantos*, to let the narrative return, until the last few pages, to the independent, unlocatable source of speech he had marked out in the first thirty cantos. Once his personal voice has been established in all its specificity, it can return to the margins of the text, letting the structural relations which Pound has discovered in history reassume their independent narrative status. A technique based on the juxtaposition of autonomous, culturally significant, details, one which can sustain the fiction of presenting the tribe's history as "a process without a subject,"[14] still remains the single most powerful way of creating an adequate structure for an epic.

In this sense, Pound is right to claim "it all coheres all right / even if my notes do not cohere" (CXVI:797). Coherence in *The Cantos* never really resided in "the notes" themselves (the actual situations presented in the poem)—it was always posited outside the text, in the realms of history, nature, and myth. Pound's own voice, joined to that of all the other characters in the poem, initiates a discourse which only the fullness of history itself can complete. Only the entire tribal heritage can unite all of the work's juxtaposed details as part of its larger, all-encompassing tale. But, in trying to understand both the unspoken logic governing the selection/juxtaposition of the poem's *exempla*, as well as the relationship between those *exempla* and the larger heritage from which they are drawn, the audience is also brought to the poem, almost like an active participant in its search for a meaningful history. Perhaps, if the poem had not also included evidence of Pound's private, and at times even despairing, search for the right relationship to his material, readers would never have become so engaged with making sense of the historical material *for its own sake*. Perhaps, that is, the very presence of a personal element, although *structurally* undermining *The Cantos'* central intentions, *affectively* helps sustain their force as an epic poem "including history" for the instruction of the tribe.

When I listed four propositions characterizing epic verse, I said they located a "family resemblance," not a set of Aristotelian categories. *The Cantos*, as we have seen, clearly violate some of the criteria described in the Introduction. But if this rupture indicates the limits of their success as an epic, it also reveals the "familial" adjustments and compromises enforced by the absence of a "coherent" (i.e., ethically and culturally united) audience. Pound's different narrative strategies are one response to that dilemma, and, for all their limitations, they did resurrect the epic as a genre that modern poets could again attempt. Much of the richness of *The Cantos*, and a large part of their immense legacy to subsequent writers, arises directly from Pound's struggle to unite two narratives—the personal and lyric affirmations of a single voice with the "objective," communally guaranteed certitudes of traditional epics—in a new kind of text, a poem whose precise modes of coherence we are still only beginning to know, and, in Williams' sense, adequately "measure."

CHAPTER SIX

· · ·

THE ARTIST WHO DOES
THE NEXT JOB

"Because the very nature of the quest is
apocalyptic . . . it the poet fails, his failure
has tragic (noble) implications; if he succeeds, his success is of the universal dimension beyond tragedy."

—L. S. Dembo[1]

"Are not Hardy and his successors right in
severely curtailing for themselves the liberties that other poets continue to take? Does
not the example of the Hardyesque poet
make some of those other poets look childishly irresponsible?"

—Donald Davie[2]

In 1971, the same year in which Hugh Kenner's brilliantly
partisan study, *The Pound Era*, appeared, one of the most distinguished contemporary English poets published an equally
partisan, although far more obviously pugnacious, account of
modern verse. For this occasion, an introduction to John
Betjeman's *Collected Poems*, Philip Larkin adopted a distinctly belligerent posture: the tough-talking, anti-American,
equally contemptuous of the "culture-mongering activities of
the Americans Eliot and Pound" and of the "pompous,
pseudo-military operation of literary warfare"[3] which has secured their reputation.

To Larkin, "modernism" is largely a bankrupt fraud, and,
instead of joining in any homage to the Poundian "vortex,"
Larkin asks (with obvious hope), "Can it be that, as Eliot
dominated the first half of the twentieth century, the second
half will derive from Betjeman?"[4] Some of Larkin's specific

arguments are so deliberately outrageous that one hopes he is simply trying to shock his readers into a new recognition, to make them at least consider the possibility of a very different and insufficiently acknowledged kind of excellence. (Ironically, this is one of Pound's own favorite critical strategies, as is Larkin's whole tone of sweeping, and often deliberately brutal, assertions.) Indeed, for all its eccentricity, Larkin's polemic cannot be dismissed as pure fatuousness, in part, as Pound would have agreed, because any statement by a man who has fashioned several of the most lucid and technically accomplished poems of the last twenty years deserves careful attention, and in part because Larkin is only stating more aggressively a suspicion increasingly voiced by many other, especially British, writers. The poet-critic John Press concludes his "General Introduction" to *A Map of Modern English Verse* (1969) by at least being tempted to judge "the course of true poetry in our century" as deriving "from Thomas Hardy through Edward Thomas, W. H. Davies, Norman Cameron, and Alun Lewis, to finish in Graves himself."[5] Even Donald Davie, whose writing includes some of the most balanced overall assessments of Pound's strengths and limitations, shows a distinct and seemingly increasing unease with the "liberties" poets like Pound have taken. Although Davie would presumably exempt Pound himself from the charge of being "childishly irresponsible," it is clear that he shares at least some of the anxieties of Larkin and Press about the dangers—both moral and aesthetic—incurred by an American poetics that is often openly "totalitarian" (*GK*:121) in its ambitions, and imperialistic in its rapacious willingness to treat the entire world as suitable *materia poetica* for its own texts.[6]

Moreover, American verse has often been ill served by its most enthusiastic admirers. Frequently a poem's intention is equated with its actual achievement, or, when this becomes manifestly impossible, the grandeur of the struggle is regarded as sufficient proof of the work's merit.[a] L. S. Dembo's

---

[a] American art-history of the late 1940s to 1960s exhibits the same vocabulary and attitudes. The rhetoric of grandiose failure became one of the standard conventions by which both critics and painters "justified" Abstract Expressionism. There is a myth of heroism in contemporary discussions of de

lines, quoted above, crystallize this critical strategy, one which rightfully leaves many readers unconvinced. (Dembo is, in context, referring to *The Bridge*, a poem that has often been defended along just these lines. Yet, as one of Crane's letters to Yvor Winters reveals, this is a defense he himself had anticipated and feared as much as any full-scale condemnation: "One may be doomed to the kind of half-success which is worse than failure.")[7]

In its strong version, of course, no one really believes such an argument: critics today hardly regard the failure of "epics" like Joel Barlow's *The Columbiad* or Archibald MacLeish's *Conquistador* as having "tragic (noble) implications." Clearly, for its failure to be "heroic," the poem must be in large measure a success, must achieve much, although not all, of its announced intentions. But even this second, weak version of the argument of excellence-from-ambition, commands no universal respect. For many writers a literary text can be evaluated only on its specific accomplishments—any considerations of its larger unrealized claims are dismissed as either irrelevant or a mystification.

It seems only honest to admit that, while I find much justice in the latter view, I regard it largely as a much-needed corrective to the excessively naïve and hectoring rhetoric of critical special pleading. I think it is impossible to disregard completely the intended scope of any work of art, either in our immediate reactions, or in our subsequent assessments of its significance. A poem's intention is not something external, known only from its author's outside statements; instead, it determines much of the text's fundamental structure and should logically figure in any analysis of the work, even if our judgment includes a sense that the intention has never found an adequate realization. I suppose it is unnecessary to confess as well that, for all its faltering, I do regard Pound's attempt to create a modern verse epic as one of the most significant ventures in twentieth-century literature. Because Pound did succeed in "yanking and hauling" so much of his world "into

---

Kooning or Pollock which obscures their real artistic merit as much as it dramatizes the fascination of their careers.

some sort of order (or beauty), aware of it both as chaos and as potential" (*LE*:396), it is hard not to be impressed by the magnitude of the effort, and to be moved by the poet's own confessions of failure. In the Introduction, I spoke of Pound's fear that, unless such an effort were made, poetry itself, "like the art of dancing in armour" might decay into obsolescence (*LE*:55). One of Pound's major legacies is simply that other poets, in part because of the very existence of works like *The Cantos*, no longer confront such an anxiety. As Hugh Mac-Diarmid realized, "to take the whole field of knowledge and to assimilate all the diverse components into a general view—establish a synthesis, in fact—is clearly a Herculean undertaking scarcely to be attempted by anyone, and hardly more likely to be understood by anyone else. Yet it is a task of paramount importance . . . on which the whole future of poetry depends."[8] Thus far, I have tried to analyze the structures, intellectual as well as artistic, governing Pound's "Herculean undertaking," without, I hope, either mistaking the poem's ambition for its accomplishment, or denying its genuine achievement because of its equally real flaws.

Hans Robert Jauss, unconsciously echoing Pound's 1922 review of *Ulysses*—"The best criticism of any work . . . comes from the creative writer or artist who does the next job" (*LE*:406)—recently said that "a subsequent work solves formal and moral problems that the last work raised, and may then itself present new problems."[9] By the same logic, rather than concluding this exploration of *The Cantos* with any general summary or synthetic overview, I prefer to turn to two other poems, *Paterson* and *The Maximus Poems*. Each of these offered "solutions" to the "formal and moral problems" of writing a modern verse epic substantially different from Pound's own, and yet intimately associated with, and to a significant extent influenced by, *The Cantos*. From an examination of their own artistic strategies, both as independent achievements, and as reactions to Pound's example, one can, I think, derive a clearer sense of the tradition of the modern verse epic—and of Pound's central contribution to that tradition—than from any isolated critique. Towards the end of his book, *Ezra Pound: Poet as Sculptor*, Donald Davie wrote,

Whatever more long-term effect Pound's disastrous career may have on American and British poetry, it seems inevitable that it will rule out (has ruled out already, for serious writers) any idea that poetry can or should operate in the dimension of history, trying to make sense of the recorded past by redressing our historical perspectives. . . . History, from now on, may be transcended in poetry, or it may be evaded there; but poetry is not the place where it may be understood.[10]

Davie uses Charles Olson's critique of Pound's "arrogant Bohemianism" to "ground" his argument, but I think he is fundamentally mistaken, not only about the "long-term effect" of Pound's career, but also about Olson's complex reaction to *The Cantos*. Most important of all, however, I think that the last twenty years of American verse indicate that Pound's ambition has by no means been discarded, that even writers with different literary and intellectual perspectives have wanted neither to "evade" nor to "transcend" history, but, instead, have sought to maintain the authority of poetry as a crucial site in which "history . . . may be understood." Olson himself spoke of "history as the one way to restore the familiar to us;"[11] to abandon it would entail surrendering not merely one theme among many, but the very context in which our lives as citizens as well as individuals have been formed. This is an abdication Pound himself resisted for over five decades. Among contemporary poets the resistance still continues today.

B · *PATERSON*

"For a very long time everybody refuses
and then almost without a pause almost
everybody accepts. In the history of the refused in the arts and literature the rapidity
of the change is always startling. Now the
only difficulty with the *volte-face* concerning the arts is this. When the acceptance
comes, by that acceptance the thing created
becomes a classic."

—Gertrude Stein:
"Composition as Explanation"[1]

"and as for the solidity of the white oxen in all this
          perhaps only Dr. Williams (Bill Carlos)
                              will understand its importance,
     its benediction. He wd/ have put in the cart."
                                   (LXXVIII:483)

CHAPTER SEVEN

A LOCAL WAR?

"Exemplum docet, exempla obscurant"

To judge a poem, even in part, by the responses it helped to
provoke in subsequent texts is obviously a dangerous practice. Not only may the responses be irrelevant to the actual
accomplishment of the initial work, but the discussion of
these other writings is bound to be one-sided in its emphasis.
Yet if one acknowledges that Pound's argument about "the
artist who does the next job" suggests a valuable, if rarely
used, critical method, then my own procedure in the following two sections will appear far from arbitrary. Not only did
Williams and Olson offer many of the most searching direct
criticisms of *The Cantos* in their prose writings, but I believe
their criticism also finds implicit expression in the structure
and argument of *Paterson* and *The Maximus Poems*. Since I intend to explore these criticisms in detail and to examine the
specific contribution that Williams and Olson made to the
tradition of the modern verse epic, it is important to keep in
mind that my comments do not pretend to a full reading of
either work. Admirers of *Paterson* and *The Maximus Poems* are
likely to be troubled by all the specific qualities left unmen-
tioned, as well as by the apparently reductive critical horizon
imposed on the two poems. In a study devoted primarily to
Williams and Olson, rather than to the modern verse epic, the
discussion's focus would have been significantly adjusted and
its range of concerns correspondingly expanded. Although I
think the categories developed in the analysis of *The Cantos*
could be applied in equal detail to *Paterson* and *The Maximus
Poems*, my present intention is primarily to examine each of
these works for their suggestions about other, though closely
related, solutions to the problem of writing the tale of the
tribe. My comments on Williams and Olson are largely a continuation of what I have already said about Pound; they form,

as the Scholastic maxim quoted above counsels, part of a single, extended *exemplum*, not a series of new *exempla*.

Precisely because my intention is not to arrive at a single, fixed "theoretical model," but rather "to free a coherent domain of description,"[2] an analysis of other works from the vantage-point of their relationship to the modern verse epic is particularly useful. Poems like David Jones's *In Parenthesis* and *The Anathemata*, Pablo Neruda's *Alturas de Macchu Picchu*, or St.-John Perse's *Amers* could easily have been included here alongside *Paterson* and *The Maximus Poems*. However, restricting the analysis to Williams and Olson offers the immediate, "local" advantage of bracketing more purely abstract, indirect lines of affiliation and contiguity. To trace the shared concerns of Pound, Williams, and Olson, does not require any appeal to a *Zeitgeist* or a cross-cultural "modernist dilemma." Instead, there exists abundant evidence of an immediate and acknowledged influence that goes far beyond questions of literary genealogy and shared ambitions. Although Williams and Olson each rightly insisted his work differed in its inspiration and idiom from Ezra Pound's, their correspondence, essays, and poetry itself all indicate that Pound remained by far the most important contemporary influence/rival, a model to emulate, and, if possible, to surpass.

•   •   •

Pound and Williams met while both were undergraduates at the University of Pennsylvania in 1902, and though Pound soon left Philadelphia to attend Hamilton College, they continued to exchange visits and letters and to discuss one another's writings. Even in 1958 Williams was ready to admit that, "Before meeting Ezra Pound is like B.C. and A.D."[3] After Pound moved to Europe in 1908, their correspondence continued, and eventually Williams' first commercially published volume of poetry, *The Tempers*, was printed in London by Elkin Mathews (1913), largely at Pound's insistence and with a guardedly laudatory introduction by him.

Pound also reprinted Williams' "Portrait of a Woman" in his 1920 volume *The Instigations of Ezra Pound* and accompanied the text with a favorable commentary: "It is a poem that could be translated into French or any other modern language and hold its own with the contemporary product of whatever country one chose."[4] In 1928, when Williams had already written *Al Que Quiere* (1917), *Kora in Hell* (1920), *Sour Grapes* (1921), *The Great American Novel,* and *Spring and All* (1923), as well as his most significant prose meditation upon American history and culture, *In the American Grain* (1925), and had won the 1926 Dial Award for poetry, Pound once more reviewed "Dr. Williams' Position." This time he found much to commend, although the tone is again far more restrained than in Pound's championing of writers like T. S. Eliot, Remy de Gourmont, or even Jean Cocteau.

Pound recognizes that while he and Williams share many of the same literary and social criticisms of America, their reactions are quite different.

> If he wants to 'do' anything about what he sees, this desire for action does not rise until he has meditated in full and at leisure. Where I see scoundrels and vandals, he sees a spectacle or an ineluctable process of nature. Where I want to kill at once, he ruminates, and if this rumination leads to anger it is an almost inarticulate anger, that may lend colour to his style, but which stays almost wholly within the realm of his art. I mean it is a qualificative, contemplative, does not drive him to some ultra-artistic or non-artistic activity.
>
> (*LE:*392)

There was, however, never any question of Williams exerting a reciprocal influence on his younger friend. Pound, from the beginning, took on the role of adviser, judge, and, at times, of editor. He continued, even during his confinement at St. Elizabeth's to send Williams long reading lists, one of which is reproduced in Book Three of *Paterson*:

> re read *all* the Gk tragedies in
> Loeb.—plus Frobenius, plus
> Gesell plus Brooks Adams
> ef you ain't read him all.—
> Then Golding 'Ovid' is in Everyman lib.
> (III,iii:138)[5]

Williams, of course, often felt stung by Pound's condescension, and in 1940 complained bitterly to James Laughlin that "He [Pound] wants to patronize me. Don't tell me this isn't so, for I know better" (*SL*:192).[6] During the next few years, Williams began to express his resentment in increasingly stronger terms. It was an anger based largely upon the quite justified assumption that Pound had never been willing to consider him a serious rival, had never realized that it was Williams' work, and not that of T. S. Eliot, which embodied the most radical alternative to his own poetics. Even in an essay on "Ezra Pound's Present Position," written shortly after the tragedy of Pound's nervous breakdown and imprisonment, Williams is unable to repress a note of intense personal grievance: "He has never recognized me as an equal on a different but just as legitimate poetic basis as his own. He has wanted to make me 'like' him and therefore always inferior. . . . But he is less than I on many counts. That he has . . . never been capable of acknowledging."[7] Yet Williams decided not to publish this outburst, almost as though the act of having once given voice to his intense and frustratingly unreciprocated rivalry made a public declaration irrelevant: "I know that I feel much relieved having written the above . . . but it does not completely resolve the matter . . . of Pound's absolute worth as a poet."[8] Later, as Williams himself began to receive widespread critical recognition and public honors, the resentment diminished until he was able to deflect Pound's continued assumption (presumption) of a tutor's role with graceful equanimity: "Dear Ez: Ain't it enough that you so deeply influenced my formative years without your wanting to influence also my later ones" (*SL*:327). Thus, in spite of formidable strains on their relationship and periods of profound mutual incomprehension, their dialogue continued unabated, and itself constitutes one of the major themes of Williams' answer to *The Cantos*, the "local pride" called *Paterson*.

By 1917 Pound had already published the early drafts of Cantos One to Three and, after the false starts and revisions discussed in Chapter Five, he continued to work on his epic uninterruptedly for the next forty-five years. In 1926 *The Dial* printed the single prize-winning poem, "Paterson." Until the appearance of *Paterson Book One* in 1946, Williams kept returning to his theme only in small fragments and isolated sections published unconnectedly in collections like *New Directions No. 2* (1937), *The Broken Span* (1941), and *The Wedge* (1944). The long gestation of *Paterson* was due partially to Williams' tendency to "meditate in full and at leisure," but, perhaps more centrally, the delay gave Williams an opportunity to watch Pound elaborate the verse techniques for a modern epic poem. He was thus able to measure the precise extent of Pound's success; he was at liberty to learn from the accomplishment of the first seventy-one cantos, and, equally important, could assure himself that the articulation of the tale of *his* tribe, "the lifting of an environment to expression" (*SL*:286), had not yet received an adequate realization, that there remained a task of paramount importance for American poetics which no one else seemed ready to undertake.

Williams' correspondence from the mid 1930s until the publication of *Paterson Book One* is full of references to the agonizing gestation of "that magnum opus I've always wanted to do: the poem PATERSON. . . . I've been sounding myself out in these years working towards a form of some sort" (*SL*:163).[a] But, if one compares Williams' outcries to Pound's hesitations during the composition of the first few cantos, two closely related differences become apparent. The first and most significant is that, unlike Pound, Williams felt no need to justify the very desire to write so extended a poem. He was often angered at his own inability to begin serious work on *Paterson* (*SL*:216), and uncertain about what form could be adequate to the demands of so complex an undertaking (*SL*:257), but at no time did the project itself seem an anachronism. The tone of Pound's 1916 letter to John Quinn, "Am at work on a long poem. Which last two words have an awful sound when they appear close together"[9] is completely absent, in part, I suspect, because during the intervening years

---

[a] Characteristically, the poet who was to close *Paterson* Book Three with the defiant assertion, ". . . write carelessly so that nothing that is not green will survive" (III,iii:129), spent two decades and countless discarded fragments searching for a language and form sufficiently "careless" in their calculated balance of design and accident to ensure his work's survival.

the creation of *The Cantos* themselves had largely removed such doubts from Anglo-American poetics. Williams, that is, might consider Pound's epic as at best a qualified success, but its very existence had decisively shifted the terms of accepted literary possibilities.

Directly related to this distinction is Williams' conviction that American literature *required* a poem like *Paterson*, that "P.[aterson] I know, is crying to be written; the time demands it" (*SL*:214). His own epic, in other words, must succeed, not in order to reclaim the modern world from the domain of the novelist, but to rescue American verse from the "formalism" imposed upon it by the triumphant example of other *poets*. Williams' sense of *Paterson* as a kind of moral-aesthetic obligation to the idiom of his own nation, his desire to ground a new epic in the speech and daily circumstances of one specific locality, gave him a far more precise focus than Pound had reached in 1917.

I am not arguing that *The Cantos* in some way encouraged Williams to consecrate a major text to the life of his own region. Williams clearly needed very little stimulation to work on such a project, and, in any event, American writing during the 1930s would have provided him with a plethora of analogous undertakings. The Federal Government's Works Projects Administration employed numerous artists to undertake detailed regional studies of different areas of the United States, and Williams himself was invited to lead the New Jersey section. Although he declined the burden, he did cooperate closely with the W.P.A. writers and drew heavily upon their *Studies of New Jersey* (1939) and *History of Bergen County, N.J.* (1941) for background material to *Paterson*.[10] What *The Cantos*, more than any other model, made possible was to conceive of such a work *as a poem*. Pound had decisively widened the domain of poetry's rightful subject matter, and Williams was free to apply Pound's lessons to areas of experience ignored in *The Cantos* themselves. Williams' comments on the genesis of *Paterson* reveal his confidence that a readership already existed which could be won over, an arena already demarcated in which his achievement could be effectively recognized. This sense of his career as an *agon*, of his verse as a direct challenge to the dominant poetics of his day, is precisely intended. Already in the 1918 "Prologue" to *Kora in Hell* Williams attacked Pound and Eliot for, in his eyes, having "run away," for having given up the struggle to find a new and fitting idiom for the modern world:

> But our prize poems are especially to be damned not because of superficial bad workmanship, but because they are rehash, repetition in another way of Verlaine, Baudelaire, Maeterlinck—conscious or unconscious— just as there were Pound's early paraphrases from Yeats and his constant later cribbing from the Renaissance, Provence and the modern French : Men content with the connotations of their masters.[11]

The repeated accusations of "conventionality"[12] are especially telling, because at the time Williams formulated his complaint, both Pound and Eliot were still regarded as the major exemplars of avant-garde, experimental verse. From the start, however, Williams felt that by setting so much of their writing within the context of an "exhausted" culture, both writers had avoided the real challenge of their own epoch. They had failed to find a language and metrics able to engage contemporary reality without either the mediation of irrelevant cultural models—irrelevant, precisely because, at the time of their first articulation, these models were themselves responses to specific, contingent, and local conditions—or a passive surrender to impressionistic formlessness. While it is true that at least since Joel Barlow the theme of celebrating the United States has been part of the country's literary tradition, this was far from the solution that Williams envisaged to the work of his expatriate rivals. Indeed, one of the characteristics most strongly differentiating Williams from poets like Carl Sandburg or novelists like Thomas Wolfe was his detestation of a rhetorical listing of American place-names in an attempt to gain epic breadth. The care for exact and sharply articulated description upon which Pound had always insisted was never abandoned by Williams, and, in the *Little Review* of August 1919, he condemned " 'chance, lovely singers' who pipe up and do conventional ditties in Wyoming or Texas or Dela-

ware or Nebraska, taking in the ready scenery of the place.
. . ."[13] American subjects, Williams realized, could be treated
just as emptily as any other theme. Throughout his career he
rejected the unstructured exuberance of Whitman or
Sandburg. Instead, he hoped to find a poetic idiom which
would be flexible enough to include new material, but one
which retained enough discipline to prevent an easy descent
into bathos or pomposity.[b]

Yet, although he longed to endow American verse with a
firm internal structure, Williams was convinced that the *same*
poetics could never be adequate to both Europe and the
United States. In Williams' judgment, the attempt by Pound
and Eliot to find a syncretistic language, true to each world
and every epoch, had distorted the very particularity of their
subject matter, had renounced the accuracy of response upon
which a genuine perception must be grounded. When Williams insists that "Europe is nothing to us. Simply nothing.
Their music is death to us. We are starving—not dying mind
you—but lean-bellied for words"[14] his violence is not directed against the art of England or France, but against those
who would impose that art as part of a cultural hegemony
upon a radically different setting, men like the Puritans of *In
The American Grain* who "have . . . in themselves nothing of
curiosity, no wonder, for the New World,"[15] and insist upon
mis-translating each new experience into the idiom of a alien
dispensation.

The Puritans, the academics, and the expatriates: three
figures embodying the rejection of America, united in Williams' imagination as a single, triple-headed antagonist, to be
met by the "trinitarian" local hero, Paterson—eponymous
giant (Myth), New Jersey city (History), and struggling
poet-doctor (Autobiography), in a combat for the still speech-
less conscience of his land.[16]

[b] In his effort to find a new structure for verse, Williams was in much the
same relationship to the writing of Whitman as Cézanne had been to the
work of the French Impressionists. Cézanne always said that his goal was to
make of Impressionism, "quelque chose de solide comme l'art des musées."
Although Williams' ultimate success is far less certain, the struggle with an
artistic legacy which had itself once been liberating, but had deteriorated into
careless and shallow mannerisms, was the same for both artists.

Nonetheless, while Eliot's spectacular success seemed to Williams to personify all the forces of academic repression, the return of American poetry "to the classroom just at the moment when I felt that we were on the point of an escape to matters much closer to the essence of a new art form itself— rooted in the locality which should give it fruit,"[17] Pound represented a far more problematic challenge. Not only did the two men continue to share numerous economic and aesthetic convictions, but, more centrally, Williams was forced to acknowledge that Pound's actual practice, *The Cantos'* uncanny ability to absorb the most recalcitrant materials, effected a decisive breakthrough in the very direction he had always marked out as his own. It is the scrupulous attention to the individual, specific nature of his different historical subjects, the participation in "the principal move in imaginative writing today—that away from the world as symbol toward the world as reality" (*SE*:107)[18] which Williams repeatedly praises in his reviews of Pound's epic-in-progress. Pound had learned how to incorporate into verse precisely those American documents and histories that Williams himself had hitherto been able to utilize only in his prose meditations:

> Thus, searching among the writings of the American patriots of 1775 and a little later—Adams, Jefferson, and some others— . . . Pound has not modified the flavor, the *full* meaning of his colonial matter. . . . He has not "modified" it to fit his preconceived—or any preconceived metrical plan. He has kept his own plan fluid enough to meet his opportunities. He has taken, laudably, the speech of the men he treats of and, by clipping to essentials, revealed its closest nature—its pace, its "meaning." And this is his poetry.
>
> (*SE*:167-9)

As a result, even during the Second World War, although deeply disturbed by the Rome radio broadcast (which resulted in a brief investigation of Williams, a known friend of Ezra Pound, by the F.B.I.), he could write to James Laughlin:

> It is impossible to praise Pound's line. The terms for such praise are lacking. There ain't none. You've got to read

the line and feel first, then grasp through experience in its
full significance HOW the language makes the verse live.
It lives; even such unpromising cataloguing as his *Cantos*
of the Chinese kings, princes and other rulers do live and
become affecting under treatment.

(SL:191)

Yet, in the same letter, Williams also insists that "my perceptions overtook him [Pound] twenty years ago—not however
my accomplishments. When I have finished, if I can go on to
the finish, there'll be another measuring" (*SL*:192). Williams
clearly recognizes the authority of Pound's "line," of his astonishing expansion of the technical resources of modern
verse. And yet, because the root "perceptions," the relationship between poet and world, upon which *The Cantos* were
grounded remained inadequate, the poem itself was ultimately no more than "a medieval inspiration, patterned on a
substitution of medieval simulacra for a possible, not yet extant modern and living material" (*SL*:135). Instead of a modern verse epic, *The Cantos* offered only "a pre-composition
for us. Something which when later (perhaps) packaged and
realized in living, breathing stuff will (in its changed form) be
the thing" (*SL*:135). Thus, when Hugh Kenner describes
Paterson as "Pound's war applied to a local case,"[19] he ignores
the decisive ways in which Williams also intended his poem as
an anti-*Cantos*, a text designed not so much to *apply* Pound's
lesson to a particular setting, but rather to *contest* the fundamental priorities, the entire hierarchy of values, celebrated in
The Cantos. The "modern and living" epic for which Williams was contending, the poem whose realization he had
meditated and postponed for so long, would owe much to
Pound's prior efforts, but it would also hurl a challenge directly at the heart of his friend's whole project, would offer, as
the invocation to *Paterson* announces:

a reply to Greek and Latin with the bare hands

(2)

CHAPTER EIGHT

• • •

A DELIRIUM OF SOLUTIONS

"My whole intent, in my life, has been . . .
to find a basis (in poetry . . .) for the actual."
(*SL*:257)

"Art is local." As a slogan, these words ring more like "an identification and a plan for action" (Invocation:2) than a critical absolute. Even though the phrase was originally attributed to the Flemish painter Maurice Vlaminck, widely repeated in the circle gathered around Alfred Stieglitz, and quoted by Williams' friend Marsden Hartley in his 1921 memoirs, *Adventures in the Arts*,[1] today these words seem uniquely associated with the aesthetics of William Carlos Williams. Like John Dewey's article, "Americanism and Localism," which appeared in *The Dial* in June 1920 ("We are discovering that the locality is the only universal"),[2] Vlaminck's assertion was appropriated as part of the prolonged struggle against American subservience to European models, a struggle in which *Paterson* constitutes perhaps the last, belated skirmish. Yet the triumph of Williams' wider principle, the acceptance of his conviction that there can be "no general culture unless it is bedded in a locality . . . no universal except in the local" (*SL*:224)—hence, of course, the inherent self-contradiction of any international(-izing) *Guide to Kulchur*—has become so much a part of our artistic heritage, is so embedded in the discourse of American culture, that the particular claims Williams made for Paterson, New Jersey, as a historically significant setting have never been sufficiently questioned. The assertion that art must maintain an intimate "contact" with the "environment it is intended for" (*SE*:37) is quite different from saying that *any* site can, under careful scrutiny, yield equally rich information about the terms, both historical and contemporary, of American life. This later claim—a kind of extravagant extension of Frobenius' *Kulturmorphologie*—was not one made by Williams himself, although *Paterson* has often been discussed as if this were the poem's governing premise.

Far from arbitrarily choosing any "local" community, Williams devoted much thought to selecting an appropriate setting for his epic. The site would have to be both specific and privileged; it would, that is, already have to contain qualities uniquely suited to Williams' project. In 1958, the poet explained in considerable detail why he had decided upon Paterson:

> I had known always that I wanted to write a long poem but I didn't know what I wanted to do until I got the idea of a man identified with a city. . . . The problem of the poetics I knew depended upon finding a specific city, one that I knew, so I searched for a city. New York? It couldn't be New York, not anything as big as a metropolis. Rutherford wasn't a city. Passaic wouldn't do. . . . Paterson had a history, an important colonial history. It had, besides, a river—the Passaic, and the Falls. I may have been influenced by James Joyce who had made Dublin the hero of his book. I had been reading *Ulysses*. But I forgot about Joyce and fell in love with my city. . . . I took the river as it followed its course down to the sea; all I had to do was follow it and I had a poem.[3]

Like many of Williams' retrospective *apologias*, this passage unites a bewilderingly inventive mixture of self-revelation and calculated mystification. It also contains, in miniature, a remarkably precise account of some of the major problems in the final text of *Paterson*.

The first and most obvious difficulty lies in Williams' idealization of Paterson's real historical significance. Except for a short period during the American Revolution, Paterson played no important role in the colonial history of the United States. During Paterson's early years, in fact, the town was historically far less important than several other New Jersey communities such as Princeton or Trenton. Indeed, the city itself arose only *after* Alexander Hamilton's "Society for Useful Manufactures" had been established in 1791. When Hamilton first projected his federal industrial city to make the new nation independent of foreign manufacturers, there were only a few settlers in the district: a total of ten buildings and a single church near the Falls. Paterson's commercial importance—the only real fame it ever attained—did not begin until the nineteenth century, when it prospered rapidly and, for a while, was called the "Cotton Town" of the Northern States. Silk, for which the area ultimately became most renowned, was not even a major industry until 1840. By 1946, the date of *Paterson Book One*, the city carried few associations in the minds of even its American readers.[a] It was known, if at all, largely as a once beautiful site ravaged by industrialization and deprived of any notable "local" characteristics by the cultural and economic dominance of nearby New York and Newark. In effect, the extent of Paterson's dependence upon the nearby metropolis was so extensive as to make the notion of an autonomous "local" community as deceptive a myth as any nostalgia for a golden age. Since Williams is acutely aware of the shabbiness and banality of life in Paterson, readers have rarely noticed that the very "ground" of the epic is naïvely romantic, that the poet has chosen to discuss the life and history of a community as if, in everything but the industrial despoliation of the landscape, it were still a self-sufficient nineteenth-century town. Nor is the problem merely one of the size and wealth of the community. Olson's Gloucester, Massachusetts, for example, is both a smaller and poorer town than Paterson, but it was able to retain its own character and customs far longer, and Olson makes the gradual decline of Gloucester's independence itself a central theme of *The Maximus Poems*. Williams always insisted that the universal must be expressed through the concrete details of the artist's

---

[a] How obscure Paterson was before Williams made it the setting of his most important poem, and, equally interesting, how little English critics cared about sources of such an artist's work, are both revealed in a 1965 article in the *London Times* (7 January) in which one is told. "Paterson is an imaginary town in New Jersey which Williams created as a symbol of America" (*William Carlos Williams*, ed. Charles Tomlinson, Harmondsworth, 1972, p. 205).

own surroundings, but too often in *Paterson* there is little awareness of the modern city's role as part of a monolithic industrial and financial network whose control is effectively centered *elsewhere*. Unlike Olson, who rails against the evils of absentee ownership throughout *The Maximus Poems*, Williams largely ignores Paterson's similar plight, and is thus unable to find a coherent basis for the economic reality of his town, for the region's actual influence upon the daily life of its citizens.

Still more unsettling, however, is the fixed series of naturalistic "identifications"—between narrator(s) and town, and between the course of the Passaic and the unfolding of the poem—which Williams names as the determining structure of his epic. Sympathetic critics have so delighted in tracing the detailed textual ramifications of his schema—a task facilitated by the ease with which each "new" development can be absorbed into the dominant codes—that often its intellectual and methodological naïveté, its "original" acquiescence in the very cultural equations that the poem subsequently means to challenge, has been passed over. *Paterson* is traversed by and grounded upon a sequence of thematic metaphors, beginning with the celebrated:

> A man like a city and a woman like a flower
> —who are in love. Two women. Three women.
> Innumerable women, each like a flower.
>
>   But
>
> only one man—like a city.
>
>   (I,i:7)

most of which are so culturally overdetermined that it is difficult not to recognize the poem's symbolic code as a "patch"-work of Romantic commonplaces. Yet it is also true that Williams at once undercuts the condescending man-city / woman-flower metaphor with the first fragment of Cress' (Marcia Nardi's) letters. As James Breslin aptly remarks, "the voice of an actual woman in distress accusing him of personal remoteness" interrupts the self-indulgence of Williams' "dream."[4] In the next chapter I will explore the ways in which the poem succeeds in spite of, and even by reacting against, its own symbolic structure. For the present, however, I think it is useful to restrict my analysis primarily to the poem's symbolic ordering, in part because this aspect of the work has received so much inattentive praise, and in part because an examination of *Paterson's* "identifications" reveals the kinds of dilemmas facing any modern epic poet who tries to assure the coherence of his text by relying upon a programmatic chain of unifying symbols. My chapter division may appear somewhat artificial—especially since the judgments in this first section will be almost entirely negative—but I consider it crucial to understand the ways in which Williams' *apparent* solution to the problem of structuring an epic is essentially inadequate, so that the real terms of his contribution can be appreciated properly.

Paterson, I believe, has been admired for its defects more than for its own, only partially successful, attempts to restrict the scope of those limitations. Much of the typological structure and imagery violates just that specificity of surface detail which had given Williams' earlier writing its energy and sharpness of focus. Between the realization of the "Author's Introduction" to *The Wedge* (1944): "A poem is a small (or large) machine made of words,"[5] and the assumption that "all I had to do was follow it [the Passaic] and I had a poem," lies what seems to me a profound and unsettling shift in Williams' practice. For all his vehement anti-academicism, *Paterson* has proved an exegete's delight. Its generative equations—the thunder of the Falls and the inarticulate language of Paterson's citizens; the death of Sam Patch and the failure of expatriate authors; the 1902 fire that burned down the Danforth Library and the poet's violent, anarchic imagination; the Curies' discovery of radium and Williams' invention of the "variable foot"—all function with a formulaic regularity that makes it easy to "explain" the poem, to trace a coherent symbolic pattern which surreptitiously becomes both a justification of the critic's effort and a validation of the poet's skill. Yet Williams himself had already explicitly rejected many of the same metaphors upon which he was to place so great a burden of meaning in *Paterson*. The 1932 text, *A Novelette*, for example, scorned as irrelevant the very equation between modern verse forms and the Curies' scientific research which "figures" so heavily in *Paterson* Book Four: "The analogy with radium is inadequate. So is the analogy with essences."[6] In more general terms, both *The Descent of Winter* (1928) and Williams' enthusiastic review of Charles Sheeler's paintings (1939) had declared that elaborate, analogical structures were no longer a suitable foundation for contemporary aesthetics: "That thing, the vividness which is poetry by itself makes the poem. There is no need to explain or compare."[7] The artist

> must possess that . . . perception of [his materials'] uniqueness which realizes in them an end in itself, each piece irreplaceable by a substitute, not to be broken down to other meaning. Not to pull out, transubstantiate, . . . not even to distill but to see and keep what the understanding touches intact.
>
> (SE:233)

As Breslin said, in all of Williams' best texts, "details do not combine into symbolic clusters but instead create a literal specificity."[8] *Paterson*, however, violates this principle at every turn. Although a catalogue of the different meanings that Williams' metaphors acquire undeniably confirms the poet's drive to order his heterogeneous material, in the end he simply makes too many demands of his figures; he allows them to stand for so many different emotional nuances and intellectual perceptions that their literal specificity is cripplingly undermined. The "symbolic structure" of *Paterson* is built upon an almost arithmetical progression of senses. Each image is simply superimposed upon the one developed earlier, until, for example, the Falls represent not only the unordered, wild words out of which the poet must "comb" his meaning, but are identified with the destructive fire of Book Three, the "Beautiful Thing," Madame Curie's experiments, and even Social Credit fiscal theories.[b] By concentrating ex-

[b] In one of his notes, now in the Beinecke Library, Williams even reminds himself to use the Falls "as background to everything else, to heighten everything else and to stitch together every other thing." Such instructions come dangerously close to being a parody of the "new criticism's" demands for a

clusively upon individual instances of such metaphoric "fus-ings," commentators, not surprisingly, have been able to cel-ebrate Williams' technique. Considered in turn, the different metaphors are often thematically well deployed, even if somewhat too "ready-at-hand." Yet read together, as they collect ever-increasing clusters of signification, it is evident that their value as signifiers becomes deflected, that they are made to carry too large and unsubstantiated a weight of narra-tive and thematic development.

Directly related to Williams' search for a symbolic frame-work is the fact that, in spite of subsequent denials, he was never able entirely to "forget about Joyce and [fall] in love with my city." Instead, he appropriated and simplified the imaginative constructs of the very tradition *Paterson* was in-tended to subvert. Williams himself, of course, acknowledged that he had "been reading *Ulysses*" at the time of the poem's genesis, and was impressed with Joyce's success in making "Dublin the hero of his book." But Joyce's influence runs deeper than even this affiliation. Behind the motif of Paterson the sleeping giant, the primal father-son whose bride is the very landscape of the poem and whose dream-thoughts be-come the characters inhabiting that landscape—"The giant in whose apertures we / cohabit . . ." (I,ii:34)—stands the direct model of *Finnegans Wake* and the more distant example of Blake's "prophetic" poems such as *The Four Zoas* and *Milton*. The early drafts of *Paterson* show that initially Williams in-tended the figure of a mythical giant to assume a central role in the poem's symbolic hierarchy. In one such fragment, he even appeals to Norse sagas, to the myth of "Ymir's flesh" creating the earth, and his thoughts giving birth to "all the gloomy clouds," in order to lend a richer context to *Paterson's* borrowed image. One critic makes the plausible suggestion that these fragments were removed "to assure that his giants would not be merely, or too much creation-story—pre-history instead of present situation."[9] But what function, if not "merely creation-story," do they serve in their present,

---

highly wrought, metaphoric structure, and it is fortunate that, in the event, Williams was unable to follow his own program with total consistency.

truncated appearance? The sleeping titan scarcely figures beyond the opening pages of the revised text, yet Williams also proved unwilling to eliminate entirely what had become a purely formal, schematic gesture. The giant is a presence asserted rather than realized, an incarnation of place designed to endow the descriptions with a mythological resonance that the poem's own structure is able neither to develop with any rigor, nor to discard completely. Moreover, this ambivalence, this use/refusal of canonic literary models, is not restricted to a single paradigm. Even T. S. Eliot, the great antagonist of Williams' entire poetic career, is constantly, and sometimes unconsciously, evoked, as though in composing *Paterson* Williams needed to draw upon all the resources of modern verse, the inimical as well as the familial, to proceed with his own work. For all the bitter humor of lines like "Who is it spoke of April? Some / insane engineer" (III,iii:142), there are countless moments when Williams simply takes over one of Eliot's characteristic formulations without improving upon it or contextually justifying the dependency: "For the beginning is assuredly / the end" ("Preface":3); "up hollow stairs among acrid smells / to obscene rendezvous" (I,ii:28); "For there is a wind or ghost of a wind" (III,i:95), etc. A more detailed series of juxtapositions would, I believe, reveal that the Eliot of *Four Quartets* must be included, along with Pound and Joyce, as one of the essential sources, both for specific images, and, heretical though this may appear, even for some of the rhythmic configurations underlying *Paterson*.

Considered atomistically, it is clear that none of my comments isolates a decisive and necessarily fatal lapse in Williams' text. Yet, experienced together, in their interaction throughout the poem, these kinds of decisions do indicate a certain failure of nerve: an ill-ease before the enormity of his undertaking, and a confusion about how to give his epic both a convincing, objectively demonstrable structure and a sufficient aura of significance. Nonetheless, had *Paterson* succeeded in genuinely *locating* its own specific horizon, had Williams been able "not to talk in vague categories, but to write particularly, as a physician works upon a patient, upon the thing

before him, in the particular to discover the universal,"[10] all
the structural deficiencies (or, more accurately, structural *excesses*) would constitute only an uncharacteristic technical regression amid one of the decisive achievements in modern
American poetics. Instead, however, Williams faltered precisely where success was most crucial, where the chance to
provide a counter-model to *The Cantos* seemed to lie most
readily within his grasp.

In the same letter in which Olson weighs the achievement
of Pound's epic, he also offers a brief, but acutely perceptive,
comment upon *Paterson*:

> . . . after that date, [1917] the materials of history which
> he [Pound] has found useful are not at all of use (nor are
> Bill's, despite the more apparent homogeneity: date
> 1917, not only did Yurrup (West, Cento, Renaissance)
> go, but such blueberry America as Bill presents (Jersey,
> dump-smoke covering same) also WENT (that is, Bill,
> with all respect, don't know fr nothing abt what a city
> *is*).[11]

It is the political, historical, and economic reality of Paterson,
its existence *as a city*, that is curiously missing, a virtual blank
at the poem's core. The prose insertions from the region's
history are meant, in Sister Bernetta Quinn's description,
to offer "a study in sources, an ignorance of which is one of
the main causes why the citizens of Paterson walk around
asleep. . . ,"[12] but it is difficult to see how these fragments
could ever effect a significant awakening.[e] They contain virtually no historical *analysis*, presenting instead only a fixed,
unchanging opposition between natural beauty (of landscape

---

[e] Although Williams "places" his prose fragments with great skill, and
often with remarkable wit, technically I wonder whether his strategy does
not represent a regression from Pound's practice. In *The Cantos*, Pound is
able, as Williams himself acknowledged, to make convincing *poetry* out of the
most intractable factual and documentary material. Yet *Paterson*, although it
does absorb certain records of New Jersey history into its overall fabric,
maintains a clear distinction between verse and prose details. Thematically,
the two complement and reinforce one another, but Williams largely abandons Pound's experiment to treat historical and economic data *in the same form*
as his lyrical and reflective passages.

or human desire) and economic-sexual despoliation. Moreover, by locating the rape of Paterson exactly contemporaneous with, and as the direct consequence of, the very organization of the town as a distinct economic and political entity (the primal fall into Alexander Hamilton's "Society for Useful Manufactures"), Williams is prevented from finding any historically grounded alternatives in his own "sources." Presumably the industrialization of Paterson could have proceeded without the brutal disregard for natural landscapes or human decency that characterized American expansion throughout the nineteenth century, but, beyond lamenting the tragedy, Williams offers little guidance.

The element of "instruction," the epic's obligation to present not only models of "the good," but also a demonstrable technique by which that good can be realized and imitated, is largely absent from *Paterson*. One can defend this absence by reading *Paterson* as a poem about the impossibility of writing an epic, as the evidence of Williams' growing recognition that to assume an epic poet's authority is inherently fraudulent. Such a reading is partially justified, and in the next chapter I will explore how Williams' complex responses to his predicament significantly enrich the text and help to form his real contribution to the tradition of the modern verse epic. But, at the same time, the limitations of this type of justification should be acknowledged, since (1) Williams' symbolic structure is clearly intended to give the poem the authority and coherence of a genuine epic, and (2) he does *try* to offer an entire series of explicit and implicit lessons in what the community requires. The problem, however, is that, first, as we have seen, *Paterson's* symbolic structure is inadequate to its purpose, and, second, the solutions Williams proposes for his town's dilemma are so abstract and general ("invention," "credit," respect for nature, etc.) that he unwittingly succeeds in making the terrible waste seem historically both inevitable and irreversible, grounded in human weakness rather than in specific and changeable social circumstances. History itself, the vital "ground" which Williams is attempting to recover from communal neglect, thus becomes largely a series of unexamined *anecdotes*, a numbing repetition of archetypal disasters from which no really useful instigations can arise.

In a sense Williams has replaced Pound's quest for the right *audience* with the question of *auditing*,[13] with the poet's obligation to hear properly the voices of his fellow citizens, his environment's natural phenomena, and its historical records: "untaught but listening, [he] shakes with the intensity / of his listening" (I,iii:81). At its best, there is a subtle and distinctly un-Poundian movement here: a flow of sounds from the community to the poet which are then returned to that community, not in a "purified" form, but in testimony to their inherent significance. In such a movement, the real lesson comes, not from the poet's conclusions and judgments, but from his example as auditor, from the seriousness with which he is willing to become engaged in the language of his tribe as it actually exists.

Insofar as this movement accurately describes *Paterson*, however, Williams' criticism of *The Cantos* as a "precomposition" would apply more to his own work than to Pound's. In such a schema, that is, *Paterson* becomes a series of steps towards a (perhaps unrealizable) epic, one which could build upon the record of the first poet's listening to uncover the full meaning—and potential for a different dispensation— implicit in his data. Yet even strictly within *Paterson's* own terms, Williams' success as an auditor is far from certain. If one of *The Cantos'* central problems is the issue of Pound's selection of his *exempla*, his degree of perception in defining the tribe's predicament and offering the appropriate counsel, then the analogous difficulty with *Paterson* is the gaps in Williams' auditory range, the limitations in his knowledge of who and what must be heeded to comprehend the full life of his town. History, as we have seen, is simply not "heard" with sufficient clarity to become more than snippets of anecdotal and antiquarian lore. More disturbingly, however, even the present life of Paterson is not realized with much greater specificity than the town's past. The narrative almost entirely neglects the actual political and social organization of the community, and the profusion of prose episodes and verse images accumulating ever more evidence of industrial pollution and sexual-cultural repression cannot, in the absence of concrete analysis, sufficiently particularize the narrative. For much of the poem, Williams simply fails to confront the most

revealing sounds of his city. He is so caught up in the fascination of his metaphorical equations that the pressures of Paterson's real circumstances do not register in the text.

And yet, at the last moment, Williams does manage to re-
trieve his missing context. Fascinatingly, all of the suppressed
details do enter the poem once, and in a form that reveals with
uncanny precision just what *Paterson* had hitherto failed to
confront. In Book Four Williams reprints a long letter from
Allen Ginsberg, the symbolic heir (Pater-son) who was to
confirm the justice of Williams' battle for a new poetics. The
passage is worth quoting in full because, for all Ginsberg's
deep sense of kinship with Williams, his questions strikingly
parallel the worst misgivings expressed in Olson's *Mayan
Letters*:

> Dear Doc: Since I last wrote I have settled down more,
> am working on a Labor newspaper (N.J. Labor Herald,
> AFL) in Newark. The owner is an Assemblyman and so I
> have a chance to see many of the peripheral intimacies of
> political life which in this neighborhood has always had
> for me the appeal of the rest of the landscape, and a little
> more, since it is the landscape alive and busy.
>
> Do you know that the west side of City Hall, the
> street, is nicknamed the Bourse, because of the continual
> political and banking haggle and hassel that goes on
> there?
>
> Also I have been walking the streets and discovering
> the bars—especially around the great Mill and River
> streets. Do you know this part of Paterson? I have seen so
> many things—negroes, gypsies, an incoherent bartender
> in a taproom overhanging the river, filled with gas, ready
> to explode, the window facing the river painted over so
> that the people can't see it. I wonder if you have seen
> River Street most of all, because that is really at the heart
> of what is to be known.
>
> (IV,iii:194–5)

Like Pound, Williams wanted to reclaim for poetry the
breadth of vision and capacity for historical judgments it had
once possessed: "I cannot swallow the half-alive poetry which

knows nothing of totality. . . . Nothing is beyond poetry.
. . ."[14] But, after the example of Joyce's Dublin or Alexander
Döblin's *Berlin Alexanderplatz*, an epic set in Paterson, New
Jersey, which excluded "the west side of City Hall" and "the
great Mill and River streets," was far too narrow a basis for
any convincing "tale of the tribe."[d]

Fundamentally, Paterson really is a "mythical" city, but
largely in the sense of an imaginary site in which the poet's
desires for coherence and meaning are tested. It does become
"anywhere," but only by the instant generalizability of all its
constituent features, and not because it has been firmly seized
in its irreducible singularity. And the moment personification
replaces characterization, the setting becomes only a private
theatre in which hope and despair struggle for dominance in
the poet-hero's consciousness. Throughout four books, *Paterson* enacts a nostalgic search for a natural language, an idiom
which can recover the lost innocence of full communication
between landscape and mind, and between artist and world.
As we shall see subsequently, it is also Williams' greatest
triumph to have resisted for so long the claims of any
plenitude, to have kept his perception so firmly fixed upon
the "blockages" that separate desire and act, and fracture the
wholeness of a mythical origin into the "nothing, surrounded
by / a surface" (III,ii:123) of lived, intersubjective discourse.
Yet it is just this perception that Williams seems eager to
abandon in Book Five, the "Coda" to *Paterson*. Few sections
of the poem have received so much detailed attention and
critical praise. But, for all the skill with which Williams de-

---

[d] Williams himself seems to have felt the force of Ginsberg's implicit criticism. Part of the evidence is his very decision to reprint the letter, but there is
another, external sign that Williams was uneasy about how much of Paterson
had escaped his vision. In February 1952, Williams wrote Louis Ginsberg:
"What I want of your son is for him to take me to a bar on River Street . . . I
don't know what the joint is like . . . but if it's something to experience . . . I'd
like to see it for I want to make it the central locale for a poem which I have in
mind—a sort of extension of *Paterson*" (Beinecke Library; cf. *Twentieth-Century Literature*, Vol. 21, No. 3, October 1975, p. 300). In the event, Williams was indeed to write his extension of *Paterson* but, instead of the bar on
River Street, the central setting was to be The Cloisters, a Museum in New
York!

ploys his new "identification," the Unicorn of the sixteenth-century Franco-Flemish tapestries in The Cloisters, and for all the passionate grace with which he confronts his own old age—"Though he is approaching / death he is possessed by many poems" (V,iii:231)—it is equally obvious that the poet has finally abandoned any attempt to approach the citizens and life of Paterson, New Jersey. (In what way, for example, is the Museum fundamentally different from the Library Williams had found so oppressive in Book Three?) In Book Five, Williams seems further than ever from the communal goals announced in the "Invocation," and all the triumphant affirmations that "A WORLD OF ART / . . . THROUGH THE YEARS HAS *SURVIVED!*" (V,i:209) scarcely effect the "marriage" between word and world, between art and the reality of daily American life, which *Paterson* was intended to consummate.

As is true of Pound in *The Pisan Cantos*, beauty is now "in the mind, indestructible." But to Williams such a shift no longer carries with it any sense of loss, any regret at a narrowing of horizons. In a world where his townsmen continue "neither [to] know their sources nor sills of their / disappointments" (I,i:6), in which "They may look at the torrent in / their minds / and it is foreign to them" (I,i:12), the poet's new-found certainty—"It is the imagination / which cannot be fathomed. / It is through this hole / we escape" (V,i:212)—seems like a purely abstract, almost solipsistic, victory. The idealization of art and memory which critics have, falsely, I believe, read into *The Pisan Cantos* and *Drafts and Fragments*, does accurately characterize Book Five of *Paterson*. In Pound's epic the *enforced* separation between the poet's imagination and the realm of communal affairs is felt as a tragedy; it represents the shattering of his deepest wishes, and unfolds as the logical consequence of the poem's initial premises. But Williams' "retreat into art" has no such internal necessity, and is, accordingly, much harder to explain. The aesthetic pressure to give his poem an apparently "triumphant" resolution, his sense that perhaps the only "lesson" he could honestly bequeath his audience was a personal record of his own imaginative powers quickened by the art of the past, or, possibly, his belated realization that *Paterson*'s "tribe" was really not the citizens of the town, but the community of poets and readers of poetry who might be encouraged by his example, are all plausible motives for the change in attitude. But none of these reasons is consistent with *Paterson*'s announced intent, or engages the task defined in the first four books. Indeed, the coda unwittingly "solves" the very problem upon which the poem itself was grounded merely by claiming one of its initial components as the long-sought answer. In the "Preface" Williams had asked, " 'Rigor of beauty is in the quest. But how will you find beauty / when it is locked in the mind past all remonstrance?' " (p. 3). Now, at the quest's end, a beauty that exists *only* in the artifacts of culture and the poet's private consciousness is suddenly and surprisingly upheld as an adequate testament. Instead, to adapt Leo Bersani's arguments from their own context, "They are solutions to a problem which deserve to be treated as symptoms of the same problem, since they essentially involve the suppression of the problem and its disguised repetition."[15] In a letter written to Cid Corman in March, 1960, Williams himself expressed serious doubts about the validity of the entire fifth book,[16] and his working notes indicate plans for a further volume in which the poem would have returned to its historical setting as part of an effort to uncover a more specific ground for Paterson's dilemma: "John Jay, James Madison. let's read about it!" (243)

Accordingly, I think it is more accurate to read Book Five not as, in any sense, the "resolution" of *Paterson*, but only as one more amid the "delirium of solutions" (I,ii:28) with which Williams experimented in his struggle to find a convincing poetic structure. By seeing how many, and how different from one another, these solutions are, we come closer to understanding Williams' achievement than by privileging any particular strategy—including even the ones he himself clearly valued most.

It was Olson who first pointed out that Williams had been unable to come to grips with a modern city, that at the level of articulating a new epic argument *Paterson* provided no viable alternative to the model of Pound's *Cantos*. However, in the same *Mayan Letters*, Olson also says why, for all its thematic and intellectual naïveté, *Paterson* remains a crucial experiment, one from which any subsequent effort at a modern verse epic would have much to learn: "the primary contrast, for our purposes is BILL   his Pat[erson] is exact opposite of Ez's, that is, Bill HAS an emotional system which is capable of extensions & comprehensions [Pound's] . . . is not."[17] It is also with this paradox, the success-in-defeat of Williams' project, *Paterson*'s "partial victory" (I,iii:30) over its own symbolic coherence, that our investigations must come to terms. In Book Four, Williams "waken[s] from a dream, this dream of / the whole poem" (IV,iii:200). If the illusion of a "whole poem," even more than the Passaic Falls, is the rock upon which *Paterson* grounds its self-mystification, that "dream" is nonetheless shattered by Williams' constant "awakenings." It is from those dizzying and fruitful descents *beneath* its symbolic structure that the text's real virtues arise, virtues that remain, as Williams himself knew, both "complex" and, unlike his own metaphoric equations, essentially "unpredictable" (IV,iii:188–90).

CHAPTER NINE

• • •

SPEED AGAINST
THE INUNDATION

"I shall not try to construct a systematic answer to this question by starting with a
dogmatic principle. Rather, I shall proceed
by a series of *approximations*, wherein the
solutions reached at one level will be rectified by bringing the initial problem back
into question."

—Paul Ricoeur,
History and Truth [1]

Paterson, as J. M. Brinnin rightly observes, has "an all-of-a-
piece consistency on an intellectual level, but on an emotive
level the poem is vastly uneven." [2] Accordingly, much of the
critical energy devoted to Williams' poem has centered on an
explication—and implicit celebration—of the work's "intellectual consistency," combined with a nervous awareness of
how difficult it is to reconcile that reassuring surface coherence with its unstable and shifting bases. Yet, I suspect that
Paterson succeeds only when it abandons its symbolic structure, when, in place of the eponymous hero and his metaphoric landscape, the text directly confronts the "delirium of
solutions" discussed in the last chapter *as a delirium*. Beneath
Williams' "dream of the whole poem" there is, in Breslin's
phrase, the violent intrusion of "modern actuality," [3] the
stubborn surplus that will not be absorbed into any holistic
explanatory framework. The emotional structure of *Paterson*,
its incomplete and fragmentary dialectic, "moving from
ground toward form to release a spark of beauty but then falling back," [4] has little connection to the poem's reductive archetypes, and only in the disparity between the two types of
organizational schemas does the text's own specificity, its real

"local truth," emerge. In the desperation of Williams' search for a stable poetic form, for a secure ground to his dream of primal unity, every possible source is tapped, from the landscape of Mount Garrett to the "roar of books / from the wadded library" (III,i:100), and though, for an instant, each can provide him with a glimpse of some possible wholeness of perception—an icon of "flagrant beauty"—that glimpse is immediately challenged. The temporality of experience itself dissolves each triumph, not because of any inherent limitation in the object of vision or desire, but because that object is already part of a context that can never be either wholly transcended or immobilized. Even the most seemingly perfect and self-contained icons are inadequate because, in the face of so large and wide-ranging a need, they cannot incarnate more than another "partial victory." Undeniably, the "beautiful thing" or "the sweet white locust" can reward the poet's (im-)patient attentiveness. They can give him the strength not to "put myself deliberately in the way of death" (I,ii:20), and the confidence not to "run off / toward the peripheries— / to other centers, . . ." (I,iii:36), but they can never provide "the total intelligence" both Williams and his town so desperately require. The next instant, the moment *after* the vision, always returns Williams to the roar of quotidian reality so that only the quest—encompassing both the insights and the despair— is fully real, becoming the very condition of his own self-representation and of the poem, *Paterson*.

Until the retrospective calm of Book Five, Williams knows that it is futile to pray, "Verweile doch, du bist so schön," because beauty itself is acknowledged as radically historical. Paradoxically, history does not enter the poem via the prose accounts of New Jersey lore. Rather, it is present in a more subtle way: as the historicity of human consciousness itself, as a process that can never be stayed within any single realization or patterning, no matter how convincing in itself and painfully won. It is in this sense that Williams, far more than Ezra Pound, lived the truth of Dilthey's insight: "The first condition for the possibility of the study of history is that I myself am a historical being."[5] In *Paterson* no ideal form, whether of individual human relationships or of communal ethics, is allowed to stand unchallenged by time and, whenever the poem seems to arrive at a fixed position, that certitude is dissolved in the continuing flux of lived experience. This is as true of Williams' own moods, constantly shifting from self-mockery, to despair, and then to triumphant, if short-lived, exultation, as it is of the larger historical and didactic motifs presented in the epic. Unlike *The Cantos*, however, Williams' poem accepts such dissolution, not as signs of human frailty, or an inadequate will to order, but as the very condition of life. Williams clearly believes in the need for a sweeping change in Paterson's circumstances, but he does not think there is any one unique economic and social system, any single model of governmental behavior, which can, by legislation alone, guarantee an equitable social order. The "solutions" proposed in *Paterson* are, as I argued in the previous chapter, too vague and generalized to serve as adequate instigations, but they are, nonetheless, recognized as subject to the same pressures of time and decay as the initial "problems." This is a crucial difference from Pound's text in which the *dilemmas* of a society are recognized in their historical specificity, but where the *remedies* are all drawn from a narrow set of atemporal, absolute principles.[a]

Yet, for there to exist a negative dialectic in *Paterson*, a recurrent and thwarted movement towards a holistic synthesis which remains permanently incomplete as all the constituent elements are hurled downwards again to their original, unreconciled antagonism, the inadequate "fixed positions" must be shown as clearly as the unassimilable impulse of dissolution. This is why I spoke earlier about a fruitful gap separating the poem's two governing structures. The disparity between the text's symbolic and emotional unfolding becomes increasingly obvious until their very incommensurability begins to

[a] The two poets' favorite image of intensity and wholeness of perception reveals a great deal about the similarity/difference in their temperaments. Both are attracted to a brightness that can cut through the decay of a shabby and debased environment. In Pound, however, that clarity takes the form of an utterly transparent, unwavering *Light*, while in Williams it finds expression in the unstable, all-consuming power of *Fire*, a force that unlike *The Cantos'* neo–Platonic, crystalline radiance is always both constructive and destructive, beneficent and potentially lethal.

assume a crucial, and even a thematic, value in its own right. Williams' flexible, tentative responses, his openness to new experiences, actually challenges the very authority of his symbolic coherence, until, in a movement of unnerving textual complexity, that coherence is already effectively deconstructed within *Paterson* itself. It is almost as though the whole archetypal structure, the mystification of the trinitarian hero, were necessary to the poem as one more false solution, as the most insidious (because so tempting) form of escape and inattentiveness of all, whose inadequacy the entire rest of the poem must expose. The nostalgia for a purified origin is thus mocked—"Stale as a whale's breath" (I,ii:20)—in the very text whose generation it seemed to have determined, and in this, the most radical internal reversal of a poem's own proclaimed teleology that I know, *Paterson* does, at last, succeed in providing an alternative to the inflexible hierarchies of Pound's *Cantos*.

• • •

"There is . . . one language which is not mythical, it is the language of man as producer . . . whenever man speaks in order to transform reality and no longer to preserve it as an image. . . ."
—Roland Barthes, *Mythologies*[6]

The concrete political and economic life of Paterson is, as I emphasized in the last chapter, curiously, almost glaringly, absent throughout Williams' poem. Yet, as my own quotations indicate, such a complaint is only partially justified. The very passage used to catalogue all that Williams ignored now exists as part of *Paterson* itself, even though it takes the form of a letter from Allen Ginsberg. It is as though this insertion, this deliberate interpenetration of accident and design, text and *hors-texte*, recapitulates, in miniature, the deliberate overthrow of the work's mythical structure; as if, through an intrusion that is at once part of and yet separate from the invention of a "whole poem," a totality were indicated that could never be realized fully in a single epic or by a single man. Williams always tempered both his aesthetic and moral judgments by acknowledging "the pluralism of experience,"[7] and, in his epic, sought to create a single poem which would also be inherently pluralistic, would remain amenable to numerous different perceptions and experiences, no single one of which could be allowed a final, author-itative privilege.

Unlike traditional epics, Williams' text has no one narrative voice able to function as the unquestioned spokesman for values acknowledged as essential to the entire community's welfare. For Williams, the epic characteristics described in the Introduction are no longer attainable with any honesty. Instead, the poem must acknowledge that no one man can still speak for the tribe legitimately, that the tribe must somehow "speak for itself" and will not do so in a unified way. Such a recognition is, of course, not unique to Williams. What is striking, however, is that this realization did not lead Williams to abandon the whole project of writing a new kind of epic, that he kept searching for ways in which to integrate the very dilemma of the epic into the final text. Thus, not only does Williams, throughout *Paterson*, shamelessly appropriate images and whole lines from his contemporaries, he even reproduces, with a quite unnerving evenhandedness of attention, both flattering tributes and bitter denunciations, until the very poem, like a small town, begins to echo with a multitude of voices that cannot be reduced to the utterance of any one narrator. This network of voices that are other than and yet constituent elements of a single text, functions, I believe, much like Pound's literary citations and historical *exempla*, serving to deflect our subjectivization of the narrative into a unified, lyric utterance. But, because these "insertions" frequently *challenge* rather than merely reconfirm or authenticate the poet's own values, their effect is both more radical and more disconcerting than in Pound's usage. The trinitarian hero does not know "the west side of City Hall" and "the bars around the great Mill and River streets"; he does not realize his own potential for cowardice or self-indulgence (cf. E.[dward] D.[ahlberg's] and C.'s [Marcia Nardi's] letters), but the collective poem does, and it attains that knowledge by refusing to privilege any single realization or consciousness. Cress' letters, for example, directly show up the poet-narrator's pretensions; they reveal him as an ordinary, and morally not very scrupulous, man. Yet by containing those very assertions, *Paterson* succeeds, not in "justifying" Williams himself, but in demonstrating its capacity to speak for more than the sensibility of a single author. Williams once wrote that "the structure of the poem ties in morally . . . with the life of a man in his day among other men in the world."[8] And it is just this capacity to make his largeness of vision, his awareness of the often quite different intellectual and emotional claims of "other men in the world," part of the deep structure of *Paterson* that offers the sharpest contrast with Pound's epic.[b]

Williams realized that by fetishizing a limited number of artistic, economic, and social practices, by treating his own catalogue of "magic moments" as absolutes according to whose *a priori* standards any particular historical era can be judged, Pound's text had compromised its ability to come to grips with either a changing world or with a society indifferent to the poem's lessons. This fetishization means that the values for which *The Cantos* are contending are never actually tested; since their relevance to a contemporary setting is axiomatic there is little chance that they will ever be questioned or revised through a confrontation with the events of the poem. Value, in other words, is unidirectionally superimposed upon the narrative from above; there is never any dialogue, any mutual interchange between the two. The number of historical ages from which the *exempla* are drawn is, as Williams saw, largely irrelevant to the internal development of the poem's axes of judgment since all the criteria exist before any local instances are introduced. The proper direction for a modern epic, in Williams' eyes, is a total relativization of the poem's assertive authority; emotionally and structurally the

---

[b] Anything Williams really *sees* in his poetry, he begins, if not to love, then at least to pardon. So "Corydon," the lesbian poet of Book Four, who starts by being only a symbol of urban sophistication and corruption, gradually wins from both Williams and the reader a qualified sympathy. Pound, as we have seen, tends to concretize his villains as much as possible (e.g., Metevsky/Zaharoff). The evil-doers in Williams, on the other hand, are usually anonymous and faceless sets of unpleasant characteristics (such as "Puritans"); as soon as a character becomes particularized the poet adopts a favorable, or at minimum, an understanding tone.

text must present itself as a "testing," as an exploration which is always willing to recognize false directions and to adjust its expectations accordingly. Much as this new structure challenges the traditional scope of the epic, in order to adapt to modern circumstances the principal narrative voice (or voices) within the poem's fiction should be possessed of an ironic consciousness, a consciousness which is capable of reflecting upon previous errors and, through such self-reflection, transcending its own, earlier and incomplete forms of judgment. It is as though the "family resemblance" described in the Introduction must take on new features, must make another adjustment almost as great in its effect as the first fundamental change in the epic, from oral, formulaic poems rehearsed by numerous "singers of tales" over several generations, to written texts composed by a single author. The most appropriate archetypal model for this second transformation is, therefore, not *The Cantos' nostos* or journey home, but an "education" similar in many ways to Henry Adams' sense of the term, a learning process in which only the questions are known from the outset and in which even they are susceptible to reformulation, increased sharpening, or even abandonment depending upon a contingent and variable context. Freedom, that is, must be more than an abstractly posited goal of the epic poet; it must be shown at work as a category of the narrative itself.

Ultimately, *Paterson* is unable to locate that freedom in any historical *praxis* open to either its narrators or its readers. Its ideas are no more "in things" than they are capable of "going into" any concrete "action," beyond the generation of an isolated, richly dispersed, text. Williams, as Olson says, did let the history of his city "roll him under," but not before he had won, for both himself and his literary successors, a considerable—although still "partial"—victory. Before beginning *Paterson*, Williams had described *The Cantos* as only "a pre-composition for us" (*SL*:135). Yet, by the time of Book Four, he was ready to admit that:

> Weakness,
> weakness dogs him, fulfillment only
> a dream or in a dream. No one mind

can do it all, runs smooth
in the effort: *toute dans l'effort*
(IV,iii:191)

Perhaps it is also most fitting to end this discussion here, with the realization that, like history itself, the modern verse epic, whether it attempts the tale of the whole tribe, or the lifting to expression of a single community, must itself always be both provisional and collective, that, in the absence of an innocent origin and the perpetual deferment of a historically adequate goal, there are only "pre-compositions," only "possible, not yet extant" models which, together, provide the groundwork for the next attempt. To begin again, in yet another way:

To make a start
out of particulars
("Preface":3)

C · *THE MAXIMUS POEMS*

"nothing counts save the quality of the af-
fection"

(LXXVII:466)

"Curam ergo verborum rerum volo esse
sollicitudinem" (I want care in words to be
solicitude for things)

—Quintilian

CHAPTER TEN

· · ·

THE OLD MEASURE
OF CARE

". . . this rhetoric is real!"
—*Paterson* III,iii:145

". . . cette donnée exacte qu'il faut, si l'on
fait de la littérature, parler autrement que
les journaux . . ."[1]

Thus, in 1886 Stéphane Mallarmé sought to locate the *minimum* precondition for the creation of literature, the unbridgeable chasm which divides two essentially incompatible deployments of language. Yet the very need to insist upon so categorical a disjunction reveals that contamination is always possible, that the chasm may prove only a threshold, a shifting margin habitually traversed by the discourse of any text. There is a sense in which the poetics Mallarmé sought was haunted at its very inception by what it would most deny, by the inherent availability of language to the public rhetoric of "les journaux."

One of the very few *positive* affirmations uniting countless otherwise quite dissimilar late-nineteenth-century poems is an insistent, clamorous announcement of their difference from any idiom corrupted by the declamatory, ideological tones of public speech. Rhetorically, a characteristic feature of these poems is a violent attack upon rhetoric, an attempt to banish from the domain of literature its prosaic and parodic double. Crystallized in endless variations upon Verlaine's injunction—"Prends l'éloquence et tords-lui son cou!"[2]— poets eloquently proclaimed their abhorrence of rhetoric, without, however, providing any fixed criteria by which its presence could be recognized. The pejorative connotations as-

signed to rhetoric are almost infinitely flexible in their application. The word functions as a single, overdetermined epithet
covering excessive ornamentation; insincere, superficial, and
florid speech; and all "public" verse occasioned by events
by which the writer himself is basically unmoved, a poetry
whose intent is so evidently polemical that the particular intimacy of one individual speaking from the depth of his own
experience to a single reader is lost. But there is another, less
explicitly articulated, premise underlying such universal con-
demnations, a supposition whose implications are distinctly
troubling. Already by the beginning of the nineteenth century
the whole relationship, not merely between an author and his
language, but also between writer and audience, had become
profoundly unstable. Increasingly, poets began to think that
the only authentic verse was one composed purely out of an
inner exigency, a poetry written solely to express the private
insights or emotions of its creator. Insofar as the presence of a
reader was even acknowledged, he was addressed exclusively
as an individual, as a single man who, in his encounter with a
text, was beyond the confines of class, politics, or geography.
Only the language of politicians and editors spoke to men in
their social roles and it is that language to which the name
"rhetoric" was applied.[a]

[a] I am, of course, aware that the tradition of the great "public" poem, a
work directly commenting upon events of immediate national significance
and addressed to the entire educated community, continued to flourish
throughout the nineteenth and early twentieth centuries. Major poets such as
Tennyson, Hardy, Whitman, Kipling, and Bridges, all produced notable
examples of such writing, and in England the list of practitioners could be
multiplied almost indefinitely. (It is interesting, however, that in spite of
single efforts like Hugo's *Les Châtiments*, French poets after Baudelaire became increasingly suspicious of any such efforts. Part of the explanation for
this is undoubtedly the very different aesthetic premises governing Symbolist
and post-Symbolist poetry, but I suspect that the political situation in France
after 1848 and the *coup d'état* of Louis Napoléon in 1851 also played a key role
in encouraging a withdrawal from the sphere of public discourse.)
   Yet, even in England, I think it is also true that by the time Pound began
his literary career, the very possibility of creating an artistically valid "public"
poem was subject to increasingly categorical doubts. Nor did the strictures
always depend upon theoretical pronouncements imported from Continental
writers. In various different formulations, John Stuart Mill's dictum of 1833:

Rhetoric, to paraphrase Mallarmé's letter, is a speech addressed to the public as a collective body; literature is the one discourse incapable of such a role without renouncing its very existence. Rhetoric is not constituted by the reliance upon any specific *techniques* of writing, any set of conventional literary tropes. Rather, it is a certain stance towards both word and world, an inherent faith in the validity of a sphere of public discourse, and a reliance upon what V. N. Vološinov has called "the categorical . . . and declaratory"[3] utterance which brands a text as rhetorical. Morally and politically, rhetoric seeks to eliminate ambiguity. Although there may be many "voices" in a rhetorical text (*The Cantos, The Maximus Poems*, etc.) it is not ambiguous because one voice bears "the ultimate conceptual authority"[4] and constantly regulates and resolves the others so as to let *us* judge their validity. At its most effective, rhetoric proceeds from a confidence that certain values are beyond question, that it is one of writing's principal purposes to reaffirm and celebrate those values, and that an essential solidarity exists between author and reader once the domain of those values has been directly engaged. (This is why writers like Verlaine or Mallarmé can be so "rhetorical" once

---

"eloquence is *heard*, poetry is *overheard*. Eloquence supposes an audience; the peculiarity of poetry appears . . . to lie in the poet's utter unconsciousness of a listener," constituted a powerful and widely accepted definition of the nature of verse (J. S. Mill, *Essays On Literature and Society*, New York, 1965, p. 109).

Clearly, though, the writing of William Butler Yeats presents the most formidable counter-example to my argument for a gradual narrowing of poetry's horizons. His *Collected Poems* contain numerous examples of openly political and social polemics, texts directed toward his fellow citizens which successfully engage the most crucial public issues of the day. I suspect that Yeats's unique position at the center of both the English literary world and of the Irish national struggle gave him an opportunity to develop a more flexible and wide-ranging understanding of an artist's opportunities—and responsibilities—than that possessed by his most gifted contemporaries or immediate successors. Indeed, among the reasons he is still the single greatest English poet of our century is that his various allegiances encouraged the creation of a body of work whose accents can range from the highly personal and subjective to the public and declamatory without violating their own internal decorum. In this regard, moreover, I think it is clearly Pound who learned much from Yeats's practice, and not, as is often claimed, the other way around.

their theme is writing itself—the one topic of whose absolute worth they themselves have no doubt.) The distrust of rhetoric, then, to return to Vološinov's penetrating analysis, is linked not so much to a changed understanding of language *per se*, as it is to a "general, far-reaching subjectivization of the ideological word-utterance. No longer is it [discourse] a monument, nor even a document, of a substantive, ideational position; it makes itself felt only as expression of an adventitious, subjective state."[5] Only after the notion of public values has been undermined, and the autonomous individual—understood as existing in opposition to, not as part of, a cohesive, political and social commonwealth—has been installed as the sole originator of authentic perceptions, can the break between literature and the discourse of "les journaux" be regarded as absolute. The apotheosis of the single word or lyric, like the concept of the radically solitary consciousness of which it is the linguistic parallel, could come only with a certain renunciation of the world of shared endeavor, an alienation from any sense of community in which, as the title page of *The Maximus Poems* declares: "All my life I've heard / one makes many."[6]

During the last fifteen years the theme of the "rhetoricity of language" has become a central concern in the thought of writers like Jacques Derrida, Gérard Genette, and Paul de Man. Yet, for all their research into the formal literary and philosophical implications of language and rhetoric (or, more accurately, of language-as-rhetoric), the social and political ramifications have been relatively neglected. My own brief discussion is intended only as a supplement to their investigations, a supplement that is, however, essential to any consideration of the modern verse epic.

I have argued that poets like Pound, Williams, and Olson sought to recapture for verse the amplitude and inclusiveness of the novelist. One could go much further and say that it was the entire domain of public, ideological utterances, "the word permeated with confident and categorical social value judgement,"[7] that the epic poet was determined to rehabilitate and install at the core of his project. The original Greek conception of a ῥήτωρ, a man skilled in all forms of public discourse whose speech was intended expressly for members of a *polis* engaged in determining the important social and political issues of the day, comes remarkably close to Charles Olson's notion of an epic poet's function. And, from the definitions of the epic proposed earlier, it is clear that rhetoric, in the sense of "framing a 'pedagogic' observation in preserved and permanent form,"[8] constitutes an essential dimension of all epic discourse.[b]

The obvious difficulty facing any modern writer is that social values have themselves become highly unstable. Clearly no poet can rely upon an ethical consensus like that governing the relationship between the Homeric bards, the oral tales they narrated, and their audiences. Pound's assertion that "An epic cannot be written against the grain of its time . . . the writer of epos must voice the general heart" (*SR*:228) indicates his uneasy recognition of the dilemma facing any contemporary poet seeking to fashion a new tale of the tribe, and I suspect the shrillness of much of the rhetoric in *The Cantos* or *The Maximus Poems* is due to their author's awareness of the enormous distance separating his own values from the age's "general heart." When a broad measure of ethical-moral consensus is no longer available, what results is a will towards an epic, a necessarily stubborn resolve to find (or create) a readership with whom a renewed community can be planned. The greater the poet's sense of isolation and outside resistance, the more dogmatic and vehement his compensatory affirmations. *Paterson*, for example, avoids much of this shrillness by including numerous different, and even conflicting, voices within its own argument. The poem's emotional openness, discussed in the previous chapter, enables Williams to dispense with the hortatory tone more consistently than Pound or Olson. Yet the price of this accomplishment is a

---

[b] Jürgen Habermas, for example, examines the direct link between theories of rhetoric and political philosophy in classical thought and concludes that the primary function of rhetoric was "the purpose of attaining a consensus among politically active citizens." The rhetor, according to Habermas, was directly "engaged in the philosophical transaction of practical prudence within the specific sphere of Politics" (*Theory and Practice*, London, 1974, p. 80).

distinct blurring of *Paterson*'s capacity to sustain specific politico-ethical judgments, and a partial surrender of its authority as a source of instruction for the tribe. But whenever one of these three poems reaches for the full scope of a traditional epic, the search for a new "tribe" in a revitalized *polis*— "Root person in root place" ("Letter 3":12)—becomes a pressing concern. The question of whom to address and how to ground the narrative is, ultimately, the modern (pre-)epic's primary methodological dilemma.

"The trouble is, it is very difficult, to be both a poet and, an historian"[9] is how, at the end of his *Mayan Letters*, Olson formulates the almost insurmountable obstacles confronting the writer of any modern verse epic, of a work that would unite a range of seemingly irreconcilable discourses into the language of a new community. Yet, by the time this letter was written (October 1953), Olson had before him the example of the first eighty-two *Cantos* and all four books of *Paterson*. In many ways this proved an almost demoralizingly rich heritage. But even if the example of his two great predecessors frequently condemned *The Maximus Poems* to be "measured outside itself" according to the "music of other men,"[10] *The Cantos* and *Paterson* also gave Olson a chance to respond with a distinctly new methodology of his own, an original form which drew upon both pre-texts in order to find an adequate rhetoric for another and radically different "disposition to reality,"[11] a scrupulous act of attention uniting the lessons of history and geography into a single impetus, ready, "as a bow-sprit / for forwarding" ("I, Maximus":2).

· · ·

"olson saved my life"
—Ezra Pound[12]

". . . he
who taught us all
that no line must sleep
that as the line goes so goes
the Nation!"

—Charles Olson, "I, Mencius,
Pupil of the Master"[13]

"Belatedness," the burden of having come to artistic matur-
ity only after, and thus in the shadow of, some overwhelming
literary accomplishment, is, as Harold Bloom regularly assures us, one of the principal agonies confronting all post-
Romantic authors. Dubious as I am about the formal
schematization and universality of this Oedipology, there is
no doubt that for Olson, both Pound and Williams represented formidable *pères-ennemis*, exemplary teachers whose
influence he could neither wholly outgrow nor painlessly absorb. Olson's troubled relationship to his predecessors—"the
pathetic struggle to keep my own ego above their water"[14]—
is amply documented, especially in his letters to Cid Corman,
editor of *Origin*, and in the notes and essays written during the
period of his regular visits to Pound at St. Elizabeth's (January
4, 1946 to spring 1948). But fascinating, even embarrassingly
confessional, as these private outcries are, they do not, I believe, offer any secure vantage-point for understanding the
complex relationship between *The Maximus Poems* and Olson's two acknowledged "masters."[15] Virtually all of his
texts, published and personal, testify to the powerful influence
Pound (and, to a considerably lesser extent, Williams) exerted
upon Olson's poetics, prose style, and sometimes even habits
of mind.[16] It is easy to juxtapose statements by all three
writers in order to reveal Olson as a pretentious epigone
crushed by the more powerful voices of his "fathers," a late-
comer who, in Marjorie Perloff's words, "never stopped
running" after the riches of his betters.[17] Yet such an effort
profoundly misconceives the seriousness of Olson's attempt
to formulate a new epic structure, and grossly underestimates
the validity of his own, remarkably acute, criticism of *The
Cantos* and *Paterson*.

Significant portions of this criticism have already been
quoted in my discussion of Pound and Williams, and I have
indicated my reservations about some of his conclusions, but
Olson's essential attentiveness, his determination to locate the
fundamental intellectual structure and poetic strategy of both

texts, deserves particular emphasis. Characteristically, it is always *The Cantos'* and *Paterson's* status as epics, their solutions to the problem of narrating an adequate "tale of the tribe," that determines Olson's responses. Even in 1946, his "defense" of Pound is almost unique in insisting that *The Cantos'* historical and economic judgments, their search for a valid political and ethical order, be examined with great care, "despite all the vomit of his conclusions."[18] Rather than exculpating Pound by concentrating purely upon his technical accomplishments, his contribution to the formal problems of modern verse, or even his remarkable personal generosity to other artists, Olson praised him because "Pound faced up to the questions of our time. . . . He would be the first to stake his work as social in consequence. He is no poet to separate his poetry from society. He is a writer of purpose."[19] As Robert von Hallberg observes, "Olson was an exception among his contemporaries . . . [He] insisted that the matter of Pound's writing—'what it was about'—be taken as seriously as it asked to be taken. . . . And ultimately, Olson was sure, it was the seriousness of poetry itself and not just of Pound's work which was at stake."[20] It was this measure of care that Olson, at his best, would continue to devote to both *The Cantos* and *Paterson*, and it is from this perspective that the seriousness of his criticism derives its authority.

·   ·   ·

Like history itself, the modern verse epic is both a process and a communal task. It is a process because the tale of a living culture can never be completed, and a communal task because, from the examples of his predecessors, every new poet learns how to define the contribution his own perceptions and technique can bring to an evolving tradition. From Pound to Williams, and then to Charles Olson, an unmistakable continuity of artistic intention is apparent, a "family resemblance" linking three very different texts, each of which deliberately assumes the challenge of finding an appropriate structure and stance for a new "tale of the tribe." In his reading of Pound and Williams, Olson constantly draws attention to their methodology —"a METHODOLOGY is a science of

HOW"[21]—because the epic's significance, its real meaning, emerges largely from the point of view according to which the poet has organized his historical material.

History, for Olson, is like a perpetually changing character in search of the author who can discern, latent within the flux, a lasting form and significance. Because it is only from specific human endeavors and values that historical events derive their meaning, the poet's choice of approach, his "methodology," has ethical as well as aesthetic implications. To Olson, modern man's relationship to his fellows, to the forces of nature, and to the products of his own labor, has become so cripplingly alienated that only the lessons of history remain "as the one way to restore the familiar to us."[22] History is not a series of absolute, impersonal occurrences but "a concept denoting intensity or value,"[23] and the unique opportunity of the epic writer is, by the stance he takes towards the specific events which serve as the "plot" of his poem, to reveal "history [as] the function of any one of us,"[24] i.e., to let us see we possess the freedom to determine by what values both our individual lives and our society are governed. Olson's ideal historical poem would, in effect, demythologize history itself so that it might again become what is most familiar: the expression of our own activity in the world. Kant had argued that "I would not be able to apprehend anything as existing unless I first experienced myself as existing in the act of apprehending it,"[25] and the epic poet must enact an analogous "Copernican revolution" in our concept of history. He must let us experience history as a series of choices adopted by living men in specific circumstances. Previous historical decisions have created the social framework into which we are born, but they do not limit our own capacity to choose again, to continue earlier patterns or to change our emphasis and create new ones in their place. Because *The Cantos* and the *Guide to Kulchur* "razzledazzle History"[26] and treat it not as an irreversible and autonomous accumulation of dead facts but as an open field in which to seek lasting values, Olson calls their author "Father Pound"[27] and "the leading poet alive in the world."[28][c]

[c] In "The Kingfishers" Olson pays tribute to Pound's sense of personal responsibility and freedom:

Pound's unwavering confidence in the inherent creativity (and thus, responsibility) of human will—"Will contradicts tragedy, insists upon cause and effect in the face of stupidity"[29]—shows that every circumstance is changeable, that man can transform the conditions of his social existence by the effort of his own labor. *The Cantos*, that is, point towards a truly "human history," one responsive to a people's genuine needs and subject to their own control. And yet, according to Olson, the position from which this liberation is proclaimed fundamentally compromises its validity. Pound's privileging of his own perceptions, his confidence in the talismanic virtues of a few private tastes and doctrines, is the wedge with which he has "driven through all time material,"[30] and the resulting model is both too arbitrary and "much too late."[31] From *The Cantos* Olson can learn how to treat all ages as equally accessible to the poet's consciousness, as potential sources of insight and energy which become actual when fully penetrated by the artist's experience of the world, but the premises by which the historical material is selected and the use to which it is put must be fundamentally different from Pound's narrow and outdated "egotism." Lucien Goldman wrote that "the historical consciousness exists only for an attitude which has gone beyond the individualistic "I," and it is precisely one of the principal means of this going beyond."[32] Pound, according to Olson, had never really gone beyond that "individualistic 'I'," and one of the main goals of *The Maximus Poems* was to transcend any such limitation.

Olson praises Williams as an alternative model, and even as a corrective to Ezra Pound, because Williams' emotional generosity, his flexibility and openness to multiple truths, re-

---

But I have my kin, if for no other reason than
(as he said, next of kin) I commit myself, and,
given my freedom I'd be a cad
if I didn't. Which is most true.

The "Preface" to *Guide to Kulchur* concludes with: "It is my intention in this booklet to COMMIT myself on as many points as possible. . . . Given my freedom, I may be a fool to use it, but I wd. be a cad not to" (7), and Olson's use of these lines in his own poem reveals the degree to which Pound had earned his respect.

veals "the ego as responsible for more than itself,"[33] and thus provides the only significant methodological alternative to *The Cantos*. *Paterson* "gave us the lead on the LOCAL";[34] it showed that one way to avoid Pound's aesthetic "Bohemianism"[35] was to center an epic on the daily circumstances of a real community, to include among the poem's materials the struggles of ordinary citizens living in a single, recognizable geographic and political site. Since "the ontological basis of history is the relation of men with other men, the fact that the individual 'I' exists only against the background of the community,"[36] the poet does not have the right to populate his epic with an arbitrary selection of characters from different eras whose only purpose is to serve as *exempla* of the author's particular predilections or dislikes. In *The Cantos* it is the mediations, the connecting links between different "magic moments" in history, that are lacking, and these can be introduced into a poem only if its framework is larger than the individual consciousness of the artist, a framework such as Williams sought in the town of Paterson, New Jersey.

In its actual practice, however, *Paterson*'s "localism" was largely vitiated by Williams' abstract and sentimental humanism, by his reliance upon cultural stereotypes rather than upon specific analyses, and by the poet's reluctance to sustain a coherent historical argument. From Carl Sauer, the geologist, Olson learned that "there is a strictly geographic way of thinking of culture; namely, as the impress of the works of man upon the area."[37] In the face of Pound's restricted and hierarchic understanding of culture—"what you can pick up and/or get in touch with by talk with the most intelligent men of the period" (*GK*:217)—*Paterson* does, at least, acknowledge the vital importance of place and community, the influence of Sauer's "area" in any full definition. What Williams' text lacks, however, is the fructifying significance of "the *works* of man," and thus it merely replaces Pound's active, "totalitarian" egotism with the potentially still more deadening burden of nostalgic regret for an unspoiled nature and a contextless history. If Pound's poem is an extended affirmation of one man's will to order, *Paterson* reveals a world of passive victims, of will-less men, who, not understanding their own city's political and economic realities, are consequently unable to transform the community. Therefore Olson regarded "each of the above jobs [i.e., *The Cantos* and *Paterson* as] HALVES,"[38] and in *The Maximus Poems* attempted to make a new whole, one which would be faithful both to the individual truth of a place with its influence upon its citizens, and to the freedom of those citizens to create rather than to suffer the terms of their own history.

The very care with which Olson kept re-reading and commenting upon *The Cantos* and *Paterson* demonstrates that his reservations were no petty attempt to belittle the achievement of his "masters" or to usurp their place. He did, however, intend to establish a claim as Pound's and Williams' rightful successor in the search for a new epic discourse. In all of its central categories, Olson's polemical criticism is determinedly ideological and ethical. For him, what is at stake is nothing less than man's capacity to make sense of his own experience in history, to unlock, in verse, the energy from which a new *polis* might yet arise. In Pound and Williams, Olson was always ready to acknowledge, American verse had indeed attained:

> two now wholly acceptable
> measures.[39]

The singular contribution of *The Maximus Poems* was to be its offering of a wholly different "ground," another type of culture, for "measuring." "This is the morning, after the dispersion, and the work of the morning is methodology: how to use oneself, and on what. That is my profession. I am an archeologist of morning."[40] Or, in the distinctly Poundian rhetoric of one of the epic's last, posthumously published, fragments, once more:

> to build out of sound the walls of the city
> (*Vol. III*:194)

CHAPTER ELEVEN

THE NEW LOCALISM

"L'uomo (il suo corpo) ci avvicina
alla storia, non all' estetica. . . ."
                    —Salvatore Quasimodo[1]

Olson so often attacked conventional notions of history as an impediment to man's self-knowledge that critics like Donald Davie have been tempted to regard him as essentially anti-historical, as wanting to *substitute* a geographical notion of "space" for any sense of temporal sequence and causality.[2] Yet Olson's principal mentor in the "doctrine of the earth,"[3] Carl Sauer, himself warned that "We cannot form an idea of landscape except in terms of its time relations as well as of its space relations,"[4] and the entire thrust of Olson's polemic is towards an integration of *chronos* and *gea*, a perception, in Charles Altieri's precise notation, of history "as the successive exploration of environmental options available to a community."[5] Whether in the sphere of history or of epistemology, what Olson refused to accept was any sacrifice of the specific for the abstract, the truth of the single moment for a fixed hierarchy of universals. Like Nietzsche, Olson insisted that "truth" is only a certain response to "local" conditions, not an immutable universal category valid independent of any human act or purpose. Like Pound, Olson believed that time was permeable to the intensity of an individual's desire— "How is it far, if you think of it?" (LXXVII:465)—, that the imagination is able to recover "the intensity of the past by letting us see how past actions create energy for use by the present," and to measure the present "in terms of its ability to use the options the past has made available."[6] But, in spite of common critical misunderstandings, neither Pound nor Olson ever sought to deny the historicity of human development itself. Indeed, for Olson, "history is the new localism, a polis to replace the one which was lost in various stages all over the world from 490 B.C. on,"[7] and, unlike most of his peers at Black Mountain College, he continued to turn towards history as a source of inspiration, a unique "refreshment of values."[8] Rather than being in any way "antihistorical," Olson hoped to renew an older, and in his eyes unjustly neglected, historiographic tradition: "I would be an historian as Herodotus was, / looking for oneself for the evidence / of what is said" ("Letter 23":100-101).[a]

In *The Special View of History* Olson linked his twin themes of history and community in a particularly revealing way. "Man," he argued, "has the context of his own species for his self or he is a pseudo-creature of two kinds, Nature's, or the machine's."[9] Only an imaginative, "factive" relationship to history can generate a third term capable of resolving the antithetical limitations of an abstract biological formalism (the view of man as essentially a passive vehicle traversed and constituted by timeless natural forces) or of a crude monolithic determinism (the reification of human activity as only mechanical reactions to material circumstances). Man belongs both to the world of Nature and to the social environment his own tools and communal labor have helped to shape, and thus he is able to be at once self-creating and a participant in a larger, universal process. In *Maximus III*, Olson gives a vivid, concrete instance, drawn from his own experience, which precisely recapitulates his theoretical statements and can stand as the single best illustration of his complex relationship to the demands of land, history, and tribe:

> that forever the geography
> which leans in
> on me I compell
> backwards I compell Gloucester

[a] Nor, in this instance, is Olson's view particularly idiosyncratic. As Michel Foucault explains, describing the difference between the first Greek historical narratives and their subsequent manifestations, "the historian, for the Greeks, was indeed the individual who *sees* and who recounts from the starting point of his sight . . ." (*The Order of Things*, New York, 1970, p. 130).

to yield, to
change
    Polis
is this.
("Letter 27 [withheld]": no pag.)

    •   •   •

"object is *fact*, not symbol"
—John Cage, *Silence*[10]

    Thus far my discussion of Olson has proceeded without relying upon the by now obligatory invocation of "Black Mountain poetry." Yet such a theme is at best only peripherally relevant to the development of a modern verse epic, and, perhaps more important, the label itself seems to me both overused and largely uninformative. More than two decades after the closing of Black Mountain College (October 1956), the differences among the artists who at one time worked or studied there are far more striking than any common intellectual stance or aesthetic tendency. Olson himself, for example, considered David Allen's famous anthology, *The New American Poetry* (New York, 1960), with its separation of poets into groups based upon supposed ideological or geographic affiliations, as unfortunate and "divisive."[11]

    Even today, criticism of Olson's work still tends to emphasize his numerous pronouncements on poetic theory at the expense of detailed considerations of the actual verse. Undoubtedly, the poet's all-too-willing assumption of the role of *chef d'école*, his (distinctly Poundian) habit of offering descriptive and even proscriptive "reading lists" to other writers, as well as the sheer audacity and exuberance of his claims for the liberating potential of "Projective Verse," have all contributed to such a development. Elsewhere, I have attempted to analyze the intellectual foundations of his literary and philosophical doctrines,[12] but I am increasingly convinced that a consideration of topology, Riemannian geometry, or quantum physics, contributes surprisingly little to an understanding of *The Maximus Poems*. In his prose essays, Olson regularly turned towards science as a valid source of inspiration for modern artists, a crucial mapping of reality which writers should learn to regard as allied, rather than alien, to their own efforts. Often he seems to be looking for a complexly "materialistic" foundation for his own intuition "that things, and present ones, are the absolute conditions; but that they are so because the structures of the real are flexible, quanta do dissolve into vibrations, all does flow, and yet is there, to be made permanent, if the means are equal."[13] As in this curious mixture of Max Planck, Heraclitus, and Alfred North Whitehead, Olson's analogies are usually more metaphoric than logical, his appropriation of scientific terminology dependent more upon parallels of resonance than upon any objectively defined reference. For Olson, science seemed to affirm both the interdependence and the permanently changing nature of reality, and he was eager to draw upon its authority, as a confirmation, not a source, of his own instinctive attitudes towards the world. Language, he felt, should somehow recapitulate the forces at work in the structure of the universe itself, and his attraction to various scientists and mathematicians seems always to have been determined by their usefulness to his own, ongoing projects in the domain of poetic theory. Indeed, at one point, Olson himself acknowledged that his various "scientific" premises might, like Yeats's visions, be no more than sources of imagery for his verse, that he valued them as much for the "stance towards reality" which they suggested to him as for any categorical accuracy.[14] Olson's wide readings, that is, gave him both a seemingly objective and externally grounded justification for his instinctive assumptions, as well as a certain markedly personal (and sometimes intentionally intimidating) vocabulary, but the success or failure of his verse is based far less upon his purely theoretical presuppositions than is usually assumed.

Curiously, the one decisive shift in modern poetics which did directly affect the very core of *The Maximus Poems* has received proportionally little attention. Unlike Pound at the time of the Ur-Cantos, Olson never doubted the potential of a verse epic to match the amplitude and inclusiveness of the novel. Precisely because of the success of his predecessors, be-

cause *The Cantos* and *Paterson* had already fashioned a sufficiently flexible and absorptive poetic idiom, Olson was able
to begin his own major work without any uncertainty about
the authority of verse to narrate the tale of the tribe. Indeed,
among the artists at Black Mountain, the prevalent assumption was that the novelists had fallen behind the poets, had
failed to learn enough from Pound and Williams, and were
therefore no longer the dominant literary figures. Olson was
confident that "today, now, it is not fiction, any longer, leads
out, the dance,"[15] and, in 1951, he warned Cid Corman not to
expect many significant prose contributions to his new maga-
zine.

> I mean, literally, that the *forms* of narrative have reacted
> back from the advances of Joyce. . . . Narrative writing
> is, at the moment, wholly waiting for the advance of
> verse. Only the poets now can pull the narrative writers
> ahead. The situation of 1910 (post-Flaubert) is reversed.
> . . . The proposition now is, that prose must handle nar-
> rative by juxtaposition as accurate as verse.[16]

In writing *The Maximus Poems*, therefore, Olson was able to
rely upon at least enough of an acquaintance with *The Cantos*
and with *Paterson* by his readers to ensure that the seriousness
of his enterprise would be recognized, that the existence of a
valid modern epic tradition would itself serve as a shared assumption between author and audience. It was up to Olson to
make a meaningful contribution to this tradition, and critics
were free to question both his methodology and his technique, but at least the poet did not have to begin from an isolated and embattled position, his very ambition no longer
arousing an *a priori* dismissive hostility. The "long poem including history" had again become an accepted undertaking,
and its successive realizations themselves began to constitute
one of the most persistent and characteristic gestures of modern American verse.

In what was probably an unconscious but quite typical echo
(and inflation) of Pound's famous dictum—"Direct treatment
of the 'thing' whether subjective or objective" (*LE*:3)—Olson
wrote Edward Dorn that a poet must learn ". . . *to dig one thing*

or place or man until you yourself know more abt that than is possible to any other man."[17] That "thing," in Olson's case, was the first days of colonial America, and the place a small fishing village called Gloucester, Massachusetts. To treat their conjunction with all the clarity of his mentors—"Write as the father to be the father"[18]—but with a *"maximum* ('s) attention"[19] to the truth of their own, unique possibilities was to occupy the poet for the last nineteen years of his life. Ultimately, it is upon the results of this labor, the fashioning of a new and genuinely "tribal" tale, that Olson's significance really depends. As the poet himself knew, "the law there is not the past or the school but the AUDIENCE, the human ear."[20]

· · ·

In what remains his most perceptive essay on the relationship between history and consciousness, Georg Lukács wrote:

> . . . the question of universal history is a problem of methodology that necessarily emerges in every account of even the smallest segment of history. . . . The totality of history is itself a real historical power . . . a power which is not to be separated from the reality (and hence the knowledge) of the individual facts . . .[21]

Olson's problem of the one and the many, of the individual and the *polis*, strikingly recapitulates Lukács' linking of "universal history" to "the smallest segment" of localized historical knowledge, and in the figure of Maximus the poet sought a concrete embodiment of just such a fusion.

Of the real Maximus, however, we possess very little historical information beyond the fact that he lived under the Antonines in the second century after Christ and was noted as an effective teacher and as a devoted neo–Platonist. *The Dissertations* are the only writings by Maximus to survive, and these were last printed in English by the neo–Platonist Thomas Taylor in London in 1804. All of Taylor's translations have been severely criticized, but it was his version of Plotinus' *Enneads* (in G.R.S. Mead's 1895 edition) which Pound first used, and his *Maximus* that Olson studied during the late 1940s at the Library of Congress. In spite of the arguments of critics like Frank Davey, it is hard to find much in the *Dissertations* which could explain adequately Olson's preference.[22] Maximus advocated moderation in all things, a respect for the powers of nature, and an absence of greed or possessiveness in dealing with other men and the physical world. Yet much the same stance, expressed both more forcefully and with greater moral insight, occurs in numerous other philosophical writings of the same era, such as Philostratus' *Life of Apollonius* upon which Olson had already based his long prose "dance." One of the definitions of a Sophist, however, is a teacher whose instruction was "designed to fit men for their duties as citizens of a democratic state"[23] and it is primarily in this sense that Maximus the Sophist was a suitable role for the poet of Gloucester.

Olson admired the fact that philosophers like Apollonius (of Tyana) or Maximus (of Tyre) were, in their very names, always associated with one particular city. He regarded this as evidence that their teaching was also "local," was addressed primarily to the citizens of their birthplace and intended not as abstract ethical treatises but as a personal contribution to the daily welfare of their community. To Olson, Maximus is not any one particular man, but himself a "process," a part of a long heritage which reveals a way of responding to the world. In "Letter 7," for example, Olson thinks of a carpenter who left Plymouth to settle at Gloucester and there became a master shipbuilder: "That carpenter is much on my mind: / I think he was the first Maximus" (31).[b] These lines reveal that

[b] In these lines Olson is referring to William Stevens, who came to Boston in 1632 and moved to Gloucester in 1642. He was the most competent shipbuilder in New England and received an extraordinary land grant of 500 acres on the west side of the Annisquam River and a further six acres on Meeting House Neck. As J. R. Pringle, one of Gloucester's local historians, writes, "The value of such a man in instructing mechanics in the art of ship-building, especially in a community whose future lay in a maritime direction, was incalculable" (*History of Gloucester*, Gloucester, 1892, p. 28). Robert Duncan at one time thought Olson's title referred to the Renaissance *homo maximus*, the "great man" competent in every field of human endeavor. Olson admitted, however, that he "hadn't thought of it" and that it was from Maximus of Tyre that he took his poems' title (taped lecture by Duncan, July 23, 1961).

Gloucester has had more than one Maximus figure and that the modern poet, like the seventeenth-century carpenter, embodies a set of values, a code of behavior, for which the name "Maximus" serves as an antonomasia. The traits which earn Olson's approval are the specifically human contributions to, and cooperation with, nature, such as the skill of shipbuilding with the knowledge it requires both of the port's needs and of the local timber and utensils available to the craftsman. Man, community, and environment all participate in the carpenter's achievement, and Olson wants to keep his gaze—"polis is / eyes" ("Letter 6":26)—on that earlier success to inspire him in his own venture. Only by such an active labor is a true "practice of the self" attained, a complete expression of an individual's life within the conditions of his own history. A genuine poet, a "Maximus," would select his words with the same care as a shipwright his wood, and in both tasks the welfare of the entire town is at stake. By the same logic, the poem will not be divided into "cantos," a category which tells only what the artist has created ("songs"), nor into Williams' "books," which describes only the internal sequence of a work of art. Instead, the text is composed as a series of "letters," a term which immediately indicates a specific *audience* located in a definite geographic region. In calling his sections "letters," Olson abandons any claim to write solely for individual, private reasons: a letter not only presupposes a reader, but, when addressed to a whole town, its discourse should contain matters of immediate public significance. Thus, in the very name and ordering of *The Maximus Poems* Olson has indicated his opposition to the century-old chasm between artist and audience and has allowed the very needs of that audience to become a part of his poem's themes. Out of a sense of shared responsibility, "Maximus" might say, we again make rhetoric and poetry one.

• • •

"on founding: was it puritanism
or was it fish"
("Letter 10":145)

In the Mayan ruins Olson found "the oldest and purest *origin* on this continent, this hemisphere."[24] But his reading of *Paterson* had convinced him that history is always collective as well as individual, that the poet must be involved directly in the site and deeds he chronicles, and that his own life must participate in the historical themes of his verse. "The tale of the tribe," in short, can be told adequately only by a member of the tribe, one with no special powers except to render articulate what is there. Thus, in *The Maximus Poems*, Olson left the Central America of the *Mayan Letters* and the Pacific whaling expeditions of *Call Me Ishmael* and returned to New England, where he could find an "origin" both for his own life and for his country's destiny.

Robert Duncan said that for Olson "there were certain places . . . [he] thought Eleusis" and that "Gloucester was one of the holy places of this world."[25] But Gloucester offered its poet more than a purely personal mysticism of place, and one of Olson's major advantages over Williams was the far greater concrete historical significance of the New England fishing town than Paterson, New Jersey. In the people and commerce of Gloucester, Olson was able to find something not even the Yucatan offered, "a continuity of the kind of excitement and mind"[26] which had moved the first settlers, a continuity of fundamental goals and struggles through which the town's past events still expressed central elements in the consciousness of its modern citizens.

Moreover, Olson joined himself to the many artists who had used Gloucester as the subject of their work. From its earliest years Cape Ann, sometimes called the "Barbizon of American art," was one of the most often painted sites in the United States. Artists as diverse as Winslow Homer (1836–1910), John Sloan (1871-1951), Marsden Hartley (1877-1943), Charles Demuth (1883-1935), and Stuart Davis (1894-1964) often spent their summers painting the busy harbor and rugged landscape of the town. Henry James set part of *The Bostonians* in Cape Ann, and his novel contains a vivid description of the region. Other writers who drew upon the Gloucester Moors or the lives of the town's fishermen include William

Vaughn Moody and Rudyard Kipling, but the most famous of all previous literary uses of the region occurs in the work of a poet with whom Olson would seem to have no themes or sympathies in common: T. S. Eliot. In the third of Eliot's *Four Quartets*, "The Dry Salvages" are identified as "a small group of rocks, with a beacon, off the N.E. coast of Cape Ann, Massachusetts," a few miles outside Gloucester's harbor. Although he never refers to Eliot's poem by name, the funeral service in Olson's epic (152-154) contains an indignant, personal rebuke of Eliot's too generalized and abstract prayer of consolation for the town's dead fishermen.[c] Consequently, if there is indeed a "continuity" in the *history* of Gloucester itself, it is matched by the continued *artistic* significance of the town in American painting and verse. By drawing upon both these traditions, Olson was able to establish the intrinsic suitability of his theme for an epic without the difficulties Williams experienced setting his poem in Paterson. Students of early American history would be familiar with at least some of the major figures and events included in *The Maximus Poems*, and when Olson begins to offer his own highly personal interpretation of those events, he is able to assume at least a core of shared interest in many of his readers.

Nonetheless, at least in the first three sections of *The Maximus Poems*, Olson is at pains to include all of the main "facts" upon which his poem draws, and, in principle at least, it is possible for a reader to reconstruct his historical argument without any prior knowledge of the work's subject, or reliance upon external annotations. This information, however, is presented in fragments throughout the verse, its appearance mirroring the process of Olson's own, gradual discovery of Gloucester's history. In an Appendix, I have prepared a

[c] Already in 1950 Olson had written to Robert Creeley objecting to Eliot's "use of my, *my* madonna, buono viaggi, Gloucester, and how he misuses it, is riding, is generalizer" (Catherine Seelye, ed., *Charles Olson and Ezra Pound*, New York, 1975, p. 130). In fact, throughout its history the port suffered enormously from losses in men, vessels, and material resources due to accidents at sea, and Olson was unwilling to have such disasters somehow "justified" by being placed within a larger pattern of Divine redemption. In 1716, for example, Gloucester lost 15 percent of her entire male population at sea, and between 1830 and 1875 the list of fatalities often exceeded 100 lives a year.

chronological summary of the main events affecting Gloucester between 1603 and 1642 in order to assist readers in following the details upon which Olson bases his unorthodox
analysis of the port's founding. Such a summary, however,
properly belongs after a discussion of how Olson *used* his historical materials, in part because the manner of the poet's ac-
quisition of these facts itself constitutes an important thematic
element in the epic, and in part because the tale of Gloucester's
first days, briefly surveyed, can seem largely an uninspiring
account of commercial rivalries and economic accidents. Yet
Olson saw in those events a microcosm of America's entire
history, a crucial testing whose outcome determined the pattern by which the moral and political future of his land took
its shape. The importance of the struggle between the Puritans and the Dorchester Company is that of a small but characteristic experiment, one which would reveal what kinds of
institutions and values could take root in the new world, and
thus it serves as an indicator of the choices confronting men at
the very beginning of the English settlement of North
America. In *The Maximus Poems* Olson often extends his
speculations and narration far beyond the events of 1606-
1642, but, unlike either Pound or Williams, he does have a
clearly defined "plot," an "epic theme" limited in time and
geographical extent, at the core of his work to which the
other aspects of the poem can be related and from which they
rightfully take their meaning. Olson has, in effect, returned
history in the sense of a restricted sequence of deeds bearing a
communal purpose and scope to the heart of the modern
verse epic. The story of Gloucester's founding is not merely
an *exemplum* of the poet's favorite themes, as are all of
Pound's different historical figures and "magic moments"
rather it is, in itself, the full epic subject from which a meaning is derived. The "plot" unfolds its significance to the attentive poet rather than serving as another concrete instance of a
theory which the writer holds independently and for which
he is seeking historical evidence. Nor is Gloucester, like Williams' *Paterson*, important in the way that any site, any "local"
experience grasped profoundly enough, can be shown to contain universal truths. Rather, the specific history of the Cape

Ann settlement makes the port the bearer of a coherent and explicit set of historical values which arose from the unique circumstances of its founding. In *Paterson* the focus of attention is inevitably on the poet, on his reactions to a community whose significance stems only from his involvement with the city; in *The Maximus Poems,* on the other hand, Gloucester itself is revealed as a place by which the future history of America was fundamentally affected. Throughout his epic Williams vainly searches the streets of *Paterson* to "find my meaning and lay it, white / beside the sliding water" (III,iii:173), until its very absence becomes the poem's theme. In the exploits of the New England colonists, however, Olson found a subject of whose historical importance he already felt assured and from whose meaning a coherent modern epic could be written. "Time" in T. S. Eliot's "Ash-Wednesday" "is always time / And place is always and only place." Yet, for Charles Olson, the fate of a few men at a specific time and in a unique place sometimes intersects so as to alter the course of an entire people's development; the results of that intersection are what determine human history, and their telling is the true definition of a modern verse epic.

CHAPTER TWELVE

. . .

POLIS IS THIS

"I paint large in order to be intimate."
—Mark Rothko[1]

Structurally, *The Maximus Poems* are constituted by the interaction between two types of "records," two narratives
which, during the course of the text, are meant to unite and
validate a particular (even if, as we shall see, highly problematic) ethical imperative. Because history is presented through
the subjective, fragmentary responses of Olson's own daily
reactions to Gloucester—"that tradition is / at least is where I
find it, / how I got to / what I say" ("Letter 11":48)—as well as
through the objective chronicle of the town's past, the poem
contains a double plot, an impersonal "outer epic" which tells
the fate of the Dorchester Company's venture, and an inner,
subjective quest which unfolds the poet's growing knowledge
about his setting and heritage. Olson makes himself, gradually and often with great effort, the spokesman for a certain
tradition, for historical and ecological forces valid independent of his own perceptions but requiring to be "made new"
and returned to the whole community's self-understanding.

Ideally, the two narratives will complement and reinforce
one another: the degree of the poet's understanding of the
harbor's plight and the intensity of his emotional involvement
with the fate of his *polis* lends an urgency to the accumulation
of historical details, at the same time as the scrupulous care
exhibited in the reconstruction of Gloucester's first days confirms the justice of Olson's immediate perceptions and polemical exhortations. "Maximus" begins the epic by claiming an
omniscient authority to reveal "the thing you're after," to
show his hearers ". . . that which you / can do!" ("I,
Maximus":1; 4), but Olson, as only one more character in the
poem, must demonstrate his wisdom, must earn the right to

have his words heeded: ". . . tell you? ha! who / can tell another how / to manage . . ." ("Maximus, to Gloucester":5).

To very different degrees, and by quite distinct narrative strategies, both Pound and Williams sought to deflect our habitual subjectivization of poetry, sought, in other words, to locate their epics in a domain of public and verifiable "truth." Yet by the end of *The Cantos* and *Paterson* what results is largely the private testament of an individual consciousness attempting to learn from history ("the inner epic"); by placing equal emphasis upon a single, coherent, and sequential historical plot, one centered, as is the *Aeneid*, upon the founding of a new city ("the outer epic"), Olson attempted to join the self-reflective, subjective stance characteristic of modern verse to the communal, impersonal discourse of classical epics. The extent to which *The Maximus Poems* succeed as an epic is principally determined by the poet's skill in proving that his twin tales do enrich one another, that the historical records provide a valid explanation of Gloucester's "present shame" (9), and that his own artistic struggle "to be clear, to make it / clear (to clothe honor / anew" ("Letter 20":92) represents a significant contribution to the welfare of his community. Because Olson adds the sense of a single, geographically and socially unique place (the lesson of *Paterson*) to Pound's determination to "razzledazzle history" for object lessons, *The Maximus Poems* are able to proceed with a methodologically more stable foundation than that possessed by either predecessor; it can, at least at the level of theory, ground its specific conclusions in both *praxis* and *gea*, in both the deeds of men and the pressures exerted by their unique physical environment upon those accomplishments. Thus, for example, the text is able to shift effortlessly between the Cape Ann snowstorms of 1623–4 and Olson's own winter meditations.

> I sit here on a Sunday
> with grey water, the winter
> staring me in the face
>
> "the Snow lyes indeed
> about a foot thicke
> for ten weeks" John White

warns any prospective
planter
("a Plantation a beginning":102)

There is no longer any attempt to distinguish between the
poet's contemporary experiences and the conditions described
by the seventeenth-century preacher and his colonists:

John White had seen it
in his eye
but fourteen men
of whom we know eleven

twenty-two eyes
and the snow flew
where gulls now paper
the skies

where fishing continues
and my heart lies
(108)

Olson's glance follows the same trajectory as that of the fourteen men left behind to winter at Gloucester in 1624. The spatial identity and emotional identification have proved
stronger than chronological distance, but it is an objective
unity of setting and landscape—"a portion of land which the
eye / can comprehend in a single view"[2]—and not the artist's
isolated "ego" which has made past and present fuse into a
single, temporally layered perception.

The collapsing of diachronic barriers, like the connections
established between discrete elements of physical reality, is
never anchored in a purely symbolic equivalence: by constantly grounding his discourse in verifiable public documents and by maintaining a referential bond with the men
and objects of Gloucester's communal existence, Olson is able
to generate an entire series of correspondences (e.g., the
flake-racks, masts, gulls, and bow-sprit of the first letter),
each term of which continues to retain its own specific meaning. They are important in their own right, as participants in
the life of the town; the poet sees a meaning in their different

functions and activities, but, unlike Williams' metaphoric chain in *Paterson*, that meaning is only the expression of their shared characteristics, it is not an external imposition of poetic significance upon natural objects. Throughout the epic, the skill of a sailor and the craft of an artist are linked. The sailor, however, is never merely a symbol for the poet; rather, both must respond to the forces of their own place and time in order to survive and to thrive at their respective trades. Maximus is important to his fellow townsmen precisely because "by ear," his own as a poet and theirs as listeners, he can make them reconsider the significance of their common origins. In him the ancestral voices are still alive so that "from this place where I am, where I hear, / can still hear" (4), he is able to bring back a message, a token of freedom for all to apply on both their own and Gloucester's behalf. It is only the enemies of localism, the absentee shipowners and the constructors of billboards in "Letter 1," or the Puritans of the later sections, who seek to inflict external and abstract values (i.e., false universalizations) upon the specific conditions of the Cape. Olson's heroes are all those who confront their world with no preconceptions, who are willing to give themselves fully to the elements within which their lives are enacted, and it is their responsiveness, their specificity of aim, that the poem's syntax and vocabulary tries to duplicate.

Olson accepts the knowledge that "Limits / are what any of us / are inside of" ("Letter 5":17), and the thematic echo of Ezra Pound's "By this gate art thou measured / Thy day is between a door and a door" in Canto XLVII (237) shows the striking similarity in their conception of man. Olson also shares Pound's thesis that economic and verbal corruption are linked. Throughout *The Maximus Poems* he is at pains to demonstrate that the decline of Gloucester is a function of its financial dependence upon outsiders, upon men whose sole concern is private gain rather than the harbor's general welfare.

> in the present shame of,
> the wondership stolen by
> ownership
> ("Letter 3":9)

At a time when "the ships, even the wharves [are] absentee-owned" (10), it becomes increasingly difficult to define a citizen, to see who does, in fact, participate in the life of a community. To Olson the question is of the utmost importance, since only from its citizens can the port find renewal. Moreover, since it is also to those citizens that he is speaking, the definition of the poem's proper audience is, from the very beginning, shown to be identical with the broader question of Gloucester's destiny. The poem and the spirit of Cape Ann are one, not by authorial fiat but because Olson shows that his epic and his city share the same needs and are both dependent upon whoever is still capable of responsible action.

Olson is equally determined to reassert the *political* value of an open, care-ful responsiveness to the unique conditions of one's own time and setting (e.g., John White's readiness to experiment with social and economic institutions consonant with a new land), and the *aesthetic* priority of a direct confrontation with "the state of the real." In disgust at Vincent Ferrini's self-indulgent and meretricious vison of a "literary" Gloucester, a port whose waters, like Williams' Passaic, suggest the presence of "pagan gods," Olson cries out:

> Venus
> does not arise from
> these waters. Fish
> do.
> And from these streams
> fur.

It was the hat-makers of La Rochelle, the fish-eaters of Bristol who were the conquistadors of my country, the dreamless present

("The Song and Dance of ":57-58)

Gloucester needs no foreign myths, no external poetic associations to enrich its significance. Its present is "dreamless" because it is still open to the shaping force of men's *conscious* deeds, and does not point to another, hidden system of values apart from the struggles of its material existence.[3] Paradoxically, it is "Because of the agora America is, was, from the start, the moral struggle" ("Letter 14":62). This sentence effects a startling reversal of traditional notions of ethics. America is a moral struggle, not because it became the home of dissident groups such as the Puritans, but rather because its origin as an "agora," a market-place, forced the most basic questions of work, of communal labor and trade, and thus of human interdependence, to the forefront of men's consciousness. Moral categories, for Olson, are not abstract and divorced from the real conditions of a people's existence; instead, they develop in response to and as a focus for those very conditions. Words, ethical standards, and practical activity all unite in a true *polis*, and by ignoring the real demands of his position, Ferrini has objectively become one with the exploiters and debasers of Cape Ann. Olson's "battle" with Ferrini is a modern version of Captain Hewes's defense of the Gloucester fishermen against Miles Standish. The poet's violent refusal to participate in *Four Winds* announces the struggle in which he would have his fishermen engage and serves as a proof of his willingness to enter the battle for Gloucester *in propria persona* and become, not just the chronicler of his town, but also its militant champion.

In miniature, the Olson-Ferrini confrontation introduces an entire chain of positive and negative *exempla* which the poet proceeds to hold up before his audience, adding increasingly deeper layers of historical substantiation to his arguments. For all its digressions, *The Maximus Poems* is organized along clearly discernible lines, akin in many ways to the stages of a classical oration. In Part One (Letters 1 to 10), Olson calls together his proper audience and defines their mutual dilemma (the *exordium*); Part Two (Letters 11-22) introduces the historical sources and moral implications of that dilemma; Olson's own relationship to Gloucester's fate is specified and his authority as a suitable rhetor-paedagogue clearly established (the *narratio* and *propositio*). Part Three (Letters 23 to the end) presents the poem's climactic battle between Miles Standish and Captain Hewes, and in that decisive engagement Olson finds the genesis of a corruption now debasing, not merely Gloucester, but the entire land (the *partitio* and *confirmatio*):[4]

> . . . one's forced,
> considering America,
> to a single truth: the newness
>
> the first men knew was almost
> from the start dirtied
> by second comers. About seven years
> and you can carry cinders
> in your hand for what
>
> America was worth. May she be damned
> for what she did so soon
> to what was such a newing
> ("Capt Christopher Levett":134-135)

The near rhyme of "newness" and "knew" contains, in a microcosm, the fundamental argument of Olson's work. True knowledge is always an origin, but this force has been lost and its promise dissipated. The Old Testament image of America as a "coat of wonder" (135), rich and colorful like Joseph's mantle, parallels the Christian phrase "Good News" with which men heralded the Cape's discovery. Those who "knew" only how to "cash in on it" (135) are thus equivalent to the jealous "brothers" (the term of address also employed by the Puritans) who sold Joseph into slavery in Egypt. Betrayed, the New World fell into the bondage of greed and exploitation, and what appeared to its first settlers as a new Eden was soon "dirtied" into a ghastly "drugstore flattened-hillside" (135) Babylon. Unobtrusively, Olson has enriched the climax of his epic by a series of religious allusions which conveys the Biblical intensity of his denunciation without ever breaking the historical surface of the narrative. And, as in the traditional closing *reprehensio* and *peroratio*, the last letters of *The Maximus Poems* return to the present, not in a spirit of defeat but with the orator and his audience ready to apply the lessons of the past towards a new consensus for action. For the last time, Olson again rehearses the events of the first years upon Cape Ann, but he does so by linking past and present within the larger category of human freedom, refusing to view the past as irrevocably determining the possibility for a different future. Against Puritan autocrats like Endicott and Downing who "divided, April that year" control of the town (1642), Olson juxtaposes the fortitude and personal courage of individual colonists like Osmund Dutch, William South-mead, and Thomas Millward. Their spirit, Olson insists, is as much a part of Gloucester's legacy as the militancy of a Miles Standish. The final words of the epic complete the historical cycle, returning to Olson,

> to this hour sitting
> as the mainland hinge
>
> of the 128 bridge
> now brings in
>
> what,
> to Main Street?
> ("April Today Main Street":160)

Even now Olson does not pretend to foresee what the next moment will bring to Gloucester: paradoxically, he will "prophesy" about the past, but leave the future open, thus retaining the basic humility which accompanies a grateful acceptance of human autonomy. The poem ends appropriately with a question mark. Nothing has been resolved, nothing has ended, but at least the basic choices and dilemmas of modern America have been articulated and understood in the rich density of their specific historical sources. The imperative for renewed action implicit in the poem is, like the epic tale itself, not the province of any one man, be he poet or ruler, but rather of the *polis* and of all its citizens. History always leads back to "April Today," to a fresh spring moment when

> . . . the seasons
> seize
> the soul and the body, and make mock
> of any dispersed effort.
> "Variations Done For Gerald Van De Wiele"[5]

.   .   .

"The polis is not primarily a collection of habitable dwellings, but a meeting-place for citizens, a space set apart for public functions."

—Ortega y Gasset, *The Revolt of the Masses*[6]

Hitherto, my discussion of *The Maximus Poems* has been primarily descriptive rather than critical. In considering Pound and Williams I found it possible to rely upon an already extensive, and often finely nuanced, analysis of their epics. My own interpretation of the underlying structures of *The Cantos* and *Paterson*, of their narrative strategies and intellectual foundations, often differs from previous accounts but at least at the level of the text's arguments—the values for which the poems are contending—a reasonable consensus has been established, and at numerous points the reader could be directed to those studies which either challenge or supplement my particular reading. Thus far, however, *The Maximus Poems* have received very little detailed critical scrutiny, and apart from a few groundbreaking efforts, much of the writing on Olson is still centered either upon his personal influence or upon his claims as a major theoretician of "post-modern" verse. As a result, rather than concentrating exclusively upon *The Maximus Poems'* underlying codes, I have thought it necessary to include large sections of direct commentary upon the text's actual "plot," and to trace the internal logic of its narrative unfolding.

The danger of such an approach is that the exegetical space may well be out of proportion to the work's intrinsic merit, that Olson's methodological intentions may become confused with his artistic accomplishment. I have not been able to avoid such an imbalance entirely and intend the following observations less as a summary than as a kind of corrective to, and perspective upon, my previous description.

The essential problem of *The Maximus Poems* is far harder to demonstrate than that of *Paterson* because it so largely resides in the line-by-line technical execution of the verse itself. At times, Olson's "ear," upon which he himself placed such heavy emphasis, seems to me to betray him. Too many sections of the epic are written with a lack of either the metrical inventiveness of Pound and Williams, or an adequate compensatory rhetorical discursiveness of his own fashioning. Regularly, individual letters can be thematically justified, can be fully "explained" by demonstrating their contribution to the poem's meaning, but they do so in a language which is unequal to their argument. All his pleas for a precise and questioning attentiveness—"The mind, Ferrini, / is as much of a labor / as to lift an arm / flawlessly / Or to read sand in the butter at the end of a lead, / and be precise about what sort of bottom your vessel's over" ("Letter 5":23)—do not prevent Olson himself from occasionally relying upon a few, simplistic code-words to carry an unsubstantiated weight of concrete analysis and emotional conviction. Terms like "mu-sick" (3), for all its echoes of a diseased muse-mouth-myth, and its rhyme with one of the most deliberately stupefying American inventions, is hardly adequate as a metonymic shorthand for contemporary culture. As Martin Dodsworth notes, such a "galumphing pun . . . won't do . . . because it does not suggest how it [the mu-sick of our society] is tolerated."[7] Similarly, Olson's appropriation of "pejorocracy" (3) from *The Pisan Cantos* (LXXIX:487) is able only to condemn, not to account for, the all-pervasive rule of the worst. At times Olson's vocabulary seeks to browbeat his listeners into agreement, but, after a few, initial successes, his tone provokes distrust as often as consent, and leaves one as skeptical as do the claims of Williams' purely symbolic correspondences. Although it is relatively easy to unscramble the literal sense of a passage like the opening of "So Sassafras," (cf. Appendix I), it is hard, even by Olson's own theories of prosody, to find any justification for so perverse a syntax and stumbling a rhythm as governs these lines:

Europe just then was being drained swept by the pox so sassafras
was what Ralegh Gosnold Pring only they found fish not cure
for fish so thick the waters you could put no prow'd
go through mines John Smith called these are her silver

streames . . .

(109)

To a large extent, I suppose, these criticisms are really a matter of individual taste and judgment. My own ear is only intermittently convinced by either Olson's notation or his language. Yet I am also aware that poets of the stature of Robert Duncan have found much to praise in Olson's technique, and, though their comments have not persuaded me to alter my judgment, recommendations from such voices should enforce a certain wariness in readers whose negative responses parallel my own. *The Maximus Poems* seem to me to succeed best at the intellectual level of creating an effective epic structure, and, to a considerably lesser extent, at fashioning a public rhetoric capable of engaging complex historical issues and immediate political arguments. But the poem fails, I believe, at consistently finding a metre or vocabulary adequate to the possibilities opened by its own theoretical principles. Moroever, if the singular contribution of Olson's work lies in its formal methodology and historico-social instigations, it is also in this domain—the area of the text's specific values, the ideas and practices it champions—that a number of confusions arise, problems which, unlike the weaknesses of artistic technique mentioned earlier, can be analyzed effectively even in a schematic outline.

From the beginning of his career, Olson realized that the historical and political judgments of a modern epic required a firm grounding in the economic realities of daily existence. Unlike Pound, however, Olson was never tempted to believe that a single measure of fiscal probity existed by which any era could be judged, or that one unique reform was sufficient to guarantee economic justice. Olson's battle is not with the prevalent rate of interest, but, more fundamentally, with men's alienation from their own labor, with the unbridled power of large, corporate institutions over local control of the means of production and conditions of work. The gradual monopolization of Gloucester's fishing industry by the Gorton-Pew company is Olson's most effective demonstration of a broad and pernicious pattern of national economic exploitation. It is wage-slavery, "the paycheck" itself, not usury, which "intimidates" the modern world's citizens ("Letter 3":11).

But, as a solution, Olson fails to suggest any actions that could challenge the power of the monopolies. The curious fact is that, in spite of his repeated emphasis on "community," on men working together towards a common aim, Olson's economic horizon is entirely restricted to the individual, autonomous family concern as a self-sufficient enterprise. The concept of any type of "union" in which Gloucester's fishermen might work together to obtain a greater measure of control over their financial conditions is conspicuously absent in *The Maximus Poems*. Olson's heroes are not active reformers, but small, isolated entrepreneurs like "the brilliant Portuguese owners" who are praised because

> . . . They pour the money back
> into engines, into their ships
> whole families do, put it back
> in. They are but extensions of their own careers
> as mastheadsmen
>
> ("Letter 6":28)

For all its undeniable emotional appeal, such a vision fails to answer the practical dilemma. Olson never succeeds in showing how an economic system based upon small, family undertakings could be restored as a viable model for the whole society, or even how its few remaining exemplars can expect to survive much longer in the face of the financial power wielded by larger corporations. Indeed, by the very logic of his own insights, the day when Gordon-Pew will absorb the last of the privately owned vessels is not far distant. In spite of its seeming concreteness, and, paradoxically, perhaps even because the emphasis on a specific "local" instance has made its limitations all the more visible, Olson's principal model of economic "sanity" is little more than a nostalgic gesture towards a system already obsolete since the beginning of this century.

The same weakness haunts, on a much larger scale, the poem's central historico-political framework. Olson repeatedly insists that he is not advocating any merely sentimental mourning of lost opportunities:

I'd not urge anyone back. Back is no value as better. That
                                         sentimentality
              has no place, least of all Gloucester,
              where polis
              still thrives

                                    ("Letter 5":22)

But if the chance to inaugurate a truly new society had already been lost after Gloucester's first "seven years" (135), and if, except for isolated "local heroes," the region's (and indeed the nation's) history since 1638 has been one long descent into "mu-sick" and "pejorocracy," it is difficult to see how, or from where, the forces of constructive change could arise again and be marshalled effectively. Equally dismissive of monopoly capitalism and state socialism, disbelieving in the totalitarian power of one "factive" ruler to effect a decisive change in the welfare of his community and yet refusing to recommend any specific political program or party through which concrete reforms might be legally enforced, Olson has only a vaguely populist ideal of "regional control" upon which to fall back, a utopian dream that, from the exhortations he has drawn out of their past, his townsmen can be sufficiently aroused to refashion the very organization of their polis. How such a revolution in attitude alone could succeed in breaking the control of the "pejorocracy"—and given Olson's view that Gloucester's history represents 300 years of ever-increasing victimization and absentee-control, clearly some kind of fundamental, political, and economic redistribution of power would be required—is never specified, nor is the goal ever defined more clearly than as the antithesis of a debased present. These issues are directly relevant to the success of *The Maximus Poems* as an epic, and I am not merely criticizing Olson's confused economic or political ideas. Insofar as an epic attempts to provide guidance by which its audience can adjust its public customs, that counsel must effectively address the real possibilities open to the community; it must, that is, be applicable in the sphere of practical activity. This is an aspect of the epic poem's responsibility with which

Olson always agreed and which informed his comments on *The Cantos* and *Paterson*. But, as the pattern for a truly humane society, the never realized plans of a John Smith or of the Dorchester Company for the new colony are, today, absurdly inappropriate. Olson, moreover, clearly wants to argue for concrete social changes, but in the end succeeds, in spite of himself, mainly in urging an abstract transformation in the private consciousness of his hearers. His rhetoric of immediate relevance, his constant assertion of engagement with Gloucester's present fate, disguises the fact that ultimately his discourse remains, as much as Pound's, "the 19th century stance," a combination of naïve enthusiasm and sentimentality, for which it is indeed "much too late."[8]

In 1949, Olson ventured one of his most astute criticisms of *The Cantos'* political assumptions, "What's shallow about it is the deadness of it, the 18th century *lag* in it, the moan for the lost republican purity, the wish to return America to its condition of a small nation of farmers and city-state patricians. . . . Pound can talk all he likes about the *cultural lag* in America . . . but he's got a 200 year *political lag* in himself."[9] Among the cruelest paradoxes of Olson's career is that, in a more subtle way, the same "political lag" returned to compromise his own epic, that even a careful "eye . . . for what New England offered" ("Letter 11":50) was not enough to prevent the "Bohemianism" of his teacher emerging again, although in a disguised form, at the very core of *The Maximus Poems*.

Yet it is possible to argue that Olson's effectiveness as an epic *rhetor* was never entirely dependent upon the presentation of any definitive solutions. By alerting his readers to Gloucester's plight and by locating the predicaments of his own day in a coherent historical continuum, he has provided his "tribe" with the information necessary to reconsider—and reform—the town's social organization. Even if Gloucester's citizens adopt quite different tactics from those advocated in *The Maximus Poems*, the epic will still have fulfilled much of its purpose if it gathers an audience to explore common problems long considered past remedy. Perhaps in a democracy this is all an epic poet not only can, but *should*, hope to accomplish, leaving the formulation of specific programs to the very readers whose hopes and interest he has quickened. The limitations of Olson's economic and political arguments, in other words, are precisely that, limitations rather than, as in *The Cantos*, tragic contradictions tearing at the coherence of the entire vision. Olson's own peculiar combination of arrogance (derived by the poet from *rogo*—"I ask")[10] and humility, keeps him aware that a process is never completed, that other, more effective "measures," actions he himself never envisaged, may in time be proposed by any of the "citizens" he has rallied together, that, in the words of his next book:

> . . . the end of myself,
> happens, on the east side . . .
> to be the beginning of another set
> of circumstances.
> (*Maximus Poems* VI: no pag.)

. . .

> "I walk you paths of lives I'd share with
> you simply to make evident the world
> is an eternal event"
> (*Maximus IV, V, VI,*
> "For Robt. Duncan": no pag.)

Thus far I have limited my discussion to *The Maximus Poems* proper, and virtually ignored the two subsequent volumes, *Maximus IV, V, VI* and *The Maximus Poems Volume Three*. To a large extent, I feel that these later texts, although central to any evaluation of Olson's own achievement, are only peripherally relevant to an analysis of his contribution to the modern verse epic. In *Maximus IV, V, VI* the historical themes have been almost entirely replaced by the poet's private, and often eccentric, speculations in cosmology and comparative mytho-geography. Instead of the detailed descriptions of John Smith's real voyages of navigation, for example, Olson presents largely unfounded theories about the trade-routes of Phoenician merchants and Hittite travellers. It is as if he now intends to demonstrate that the initial volume contains, although only implicitly, the same materials and focus as a universal epic or theogony, and that from the core

of Cape Ann's specific significance, fields of force go outwards showing ever wider relevance.[a] The text often reads as
though Olson wished to introduce everything which the
more unified structure of the first book had excluded, as
though the epic must itself demonstrate human interdependence by becoming all-inclusive in its catalogue of themes. Accordingly, the map on the cover of the second volume en-
compasses the entire world with each area labelled by its old,
mythic name. Gloucester, whose geography was depicted in
great detail on the cover of *The Maximus Poems*, has been replaced by what Olson calls a "mappemunde," an image of the
entire globe open to man as a navigator. The individual
poems are now only infrequently "letters" addressed to
Gloucester, and as a result the rhetorical focus of the epic has
become blurred. Gloucester is still a major presence in the
work, but it is not the cynosure for which the other elements
exist and by which their significance is guaranteed. The port
has become a particular *example* of the poet's different theories;
it is no longer their *cause*, and with this reversal the characteristic
strength of *The Maximus Poems* is in large measure renounced.

Even within the "fiction" of the poem, the acknowledged
audience is no longer Gloucester's citizens, but the circle of
fellow writers and disciples for whom Olson had become
something of a culture-hero in his own right. At the end of
The Maximus Poems Olson had isolated his city's dilemma. He
had, in the words of one critic, "sought its redemption . . .
through argument and prayer,"[11] but his exhortations had effected no change and had led to no efforts at reversing the
port's decline. For all the energy and exuberance of *Maximus
IV, V, VI*, I suspect Olson's discouragement with the limited
impact of his labor helped drive him to other subjects. In a
movement strikingly similar to Pound's at the end of *The
Cantos* and Williams' in Book Five of *Paterson*, Olson's shift
from a public and historical discourse to a private exploration
of cherished themes is linked to a realization of his distance

[a] In "Proprioceptions," Olson praises Hesiod as a possible source of inspi-
ration for new works, and the "proem" to "Maximus IV" entitled
"Maximus, From Dogtown — 1" contains a very free adaption of Hesiod's
Theogony.

from the audience he had hoped to reach—and instruct—with his tale. More than either of the two epics analyzed earlier, however, *The Maximus Poems* initially succeeded in integrating the pressures of a communal audience into the poetic structure. But even for Olson, that "necessary fiction," perhaps an epic's single most important *donné*, could not be maintained indefinitely in the face of the indifference of its intended listeners.

Thus, rather than Gloucester's history and the destiny of its modern inhabitants, in *Maximus IV, V, VI* it is the poetic imagination itself, in its interaction with the landscape *of the entire earth*, that becomes the real "hero" of the poem. Olson now attempts to isolate the constitutive elements of any "epic consciousness" per se, hoping that from a sufficiently wide gathering of individual realizations a universal pattern could be both deduced and creatively confirmed. Migration alone, in all its diverse manifestations, forms the unifying "drama" of *Maximus IV, V, VI*, and Olson is less interested in any one particular narrative sequence than in the general laws of heroic action, the fundamental principles underlying all epic "forwarding."[12]

Olson deliberately turns away from the conventional "Historie," the "high fallutin' / big shot stuff" to which he had always objected in Pound, but which he began to feel also dominated *The Maximus Poems*.[13] *Maximus IV, V, VI* was intended to correct this "fault" by refusing to place its materials within any fixed hierarchy, and at times the volume seems to contain the seeds of a radically new kind of text, a topologically grounded, cross-cultural creation myth. However, the writing itself has become so idiosyncratic and the pronouncements so unchecked by the demands of either factual reliability or internal consistency, that such a new mode exists only in embryo, awaiting, perhaps, "the artist who does the next job" for its successful realization—after whose labor, of course, this foundation may retroactively seem Olson's most fruitful accomplishment!

Robert von Hallberg observes that in *Maximus IV, V, VI*, Olson's high-handed and often counter-factual appropriation of available information (migration records, archaeological and geographic findings, etc.) leaves him as vulnerable as Ezra Pound to the charge of "driving through all time-material" by the sheer determination of his own "Ego."[14] And indeed, in the posthumous *Volume Three* Olson himself retreats considerably from the wilder speculations of *Maximus IV, V, VI* to offer a personal, almost tragic "coda" to his whole *oeuvre*, a coda which, in its tone of controlled sorrow and lonely hope, is remarkably akin to the closing parts of *Paterson* and Pound's *Drafts and Fragments*. Although *Volume Three* does not, in itself, enrich Olson's contribution to the methodology of "a poem including history," it is fascinating to observe that he too, like his great predecessors, felt the need to speak in his own voice at length and almost with confessional intimacy, to conclude his work, not on a note of heroic ambition but with the passionate, lyric outcry of one individual, haunted by his own impending death while still full of a heightened alertness towards "the Real" that "goes on forever" ("The Ocean":90).

Undeniably, the most typical gesture of the modern verse epic is a stubborn attempt to tell the tale of the tribe until the pressures of an indifferent and ethically "incoherent" tribe compel a withdrawal back into the private accents of a lyric or verse meditation. Yet that withdrawal should not be taken as sufficient evidence of the entire project's futility. As I argued at the end of the discussion of *The Cantos*, the issue is one of proportion and degree. The final self-representation of the author, as a particular, limited individual, not as the authoritative spokesman for the entire tribe, has by now itself become part of the tradition of the modern verse epic. It is, perhaps, even this change in the genre's features which has permitted the tradition to continue and allowed a number of different epics to be composed side-by-side, as opposed to the few, all-powerful models of the classical heritage.

Like Pound and Williams, moreover, Olson never completely abandons his initial historical concerns. *Volume Three* returns to the themes of *The Maximus Poems* far more consistently than the intervening book, but now the accents are those of a leave-taking, at moments almost of a restrained threnody. Once, perhaps instinctively duplicating the Plotinian ending of *The Cantos* (CXVI:797), Olson even speaks of the "Aglaia of this Port" (114), as if Gloucester's "splendour" could, like Pound's "rushlight," lead him back to an experience of universal and radiant harmony.[b]

The text now contains several wonderfully realized odes, and in a study of Charles Olson, rather than "the tale of the tribe," this last book would merit much more detailed attention:

> Sweet Salmon
> from the coldest clearest
> waters. Cut the finest
> on the bone.
>   Rose
> directly from the stream straight into my greedy
> throat. And breast. A home
> for life. Wise goddess
>
> of the straightest
> sapling
>   ("Saturday March 20th 1965":72)

But even within the specific horizons of our present concern, the significance—as well as some of the limitations—of Olson's labor should be apparent. In a very real sense his synthesis of elements from *The Cantos* and *Paterson* did succeed in providing a new and workable foundation for an epic poem, and, far from being a permanently thwarted "late comer" to their triumphs, it is Olson, as much as any writer, who demonstrated the essential solidity, the decisive "pedagogic" relevance, of Pound and Williams, precisely by being able to build upon their achievements a work significantly original in its own right. *Volume Three* opens with an announcement of the book's epic intentions, almost as if it were going to become a direct continuation of the first text:

[b] Cf. also the sense of Aglaia as one of the three Graces born of Zeus and Eurynome, the daughter of Ocean in Hesiod's *Theogony*, l. 909. George Butterick points out that Olson read about Aglaia in Havelock's *Preface to Plato* and underlined the reference himself (*A Guide To The Maximus Poems*, p. 617).

having descried the nation
to write a Republic
in gloom on Watch-House Point
(9)

Yet, by the poem's end, in a passage dated June 28, 1969, and thus composed only a few months before his death in January, 1970, Olson offers a different kind of declaration, a single imperative, addressed both to himself and to his audience. It is an exhortation which can stand as a fitting epigraph both for the poet and for the tradition whose rightful heir he had indeed become: "Love life until it is / your own" (215).

To show how that love can lead men "to construct an actual earth of value" (*Vol. III*:190) is, for all the asperities of the struggle, the essential lesson of all the modern verse epics I have considered, three different poems in which objective history and private consciousness, the individual and his community, "measure the sources" ("Letter 9":42) of their heritage in an ongoing quest to "make it new," not merely in the minds of individual readers, but also in the deliberate and consciously chosen deeds of the entire "tribe." In essence, polis and the epic are this.

CONCLUSION

· · ·

REMEMBER THAT I
HAVE REMEMBERED

"And even I can remember
A day when the historians left blanks in their writings,
I mean for things they didn't know."

(XIII:60)

"All peoples who possess a history have a
paradise. . . ."

—Friedrich Schiller[1]

"History is not a 'dream from which I am
trying to awake.' "

—Ezra Pound[2]

In some ways, Stephen Dedalus' "History . . . is a nightmare
from which I am trying to awake,"[3] is the more reassuring
outcry. For, in spite of Yeats's assertion, in dreams one is responsible primarily to oneself, and no matter how enmeshing
the psychological lures, or how fascinating the specular authority of one's own demons, the chance to awake is always
potentially at hand, the movement of a radical deliverance already implicit in the very repressions that had constituted the
original terror.

History, however, provides no private awakenings. There
is no individual gesture of courage or lucidity with sufficient
force to make whole all that has been crushed in the course of
man's development, or to make good all the thwarted hopes
of history's dispossessed. In the narration of history, responsibility is always both collective and diachronic, the truths of
the past and the exigencies of the present uniting to shape a
particular tale whose spokesman is a single author, but whose
true subject matter is articulated in the labor of an entire

people. This is the essential paradox of a modern verse epic, a text that can be only the response of a particular individual writing from his own, partial and limited, perspective, but which must nonetheless give voice to historical forces transcending any single consciousness or moment. It is a problem Olson called "methodological," and its implications are as much moral as technical, and as much political (in the broadest sense) as aesthetic.

In a work which deliberately commits itself to an act of "projective commemoration," to an attentive recollection of the claims of the past on the needs of the present, the dilemma of narrative selection and ideological perspective already represents an ethical decision. Without the religious certainties of a Divine Justice governing, and thus ultimately reconciling, the vicissitudes of history, the problem becomes one of structuring a historical framework that does not deteriorate into a mere chronicle of anecdotes designed to illustrate the private obsessions of its author. The writer of a modern "poem including history" does not even have the nineteenth-century optimism that sustained epics like Lamartine's *Jocelyn* and Hugo's *La Légende des Siècles*, the faith that history will, by itself, enact its own transcendence, that somehow an inevitable, cumulative progress will bring about a radiant future in which the very categories of victim and conqueror, accident and necessity, are forever left behind.

"Only a redeemed mankind," as Benjamin knew, "receives the fullness of its past—which is to say, only for a redeemed mankind has its past become citable in all its moments."[4] And only from the vantage-point of that ultimate clarity (whether it take the form of a Messianic Last Judgment or a historicist perfectionism) can history be comprehended as a totality, a grand summary in which everything is recognized in its true value and all the earlier events are harmonized within the plenitude of a final synthesis. Until then there is no privileged horizon from which history can be seen clear and recorded whole. History does not unfold through a homogeneous time which can be surveyed *sub specie aeternitatis*, nor is it possible for a narrator to articulate the past "the way it really was," unless he acknowledges the fragmentary, inconclusive nature of that narrative. As Hans-Georg Gadamer explains:

> There is one thing common to all contemporary criticism of historical objectivism or positivism, namely the insight that the so-called subject of knowledge has the same mode of being as the object, so that object and subject belong to the same historical movement. The subject-object antithesis is legitimate where the object, over against the *res cogitans*, is the absolute Other of the *res extensa*. But historical knowledge cannot be appropriately described by this concept of object and objectivity.[5]

Whether its form be a detailed monograph, an extended chronological survey, or an epic poem, what emerges from a sufficiently intense concern for history is always something like a dynamic image or vortex, a series of intertwined crystallizations or illuminations, vitally bound to the particular concerns of the perceiver. But, far from being an index of unreliability, the very "partiality" (in both senses) of each perception is a necessary aspect of its continuing human significance. "For every image of the past that is not recognized by the present as one of its own concerns threatens to disappear irretrievably."[6]

· · ·

> "I don't know how humanity stands it
>   with a painted paradise at the end of it
>   without a painted paradise at the end of it"
>   (LXXIV:436)

In all three of the poems I have examined, splinters of a redemptory wholeness of existence are embedded, ranging from the ἀγλαΐα of Pound's undivided Light to Olson's vision of a "root person" fully at home in his "root place." This openness, or rather appeal, to a *potential* totality is what most sharply divides an epic poem from a conventional study of history, but the presence of such "Messianic" fragments, rather than negating the concrete historical judgments of the verse, acts as a pledge that "nothing that has ever happened should be regarded as lost for history,"[7] and thus preserves the collective longings through which the past retains an immediate fraternity with the deepest needs of succeeding generations.[a] What separates the irruption of a moment of visionary wholeness amid the historical details of an epic poem from its presence in a lyric or religious meditation, is the recognition that questions of individual fulfillment or redemption are ultimately not at stake, that every such privileged instant is at once the figure of a profoundly communal necessity, and the index of everything still absent from the daily activity of that community. The glimpses of a *paradiso terrestre* serve to distance the epic poet from a history inscribed solely by the world's conquerors, and, so long as the thrust of those magic moments is to alert readers to all the unrealized potential of their own heritage, to everything that remains to be won, there is nothing anti-historical or solipsistic in their deployment. Such a moment, for example, is realized by Pound amid the squalor of his confinement at St. Elizabeth's when he cries out, not for his own deliverance, but for a world in which a future innocence can flourish, unthreatened by degradation or loss:

> For me nothing. But that the child
>   walk in peace in her basilica,
> The light there almost solid.
>   (XCIII:628)

---

[a] Thus, all three epics make extensive use of direct quotations from the actual records left by the past. As was noted earlier, this practice helps to establish the poet's authority as a trustworthy historian, and serves to deflect our tendency to treat his discourse as a purely subjective creation. But Walter Benjamin saw another and more subtle purpose in such a technique, one I think Pound, Williams, and Olson also instinctively utilized. In Benjamin's eyes, the judicious use of quotations offers one of the most effective means of overcoming a historiography of pure power and political dominance. As Irving Wohlfart notes, for Benjamin, "the function of quotation is to break up the unified, totalitarian blocks that conformist historiography passes out as history," it "isolates the elective affinities between the present and specific moments of the past. To grasp such correspondences is to seize the chance of the moment" ("On . . . Benjamin's Last Reflections," *Glyph 3*, 1978, p. 181).

To surrender the energy latent in those "idealistic" shards would, paradoxically, risk capitulating to a far more dangerous counter-idealism: the reification of history as some autonomous force beyond human control or transformation, a mechanical procession whose disasters we cannot remedy, and whose "comprehension" is attained only by the assumption of a correspondingly mechanical—and hence fundamentally inhuman—moral neutrality.

The crucial dilemma, however, remains that these "magic moments" must never, in themselves, be taken for a resolution to the concrete struggles presented in the historical narrative. Somehow, the vision of an enlightened totality must remain anchored in a *praxis* possible in the daily circumstances of social existence. Thus, at various times, I have criticized some particular retreat from the historical realm into a purely private, imaginary transcendence: e.g., the apotheosis of art in Book Five of *Paterson*; Olson's nostalgia for an autonomous Gloucester; or *The Cantos'* often cavalier absorption of specific historical contexts into their own network of metamorphic recurrences and universal archetypes. Similarly, I have sensed a fundamental loss of focus in all three epics whenever the ruptures and omissions in the historical texture vitiate the essential specificity of argument upon which the poem's authority as an "instigation for certain values" depends, episodes like Pound's reductive presentation of British history at the end of *Thrones*; Williams' simplistic equation between the industrial despoliation of Paterson, its citizens' sexual frustration, and the uneasy sleep of the region's eponymous giant; or Olson's derivation of so many of the disasters in contemporary American life from the single defeat of the Dorchester Company's 1623 venture.

Yet so far in this conclusion I have emphasized the potentially "liberating" aspect of a perception "shot through with chips of Messianic time"[8]—which is, of course, beyond the confines of any purely descriptive historiography—as well as the epistemological honesty of "leaving blanks" for what one does not know, of refusing to provide all the mediations between the necessarily disconnected fragments of any individual's historical understanding. Nonetheless, I do not think there is a fundamental contradiction between my earlier judgments and present argument. Rather, the polarity between them reflects a (perhaps irreconcilable) tension at the core of any modern verse epic which does not order itself according to a universal and totalizing explanatory system. The gaps, the unexplained fissures, and even the personal distortions of perspective, are unavoidable when a single author attempts "a poem including history." Yet the sudden glimpses of an absent wholeness are also essential if the resulting text is to speak to its audience with a careful openness to the unfulfilled energy of the past and the precarious hopes of the future. If Mnemosyne is indeed the mother of the epic muse, what the modern epic poet attempts is no longer merely the remembrance of the deeds of the past, but the recollection of an almost obliterated wholeness of response to the conditions of our historical experience. It is only when the visionary intuitions foreclose any possible communal action, or when the lack of sufficiently specific historical mediations between single narrative units freezes rather than opens the historical field, that the risks inherent in a single poem's attempt to articulate a new tale of the tribe become actual contradictions, rending the very fabric of the entire project. What is demanded is nothing less than a dizzyingly complex series of adjustments, a dialectical interplay between an individual's wisdom of paedagogic selection and the whole community's past achievements, and between a personal image of a still possible redemptive integrity and the dispersal of actual human history.

Clearly, I do not think any of the poems examined here have consistently managed to negotiate that ideal dialectic, nor do they seem to me remotely equal in their respective degrees of success. By now, any attempt to summarize their relative strengths and limitations could only echo, in an impoverished form, the detailed criticisms proposed earlier, but if *The Cantos* are undeniably the principal "flawed hero" of this study, *Paterson* and *The Maximus Poems* are equally important to an understanding of the tradition of modern epic verse and to the range of possibilities—and responsibilities—

inherent in that tradition. It would be facile to claim that the very impossibility of writing a uniformly successful modern verse epic suffices to justify any particular faltering. On the contrary, the foreknowledge of the difficulties should alert readers to a corresponding attentiveness, one which does not equate intention with achievement, or deny the whole significance of the project by a careless passivity of judgment. Equally, however, the discovery of particular lapses should not be taken as an excuse to dismiss any individual contribution, let alone the essentially inter-textual endeavor— "thought is built on Sagetrieb" (XCVIII:686)—that the modern verse epic has become. At their best, all three of the poems scrupulously record their own distance from any aesthetic closure or metaphysical plenitude. They have been written not only *about* history, but from *within* it. *The Cantos, Paterson*, and *The Maximus Poems* resist severing themselves from the ongoing history of their tribe and time, and I have tried to respect this "decorum" by not presuming further than the texts will justify. Of course, "It can't be all in one language" (LXXXVI:563), or even in three poems that together offer a succession of intricately connected models for a new epic discourse. Yet by considering these three attempts, both individually and as parts of a larger movement in modern verse, we may find that some sense of that unrealized totality emerges: an ideal image, parallelling in the quite different idiom of prose criticism the splinters of a higher unity embedded in the epics themselves, without distorting the specific texts from which the criticism derives.

"Critique," we are told, "is concerned with the truth content of a work of art, the commentary with its subject-matter."[9] Perhaps this study has moved too often and unfashionably between a commentary and a critique, and in the process introduced its own unwarranted distortions of emphasis and presumptions of judgment. Without thereby intending to excuse my particular biases, I think it crucial to recognize that any full response to *The Cantos, Paterson*, or *The Maximus Poems* must include both a commentary and a critique, that unlike the self-reflexive, autonomous literary modes cherished by current critical theory, a modern verse epic explicitly appeals to our sense of a historical and public "truth" as well as to our pleasure in aesthetic "invention." In Book Ten of *The Republic* Plato twice refers (with great skepticism) to the Homeric epics as offering instruction in the *dioikesis* or " 'management' of life, social and personal, proceeding outwards from the family into the sphere of political and religious obligations."[10] To refuse to engage that same claim, even in the far more problematic and reduced version present in a modern verse epic, may well avoid some of the excesses risked by any genuine critique, but only at the cost of a far more brutal denaturing of the text, an aestheticization that simply repeats the *"gran' rifiuto"* from which *The Cantos* sought to preserve both modern verse and our historical understanding itself. Or, in the characteristic rhetoric of Williams' last great work

> It is difficult
> to get the news from poems
>   yet men die miserably every day
>   for lack
> of what is found there.
>   ("Asphodel, That Greeny Flower")[11]

• • •

In a recent review John Bayley criticized readers who insist upon discovering direct social instigations in the work of a great poet. His polemic against the vulgarities of fashionable "relevance-hunting" contains numerous accurate local observations, but the logic of his argument leads Bayley to a position against which all the poems I have examined are directly contending: "The point about great poetic genius . . . is how personal it is and how irresponsible. Therein lies its value to us, not in any sense in which it seeks to demonstrate a 'quality of seriousness.' . . . The medium is simply not designed for such a purpose; it works much more indirectly and through an ad hominem appeal, not a social one."[12] The very distinction between an "ad hominem" and "a social appeal," although self-evident to Bayley, already accepts as absolute the split between an individual and his community which the poet of a modern verse epic seeks, often desperately and with limited resources, to help to heal. Moreover, even at the formal level of describing a poem's basic rhythms, the reluctance to admit the public and paedagogic dimension that writers like Pound accepted as part of their essential responsibility can lead the best critics into serious distortions. Thus, Donald Davie, who has given us virtually the only serious technical analysis of *The Cantos'* metrics, concludes that, "For the most part the rhythms of the *Cantos* . . . are the sung rhythms of Burns, not the intoned or chanted rhythms of Swinburne."[13] Yet much of *The Cantos* explicitly renounces pure song, and in order to convey those very "ideas" whose presence in the poem Davie seems to doubt,[14] Pound quite deliberately introduced an extensive "prose element" into his epic. As Thomas McKeown observes, "the spoken word, not the song, provides the dominant rhythm for vast stretches of the *Cantos*; we may think of the letters of Sigismundo Malatesta, Jefferson, and Adams. . . , the numerous anecdotes. . . , and the long passages in French"[15] as well as the painstaking transcriptions from Renaissance, Byzantine, or Chinese history classics.

In spite of Pound's "mystical ear" (to borrow Williams' phrase)[16] for the invention of new musical and rhythmic patterns, it is the daring confidence with which *The Cantos* are able to absorb so much prose narrative and historical documentation that remains one of their most decisive technical accomplishments. Pound himself realized that upon such a strategy depended poetry's chance to "donner une idée claire et précise" (*LE*:55), and thus to compete successfully with the novel as a significant medium for the expression of social, psychological, and historical judgments. Already in his 1920 study of Arnaut Daniel, Pound warned that the musicality of the troubadours, despite its powerful attraction for his own sensibility, no longer offered an adequate basis for twentieth-century verse: "the Provençals were not constrained by the modern literary sense. Their restraints were the tune and rhyme-scheme, they were not constrained by a need for certain qualities of writing, without which no modern poem is complete or satisfactory. They were not competing with De Maupassant's prose" (*LE*:115).

Today, the lessons of Pound's warning and the example of his practice have penetrated the entire domain of poetics. Their influence is registered not only among those writers who have sought to follow him in the creation of a modern verse epic, but is immediately felt in the range of tones, the freedom to select among widely different modes of expression, available to contemporary poets. If, as we have seen, Mallarmé in 1886 insisted upon a categorical distinction between poetry and the accents of "les journaux," in 1976 Robert Pinsky, himself a distinguished poet and critic, summarized a diametrically opposed development, one of which Ezra Pound, along, perhaps, with Thomas Hardy and Ford Madox Ford, surely stands as the principal begetter:

> From the beginning, some of the most exciting, overwhelming moments in the modernist tradition have come when a poet breaks through into the kind of prose freedom and prose inclusiveness which I have tried to suggest with words like "discourse" and "discursive" . . . the poet claims the right . . . to speak . . . with all the liberty given to the newspaper editorial, a conversation, a philosopher, or any speaker whatever.[17]

In essence, the danger of a theoretical framework like Bayley's is that any strenuous insistence upon the distinction between "great poetic genius" and the *dioikesis* of public existence, or between an "ad hominem" and a "social" appeal, automatically condemns the effort to create a modern verse epic as a kind of artistic solecism and threatens the legitimacy of the discursive freedom Pinsky identifies with modernist poetics as a whole. Similarly, although Donald Davie has always demonstrated an acute sensitivity to literature's intellectual and moral dimension, his recent comments on *The Cantos'* ideas and metrics also tend, in a more subtle way, towards a strict aestheticization of the poem—perhaps in order to safeguard its brilliant fragments from the moments of appalling wrong-headedness. But it is part of the continuing fascination of Pound's work that it compels us to confront its ideas, including the "wrecks and errors," as deliberate social and historical judgments, just as it is part of the epic's aesthetic technique to base much of its rhythm on the inclusiveness of the "prose tradition." Ultimately, it is from Pound himself that the right to question the polemical content of his work on its own terms derives, since few poets have argued as forcefully against the aesthetic as a category necessarily distinct from and indifferent to the social and political spheres of human cognition. Yet I know that my own focus of attention has at times caused me to leave insufficiently analyzed those aspects of the poems, the syntactic and metrical inventions, the audacious use of patterned sounds and images, which attracted me as a reader long before questions of ethical sense or historical argument began to impose their own pressures. In many ways it would have been easier to write a quite different book, one concentrating far more exclusively upon the immediate aesthetic appeal of all three epics, but such an undertaking would undervalue just those features that separate *The Cantos, Paterson,* and *The Maximus Poems* from traditional lyrics, and impose a perspective that risks excluding the texts' specific intentions and governing conventions from scrutiny.

In a sense, perhaps the very scope of this investigation is inherently foolhardy, any single effort to locate the characteristic strategies of the modern verse epic being foredoomed to a certain insufficiency. My justification, however, lies precisely in the dangerous openness defined by that effort: an openness that is dangerous not because of its amplitude but because, in that venture, the relationship between the words of a poem and the events of our lives, both as individuals and as members of a much larger human community, a social and linguistic commonwealth, is contested. I can, at least, assert that I have in no sense invented my topic; all that I have done is to listen to the dialogues (often directly articulated, sometimes implicitly, and yet fundamentally, unmistakably present) of the poets and thinkers who have themselves wrestled with the questions I am now repeating. And although such a claim runs counter to most of our present assumptions, the effort to formulate a convincing "tale of the tribe" still seems an un-

dertaking of enormous value, one central not only to the continuing authority of verse, but to the very possibility of making sense of the conditions of our common history.

•　　•　　•

And then went down to the ship
(I:3)

APPENDIX

* * *

ON FOUNDING:
A HISTORICAL SURVEY
OF GLOUCESTER'S
SETTLEMENT

In order to assist readers of *The Maximus Poems*, I have prepared a brief outline of the early history of the Cape Ann settlement, concentrating upon those details which Olson himself mentions in the poem.

In 1603 Martin Pring, Captain of the "Speedwell" and "Discoverer," sailed along the shores of Cape Ann in an unsuccessful quest for sassafras which was believed to have medicinal powers, especially in the cure of syphilis. Instead he encountered "fish so thick" it became difficult to navigate, and, upon returning to England, Pring reported the presence of an almost unimaginable quantity of cod which had blocked his boat's progress ("So Sassafras":109).

In July 1605 Demonts and Champlain also sailed past the same region. On a subsequent voyage, in September 1606, Champlain returned alone and went ashore. He named the site Le Beauport, and became the first European to land at what is the modern town of Gloucester. However, he established no settlement and the port was quickly abandoned. In 1614, Captain John Smith explored large sections of the coastline, making the most detailed map then available and giving the land its future name of New England. He called the Cape itself Tragabigzanda after a Turkish maiden who had saved his life when he was a soldier in the Balkans, a name which was used until 1624 when Prince Charles (later Charles I) changed it to Cape Ann after his mother Princess Ann of Denmark. Smith was also impressed by the potential wealth of a site so singularly abounding in fish that he called cod-fish New England's "silver ore" ("April Today Main Street":157). Smith himself became one of the leading advocates of a permanent colony in Massachusetts and in works like *Advertisements for the unexperienced Planters of New England* (1631) offered his assistance to anyone setting out for the New World independent of the religious disputes which bitterly divided the first group of colonists. However, when the Puritans established the Plymouth settlement in 1620, one of their reasons for not employing Smith in any direct capacity was his refusal to enter into sectarian quarrels. The Puritans were interested only in farming and trade, and at first ignored the Gloucester Banks, which were still visited by independent English and Breton fishermen. One English vessel in 1619 sold its catch for £2100 and subsequent boats realized an ever greater profit.[1] In 1623, under the leadership of the Reverend John White, a group from Dorchester decided to make a permanent settlement at Cape Ann, one in which fishing and agriculture were to be fully integrated activities. The sale of fish was to raise the necessary money for the colony, while the farmers were to render assistance to the sailors and cultivate enough food to sustain the whole community. On the first trip, after the fishing was completed, most of the Dorchester men went on to Spain, then the principal market, leaving behind fourteen settlers to pass the winter on the Cape Ann mainland. But the Dorchester Company had no grant to this territory and, at the same time, Edward Winslow of the Plymouth settlement secured a patent from the Council of New England granting the Puritans extensive rights to the Cape. The Puritans had at last decided to engage in fishing and built a station at Gloucester.

However, their men did not go to sea that season and the Dorchester settlers, now reinforced with new recruits from England, took over the Puritans' unused fishing station. In 1625, Plymouth sent Miles Standish, their military leader, to retake the port and a full-scale battle between the rival claimants was avoided only by the diplomatic skill of Roger Conant, who, soon after, became governor of the Colony. The legal issue was complex and uncertain, in part because of the usual vagueness of the royal charters. The dispute was finally resolved by an agreement to have two independent forts at Cape Ann from which each group could continue to fish. In 1626, owing to unfortunate investments, to the difficulty of sustaining both a fishing fleet and an agricultural colony, and, most of all, to the closing of the traditional markets in Bilbao as a result of the English-Spanish War, the Dorchester Company went bankrupt. Many of the original colonists returned home, while Roger Conant moved to "Naumkeag" (the modern Salem) where he established a successful settlement. Cape Ann was again unpopulated, except for transient fishing fleets, until the 1630s, when men began to move back in small numbers. In 1634, the port was first called Gloucester, after the English home of many of the newer immigrants, and the final act of incorporation as a town was passed by the London General Court in May 1642, but by then Gloucester was already completely under the control of the Massachusetts Bay Colony.

In the text of *The Maximus Poems*, Olson mentions two of his major sources for the history of the Cape Ann region. The first, "the historian Babson" ("Maximus, to Gloucester":106) is John J. Babson, whose *History of the Town of Gloucester, Cape Ann* was published in Gloucester in 1860. Babson himself was a direct descendant of the "widow Babson," one of the first English settlers in the Colony. Then, while already engaged in writing *The Maximus Poems*, Olson discovered the English historian Frances Rose-Troup, whose *John White, The Patriarch of Dorchester* (New York, 1930) is still the most extensive study of the Dorchester Company's attempt to settle Cape Ann. This book offered Olson a great deal of support, since Rose-Troup's interpretation of Gloucester's early history is strikingly similar to the poet's own intuitions. Both Olson and the author of *John White* argue for a fundamental reversal in the traditional view of the Colony's first years. Olson praises Rose-Troup several times, especially in "Letter, May 2, 1959" (145-151), and both "The Picture" (115-116) and "The Record" (117) are based directly upon her research.

In evaluating Olson's use of New England history, we must realize that he is not merely presenting a new version of the story, but is actually attempting to overthrow another and widely accepted one. Until Frances Rose-Troup's careful investigation, most histories neglected the importance of the Dorchester Company's attempt to settle Cape Ann, and when they did mention the clash between Pilgrims and Dorchester men, historians invariably sided with the former. Even to local Gloucester historians like J. R. Pringle, writing in 1892, the defender of the Stage Fort was only a "captain of the semi-piratical ship . . . named Hewes" while the Plymouth forces were led by "that redoubtable Pilgrim warrior, Capt. Miles Standish," who is called "the valiant captain of the Pilgrims."[2] William Hubbard, in *A General History of New England from the Discovery to MDCLXXX* (1815), does describe Standish as being "of very little stature" and adds that because of his "hot and angry temper" he was like "a little chimney. . . soon fired,"[3] but this critique of the Puritans' military leader does not lead Hubbard to a re-evaluation of the Cape Ann fishermen against whom Standish fought.[a] Olson is thus arguing against a historical judgment that is both well known and seemingly irrevocable. Much of his repetitive, "rhetorical" insistence is a result of his awareness that *The Maximus Poems* are pleading a cause against powerful and long-established authorities. Olson's objective in tracing the confusion of values described throughout the first ten "letters" to its colonial source is thus not so much to unveil a *mystery* as it is to undo a *mystification*, to correct a false history of Gloucester which has prevented the port's citizens from understanding—and thus utilizing—the opportunities inherent in their own setting and past.[4] As the poet wrote explaining his projected research trip to Dorchester, "I want to go to

[a] Thomas Morton of Merrymount, one of the original opponents of the Pilgrims and a hero of William Carlos Williams' *In The American Grain*, described Standish as "Captaine Shrimpe" and called him "a quondam drummer" (*Tracts and Other Papers*, ed. P. Force, New York, 1947, Vol. II, p. 95). Olson introduces most of these contemporary criticisms of Standish into the text of *The Maximus Poems*. In "Letter 11" for example, he refers to Standish by saying "and the short Chimney / wld have died right there, being plugged by a fisherman if / Conant had not ordered Capt Hewes to lowr his gun, to listen / to what the little man from Plymouth had to squawk about" (48) and, "more Capt Shrimpe / from the loudness of him, quondam Drummer" (49).

England very soon to get the information to show how this city was in the mind of John White even without his knowing what she was, as a place to go fishing from. She is still a place to go fishing from. She is still le beauport. She is a form of mind."[5]

NOTES

•　•　•

INTRODUCTION • *THE TALE OF THE TRIBE*

1. Edgar Allan Poe, "The Poetic Principle" in Walter J. Bate, ed., *Criticism: The Major Texts*, New York, 1952, p. 353.

2. John Dryden, *Essays of John Dryden*, New York, 1961, Vol. II, p. 154.

3. Georg Lukács, *The Theory of the Novel*, Cambridge, Mass., 1971, p. 56.

4. Ezra Pound, "Canto I" in *Poetry* (Chicago), Vol. X, No. 3, June 1917, p. 118.

5. Stéphane Mallarmé, *Oeuvres Complètes,* Paris, 1945, p. 380.

6. Michel Foucault, *The Order of Things*, New York, 1970, p. 89.

7. *Ibid.*, p. 300.

8. Ludwig Wittgenstein, *Tractatus Logico-Philosophicus*, London, 1961, pp. 150–151.

9. Stéphane Mallarmé, *Correspondance,* Paris, 1955ff, Vol. II, p. 301.

10. Georg Lukács, *op.cit.*, p. 47.

11. Stéphane Mallarmé, *Oeuvres Complètes,* p. 367.

12. Walter Pater, *Studies in the History of the Renaissance*, London, 1910, p. 137.

13. Stéphane Mallarmé, *op.cit.*, p. 189.

14. T. S. Eliot, *The Complete Poems and Plays 1909-1950*, New York, 1958, p. 141.

15. Rudyard Kipling, "Literature" in *A Book of Words*, Vol. XXXII of *The Writings in Prose and Verse*, New York, 1928, pp. 3-4.

16. *Ibid.*, p. 4.

17. *Ibid.*, p. 6

18. *Ibid.*

19. Christine Brooke-Rose, "Lay Me By Aurelie" in *New Approaches to Ezra Pound*, ed. E. Hesse, London, 1969, p. 251.

20. Milman Parry, *The Making of Homeric Verse: The Collected Papers of Milman Parry*, Oxford, 1971, p. 8.

21. Claude Lévi-Strauss, *The Savage Mind*, Chicago, 1966, p. 58.

22. See especially: Robert Durling, *The Figure of the Poet in Renaissance Epic*, Cambridge, Mass., 1965; Albert Cook, *The Classic Line: A Study in Epic Poetry*, Bloomington, 1966; Thomas Greene, *The Descent from Heaven: A Study in Epic Continuity*, New Haven, 1963; H. T. Swedenberg, *The Theory of the Epic in England*, Berkeley, 1944; Donald M. Foerster, *The Fortunes of Epic Poetry*, New York, 1962; H. J. Hunt, *The Epic in Nineteenth-Century France*, Oxford, 1941; R. C. Williams, *Epic Unity as Discussed by Sixteenth-Century Critics in Italy*, Baltimore, 1921; E.M.W. Tillyard, *The English Epic and Its Background*, London, 1954; C. M. Bowra, *From Virgil to Milton*, London, 1945. For a very different perspective than the one taken in my study, see also James E. Miller, Jr., *The American Quest For A Supreme Fiction: Whitman's Legacy in the Personal Epic*, Chicago, 1979.

23. Milman Parry, *op.cit.*, pp. 365-375.

24. E.M.W. Tillyard, *The English Epic and Its Background*, London, 1954, p. 182.

25. Torquato Tasso, *Prose*, Milan, 1959, pp. 359-360.

26. H. J. Hunt, *The Epic in Nineteenth-Century France*, Oxford, 1941, p. 1.

27. Ludwig Wittgenstein, *The Blue and Brown Books*, Oxford, 1958, p. 17.

28. René Le Bosu, *Traité Du Poeme Epique*, Paris, 1675, p. 14.

29. For a detailed discussion of Marx's attitude toward literature, see S. S. Prawer, *Karl Marx and World Literature*, Oxford, 1976.

30. W. B. Yeats, *Essays and Introductions*, New York, 1968, p. 448.

31. Edmund Wilson, *The Triple Thinkers*, London, 1938, p. 29. Remy de Gourmont also consistently linked Flaubert to the classical epic poets, cf.: Richard Sieburth, *Instigations, Ezra Pound And Remy de Gourmont*, Cambridge, Mass., 1978, pp. 107-111.

32. Edmund Wilson, *op.cit.*, p. 34.

33. From an unpublished letter by Pound to his mother. Quoted in Noel Stock, *The Life of Ezra Pound*, London, 1970, p. 76.

34. Ezra Pound, "Redondillas . . . etc." in *Collected Early Poems*, New York, 1976, p. 218.

35. From an unpublished letter to John Quinn, 31 December 1916. Quoted in Daniel Pearlman, *The Barb of Time*, New York, 1969, p. 299.

36. J. P. Sullivan, *Ezra Pound and Sextus Propertius*, Austin, Texas, 1964, p. 134, line 4.

37. M. L. Rosenthal, "The Structuring of Pound's *Cantos*," *Paideuma*, Vol. 6, No. 1, Spring 1977, p. 10.

38. Eric A. Havelock, *Preface to Plato*, Cambridge, Mass., 1963, p. 27.

A · *THE CANTOS*

CHAPTER ONE · A POEM INCLUDING HISTORY

1. Max Horkheimer and Theodor Adorno, *Dialectic of Enlightenment*, New York, 1972, p. xv.

2. Richard Ellmann, "Ez and Old Billyum" in Eva Hesse, ed., *New Approaches to Ezra Pound*, London, 1969, p. 12.

3. Robert Creeley, "A Note followed by a Selection of Letters from Ezra Pound," *Agenda*, Vol. 4, No. 2, Oct.-Nov. 1965, p. 17.

4. William Butler Yeats, *The Letters of W. B. Yeats*, New York, 1955, p. 781.

5. From a letter to William Cookson quoted in "A Note By the Editor," *Agenda*, Vol. 8, Nos. 3-4, Autumn-Winter 1970, p. 6.

6. Donald Davie, "Sicily in the Cantos," *Paideuma*, Vol. 6, No. 1, Spring 1977, p. 105.

7. Theodor Adorno, *Prisms*, London, 1967, p. 62.

8. For a discussion of the literary tropes by which historians "emplot" their material, see Hayden White, *Metahistory*, Baltimore, 1973.

9. Agassiz, that is, belongs to the eighth heaven of the ten

making up Dante's *Paradiso* (Cantos 23-27). The fixed stars are associated with the Church Triumphant and it is there that the Divine Wisdom reveals itself through knowledge and true doctrine.

10. Quoted by Clark Emery, *Ideas Into Action*, Coral Gables, Florida, 1958, p. 26.

11. Ian Bell, "Divine Patterns: Louis Agassiz and American Men of Letters," *Journal of American Studies*, Vol. 10, No. 3, Dec. 1976, p. 373.

12. Richard Sieburth, *Instigations, Ezra Pound And Remy de Gourmont*, Cambridge, Mass., 1978, p. 121.

13. Roman Jakobson & M. Halle, *Fundamentals of Language*, The Hague, 1956, p. 80.

14. *Ibid.*, pp. 77-78.

15. John J. Nolde, "The Sources for Canto LIV: Part One," *Paideuma*, Vol. 5, No. 3, Winter 1976, p. 425.

16. Described in Noel Stock, *The Life of Ezra Pound*, London, 1970, p. 351.

17. Lucien Goldmann, *The Human Sciences and Philosophy*, London, 1969, pp. 28-29.

18. Siegfried Kracauer, *History: The Last Things Before The Last*, New York, 1969, p. 19.

19. Meng K'e, *Mencius*, Harmondsworth, 1970, p. 126.

20. Alex Zwerdling, *Yeats and the Heroic Ideal*, New York, 1965, p. 8.

21. Creeley, *op.cit.*, p. 19.

22. Charles Olson, *Letters for Origin 1950-1956*, London, 1969, p. 129.

23. John J. Nolde, *op.cit.*, pp. 419-420. See also Carroll F. Terrell, "History, de Mailla, and the Dynastic Cantos," *Paideuma*, Vol. 5, No. 1, Spring-Summer 1976, pp. 95-121, and David Gordon, "The Sources of Canto LIII," in the same issue, pp. 122-152.

24. John J. Nolde, "The Sources for Canto LIV: Part Two," *Paideuma*, Vol. 6, No. 1, Spring 1977, p. 81.

25. For a discussion of Pound's very personal appropriation of Confucian historiography, see Richard Freudenheim's unpublished Ph.D. thesis, "Canto 85," U.C. Berkeley, 1977.

26. Herrlee G. Creel, *The Origins of Statecraft in China:*

The Western Chou, Chicago, 1970, pp. 44–45. See also, Freudenheim, *op.cit.*, pp. 28–71.

27. Daniel D. Pearlman, *The Barb of Time*, New York, 1969, p. 215.

28. Quoted by Clark Emery, *op.cit.*, p. 47.

29. Michael Alexander, "On Reading the Cantos," *Agenda*, Vol. 4, No. 2, Oct.–Nov. 1965, p. 8.

30. Cf. Daniel D. Pearlman, *op.cit.*, pp. 164–165.

31. Hugh Kenner, "Ezra Pound and Money," *Agenda*, Vol. 4, No. 2, Oct.–Nov. 1965, p. 51.

32. For a discussion of how Pound differed from orthodox Social Credit doctrine, and a correction of both Earle Davis' and William Chace's reading of Pound's economics, see Dennis R. Klinck, "Pound, Social Credit, and the Critics," *Paideuma*, Vol. 5, No. 2, Fall 1976, pp. 227–240.

33. Hugh Kenner, *op.cit.*, p. 52.

34. Quoted in William Chace, *op.cit.*, p. 67.

35. Ezra Pound, "Paris Letter," *The Dial*, Vol. LXXIII, No. 3, Sept. 1922, pp. 336–337.

36. William Chace, *op.cit.*, pp. 6–10.

37. *Ibid.*, p. 8.

38. Quoted by Kenner, *op.cit.*, p. 50.

39. Ronald Bush, *op.cit.*, p. 10. Bush's entire discussion of the ideogram (pp. 9–15) is a useful corrective to critics who have over-emphasized its importance as *the* key to Pound's technique. I think Bush is correct in his analysis of the years 1916–1933, but his account leaves unexplained Pound's increasing reliance upon ideograms *in the poem*, as well as his championing of the "ideogrammic method" in the prose essays and private correspondence.

40. Ezra Pound, "Pastiche. The Regional," *The New Age*, Vol. XXV, No. 17, August 21, 1919, p. 284. Cf. R. Bush, *op.cit.*, p. 212.

41. R. Bush, *op.cit.*, p. 73.

42. *Ibid.*, p. 14.

43. Hayden White, *op.cit.*, p. 21.

44. Donald Davie, *Ezra Pound, Poet as Sculptor*, New York, 1964, and *Ezra Pound*, London, 1975. Cf. also Davie's "Ezra Among the Edwardians," *Paideuma*, Vol. 5, No. 1, Spring-

Summer 1976, pp. 3-14. Many of Pound's comments on art, such as his dislike of *chiaroscuro* and his general prejudice in favor of the early Renaissance painters—"all that Sandro [Botticelli] knew, and Jacopo [Sellaio] and that Velásquez never suspected / lost in the brown meat of Rembrandt / and the raw meat of Rubens and Jordaens" (LXXX:511)—are direct echoes of Berenson's *The Italian Painters of the Renaissance* (1898-1907). Similarly, his emphasis on line rather than color owes as much to pre-Raphaelite aesthetics as it does to Vorticism.

45. E. Badian, "Imposing Gibbon," *New York Review of Books*, Vol. xxiv, No. 16, Oct. 13, 1977, p. 9.

46. Stuart Hampshire, *Spinoza*, Harmondsworth, 1962, pp. 192-193.

47. Antonio Gramsci, *The Modern Prince and Other Writings*, London, 1957, p. 143.

48. Even Ian Bell's basically sympathetic essay on Agassiz shows how curious a choice he was for lessons on "the most modern scientific thought" in 1933, sixty years after his death! Bell, *op.cit.*, p. 350.

49. Walter Benjamin, *Illuminations*, New York, 1969, p. 255.

CHAPTER TWO · AN ETERNAL STATE OF MIND

1. Paul Valéry, *Oeuvres*, Paris, 1951, Vol. i, p. 658.

2. T. S. Eliot, "Ulysses, Order, and Myth," *The Dial*, Vol. lxxv, No. 5, Nov. 1923, p. 483.

3. *Ibid.*, p. 483.

4. Charles Altieri, "From Symbolist Thought to Immanence: The Ground of Postmodern American Poetics," *Boundary 2*, Vol. i, No. 1, Spring 1973, pp. 633-634.

5. I. A. Richards, *Mencius on the Mind*, London, 1932, p. 56.

6. Meng K'e, *Mencius*, Harmondsworth, 1970, p. 37.

7. Peter Makin, "Ezra Pound and Scotus Erigena," *Comparative Literature Studies*, Vol. x, No. 1, March 1973, pp. 72ff.

8. H. D. Smith, *Chinese Religions*, New York, 1968, p. 93.

9. W. B. Yeats, *The Letters of W. B. Yeats*, New York, 1955, p. 774.

10. Hugh Kenner, "Drafts and Fragments and The Structure of *The Cantos*," *Agenda*, Vol. 8, No. 3-4, Autumn-Winter 1970, p. 17.

11. R. L. Brown, "Saint Augustine," in *Trends in Medieval Political Thought*, Beryl Smalley ed., Oxford, 1965, p. 6.

12. R. T. Wallis, *Neoplatonism*, London, 1972. See especially chapters 1-4.

13. Plotinus, *Enneades,* ed. H. Mueller, Berlin, 1878, p. 145. I have translated the phrase myself, since MacKenna's version (p. 141) is not as direct as Plotinus' own affirmation. In fact, Thomas Taylor's much-abused translation (p. 61 of Mead's edition) seems to me in this instance as sound as MacKenna's.

14. Plotinus, *The Enneads*, trans. Stephen MacKenna, revised B. S. Page, 3rd edition, London, 1962, p. 141.

15. R. T. Wallis, *op.cit.*, pp. 89-90.

16. Henry Bett, *Johannes Scotus: A Study in Medieval Philosophy*, Cambridge, 1925, p. 70. For further discussions of Erigena, see R. T. Wallis, *op.cit.*; Peter Makin, *op.cit.*; Walter Benn Michaels, "Pound and Erigena," *Paideuma*, Vol. i, No. 1, Spring-Summer, 1972, pp. 37-54; Maieul Cappuyus, *Jean Scot Erigène*, Paris and Louvain, 1933.

17. R. T. Wallis, *op.cit.*, p. 61.

18. Considering that Pound's life-long devotion to the Medieval Light Philosophers and the neo-Platonists was combined with such hostility towards Buddhism, it is ironic that modern scholars think there is a direct link between the texts of Indian Buddhism and the Neoplatonic comparison of Divine Activity to the effortless radiation of light by the sun; Cf. Wallis, *op.cit.*, p. 15.

19. S. T. Coleridge, *Biographia Literaria*, J. Shawcross ed., Oxford, 1907, Vol. ii, p. 243.

20. *Ibid.*, Vol. i, p. 166.

21. Ezra Pound, *A Lume Spento and Other Early Poems*, New York, 1965, p. 56. Cf. Plotinus, *Selected Works of Plotinus*, trans. Thomas Taylor, ed. G.S.R. Mead, London, 1895, pp. 314-317. Recently, in "Pound's Vortex," *Paideuma*, Vol. 6, No. 2, Fall 1977, pp. 175-176, Timothy Materer has seen Pound's reading of Taylor's Plotinus and John Burnet's *Early Greek Philosophers*, London, 1892, as a major source for the image of the Vortex.

22. For a fascinating discussion of the revival of interest in neo-Platonism early in the century, see E.R.S. Dodd's autobiography, *Missing Persons*, Oxford, 1977. Dodds also reveals that it was after one of J. A. Stewart's lectures on neo-Platonism in 1915 that he persuaded a "shy American" to read his poems to a small English group, "The Coterie" (pp. 40-41). In this way, neo-Platonism was indirectly responsible for the first public European reading of "The Love Song of J. Alfred Prufrock!"

23. Plotinus, *The Enneads,* trans. S. MacKenna, *op.cit.,* p. 427.

24. *Ibid.,* p. 63.

25. *Ibid.,* pp. 617-618.

26. Porphyrius, "De Vita Plotini," in Plotinus, *Enneades,* ed. Mueller, Berlin, 1878, p. 4. I follow Wallis' suggestion in translating Plotinus' last words (Wallis, *op.cit.,* p. 40) rather than MacKenna, who renders them, "I am striving to give back the Divine in myself to the Divine in the All"(p. 2).

27. George Dekker, *Sailing After Knowledge*, London, 1963, pp. 102, 104.

28. Richard Freudenheim, "Ezra Pound: Canto 85," unpublished Ph.D. diss., U.C. Berkeley, 1977, pp. 18-19.

29. Theodore Ziolkowski, *The Novels of Hermann Hesse*, Princeton, 1965.

30. Roland Barthes, *Mythologies*, London, 1973, p. 124.

31. *Ibid.,* p. 142.

CHAPTER THREE · THUS WAS IT IN TIME

1. Ernst Bloch, *Das Prinzip Hoffnung*, Frankfurt am Main, 1959, Vol. II, p. 1628.

2. Quoted by Max Halperen, "How to Read a Canto" in *The Twenties, Poetry and Prose*, ed. R. E. Langford and W. E. Taylor, Deland, Florida, 1966, p. 8.

3. William Harmon's *Time in Ezra Pound's Work*, Chapel Hill, 1977, contains only one sketchy and rather conventional chapter on *The Cantos*. Harmon is far better on Pound's use of different temporal perspectives in the early poetry. Cf. also: Vincent Miller, "Pound's Battle With Time," *Yale Review*, Vol. LXVI, No. 2, Winter 1977, pp. 193-208.

4. Daniel D. Pearlman, *The Barb of Time*, New York, 1969, pp. 17ff.

5. *Ibid.*, p. 30.

6. *Ibid.*, p. 26.

7. *Ibid.*, p. 25.

8. See especially: Mircea Eliade, *Le Mythe de l'Eternel Retour*, Paris, 1949. Cf.: Pearlman, *op.cit.*, p. 22, note no. 32.

9. Ezra Pound, "Statecraft," *The Exile*, No. 4, Autumn 1928, p. 3.

10. John Dewey, *Logic: The Theory of Inquiry*, New York, 1938, p. 239.

11. See especially: Arthur O. Lovejoy, "Present Standpoints And Past History," *The Journal of Philosophy*, Vol. xxxvi, No. 18, August 1939, pp. 477-489; and Ernest Nagel, "Some Issues in the Logic of Historical Analysis," *The Scientific Monthly*, Vol. 74, March 1952, pp. 162-169.

12. Charles Olson, *Mayan Letters*, ed. Robert Creeley, London, 1968, p. 26.

13. *Ibid.*, p. 29.

14. Cory R. Greenspan, in "Charles Olson and Ezra Pound," unpublished Ph.D. thesis, S.U.N.Y. Buffalo, 1973, p. 64, points out that time itself is first carefully recorded in *The Pisan Cantos*, and that only in Pisa is the minute passage of individual moments scrupulously noted.

15. Theodor Adorno, *Prisms*, London, 1967, p. 58.

16. Donald Davie, *Pound*, London, 1975, p. 12.

17. Eugene Paul Nassar, *The Cantos of Ezra Pound: The Lyric Mode*, Baltimore and London, 1975, p. 30.

18. John Peck's "Landscape as Ceremony in the Later *Cantos*," *Agenda*, Vol. 9, Nos. 2-3, Spring-Summer 1971, pp. 26-69, remains the finest discussion of the last cantos. Peck recognizes the despair implicit in Pound's use of the Na-Khi ceremonies, and suggests an illuminating comparison between *Drafts and Fragments* and Baudelaire's bitter poem, "Voyage au Cythère."

19. On the last cantos see also: Hugh Kenner, "Drafts & Fragments & The Structure of The Cantos," *Agenda*, Vol. 8, Nos. 3-4, Autumn-Winter 1970, pp. 7-18; Jamila Ismail, "News of the Universe: ²Muan ¹Bpo and *The Cantos*," *Agenda*, Vol. 9, Nos. 2-3, Spring-Summer 1971, pp. 70-87;

Daniel Pearlman, "The Blue-Eyed Eel, Dame Fortune in Pound's Later Cantos," *Agenda*, Vol. 9, No. 4—Vol. 10, No. 1, Autumn-Winter 1971-1972, pp. 60-77; Donald Davie, "Cypress Versus Rock-Slide: An Appreciation of Canto 110," *Agenda*, Vol. 8, No. 3-4, Autumn-Winter 1970, pp. 19-26; Carroll F. Terrell, "The Na-Khi Documents I," *Paideuma*, Vol. 3, No. 1, Spring 1974, pp. 90-122; James J. Wilhelm, *The Later Cantos of Ezra Pound*, New York, 1977.

20. William Carlos Williams, "The Later Pound," *Massachusetts Review*, Vol. 14, No. 1, Winter 1973, p. 124.

CHAPTER FOUR · THE LANGUAGE OF THE TRIBE

1. Robert Creeley, "A Note followed by a Selection of Letters from Ezra Pound," *Agenda*, Vol. 4, No. 2, Oct.-Nov. 1965, p. 15.

2. Theodor Adorno, *Minima Moralia*, Frankfurt, 1951, p. 80.

3. Eric A. Havelock, *op.cit.*, pp. 291-292.

4. Donald Davie, *Pound*, London, 1975, pp. 73-74.

5. Charles Rosen & Henri Zerner, "The Revival of Official Art," *New York Review of Books*, March 18, 1976, p. 33.

6. *Ibid.*, p. 33.

7. *Ibid.*, p. 34.

8. Clement Greenberg, *Art and Culture: Critical Essays*, Boston, 1961, p. 171.

9. R. Murray Schafer, "Ezra Pound and Music," *The Canadian Music Journal*, Vol. V, No. 4., Summer 1961, p. 28. See also: William McNaughton, "A Note on Main Form in *The Cantos*," *Paideuma*, Vol. 6, No. 2, Fall 1977, pp. 147-152.

10. George Eliot, *The George Eliot Letters*, New Haven, 1954, Vol. II, p. 324.

11. Theodor Adorno, *Prisms*, London, 1967, p. 32.

12. Friedrich Nietzsche, *Beyond Good and Evil*, New York, 1966, p. 223.

13. R. P. Blackmur, "A Critic's Job of Work," in *Form & Value In Modern Poetry*, New York, 1957, p. 339.

14. Gerald L. Bruns, *Modern Poetry and the Idea of Language*, New Haven, 1974, p. 256.

15. Herbert N. Schneidau, *Ezra Pound: The Image and the Real*, Baton Rouge, 1969, pp. 138-139.

16. Charles Rosen & Henri Zerner, *op.cit.*, p. 36.

17. Gerald Bruns, *op.cit.*, p. 194.

18. *Ibid.*, p. 195.

19. Ezra Pound, "Pastiche, The Regional," *The New Age*, Vol. xxv, No. 18, August 28, 1919, p. 300.

20. Michael Reck, "A Conversation between Ezra Pound and Allen Ginsberg," *Evergreen Review*, No. 57, June 1968, p. 28.

21. Jonathan Williams and Tom Meyer, "A Conversation with Basil Bunting," *St. Andrews Review*, Vol. 4, No. 2, Spring-Summer 1977, p. 25.

22. Cf. Daniel Pearlman, "Alexander Del Mar In *The Cantos:* A Printout of the Sources," *Paideuma*, Vol. 1, No. 2, Fall-Winter 1972, pp. 167-180; Wendy S. Flory, "Alexander Del Mar: Some Additional Sources," *Paideuma*, Vol. 4, Nos. 2-3, Fall-Winter 1975, pp. 325-327; Steven Helmling, "Del Mar Material in Canto 97: Further Annotations," *Paideuma*, Vol. 5, No. 7, Spring 1976, pp. 53-57.

23. Max Nänny, *Ezra Pound: Poetics for an Electric Age*, Bern, 1973.

24. Jürgen Habermas, *Theory and Practice*, London, 1974, p. 42.

25. Ezra Pound, *The Classical Anthology Defined By Confucius*, intro. by Achilles Fang, London, 1974, p. xiv.

26. Allen Upward, *The New Word*, New York, 1910, p. 193.

27. Ezra Pound, *America, Roosevelt and the Causes of the Present War* (Money Pamphlet Number 6), London, 1951, p. 17.

28. Hugh Kenner, "Drafts & Fragments & The Structure of The Cantos," *Agenda*, Vol. 8, No. 3-4, Autumn-Winter 1970, pp. 14-15.

29. John Peck, "Pound's Lexical Mythography," *Paideuma*, Vol. 1, No. 1, Spring-Summer 1972, pp. 3-36.

30. Cf. Richard Freudenheim, "Canto 85," unpublished Ph.D. thesis, U.C. Berkeley, 1977. Freudenheim sees "a good deal of hostility toward the reader" in the impenetrable surface of Canto 85 (p. 135).

31. *Ibid.*, p. 135.

32. Christine Brooke-Rose, *A ZBC of Ezra Pound*, London, 1971; Suzanne Juhasz, *Metaphor and the Poetry of Williams, Pound, and Stevens*, Lewisberg, Pennsylvania, 1974.

33. Michel Foucault, *The Order of Things*, London, 1970, p. 82.

34. Frederic Jameson, "Of Islands and Trenches: Naturalization and the Production of Utopian Discourse," *Diacritics*, Vol. 7, No. 2, Summer 1977, pp. 5-6.

CHAPTER FIVE · IDENTIFICATION AND ITS VICISSITUDES

1. John Ashbery, "Grand Galop," in *Self-Portrait in a Convex Mirror*, New York, 1976, p. 14.

2. Paul Alpers, "Narration in *The Faerie Queene*," *E.L.H.* 44, 1977, p. 19.

3. William Carlos Williams, *Paterson*, New York, 1963, p. 239.

4.. Charles Baudelaire, *Oeuvres Complètes*, Paris, 1961, p. 1271.

5. Ezra Pound, "Canto One" in *Poetry*, Vol. x, No. 3, June 1917, pp. 113-121; "Canto Two" in *Poetry*, Vol. x, No. 4, July 1917, pp. 180-188; "Canto Three" in *Poetry*, Vol. x, No. 5, August 1917, pp. 248-254. All future references are acknowledged in the text.

6. Leo Bersani, "The Subject of Power," *Diacritics*, Vol. 7, No. 3, Fall 1977, p. 17.

7. Sigmund Freud, "Mourning and Melancholia," in *The Standard Edition of the Complete Psychological Works*, London, 1957, Vol. xiv, p. 249.

8. Roland Barthes, *S/Z*, Paris, 1970, p. 151. "The discourse, and not one or another of its characters is the only *positive* hero of the story."

9. *Ibid.*, p. 146. "Flaubert . . . manipulating an irony saturated with uncertainty, works a salutary discomfort of writing; he does not stop the play of codes (or stops it only partially), so that (and this is doubtless the *proof* of writing) *one never knows if he is responsible for what he writes* (if there is a subject *behind* his language)."

10. Friedrich Nietzsche, *Thus Spoke Zarathustra*, Harmondsworth, 1961, p. 162.

11. Robert Durling, *The Figure of the Poet in Renaissance Epic*, Cambridge, Mass., 1965, pp. 1-2.

12. For Flaubert's strategy of "demoralization," see Jonathan Culler, *Flaubert, The Uses of Uncertainty*, Ithaca, 1974. Culler's argument is criticized in: M. A. Bernstein, "Jonathan Culler And The Limits of Uncertainty," *P.T.L.*, 3, 1977, pp. 589-595.

13. I owe the last part of this sentence to Jean Andrews, a graduate student at U.C. Berkeley. Several arguments in this chapter were stimulated by my disagreement with, as well as admiration for, a provocative essay prepared by Ms. Andrews for a seminar on *The Cantos* which I offered at Berkeley in the Fall of 1976.

14. Cf. Louis Althusser's description of this process in Hegel and Marx, in *Politics and History*, London, 1972, p. 185.

CHAPTER SIX · THE ARTIST WHO DOES
THE NEXT JOB

1. L. S. Dembo, *Conceptions of Reality in Modern American Poetry*, Berkeley, 1966, pp. 145-146.

2. Donald Davie, *Thomas Hardy and British Poetry*, New York, 1972, p. 12.

3. John Betjeman, *Collected Poems*, Introduction by Philip Larkin, Boston, 1971, p. xxxviii.

4. *Ibid.*, p. xli.

5. John Press, *A Map of Modern English Verse*, London & New York, 1969, p. 4.

6. For a fine and witty discussion of this tendency by a noted American poet, critic, and editor, see: Theodore Weiss, "The Blight of Modernism and Philip Larkin's Antidote," *The American Poetry Review*, Vol. 6, No. 1, Jan.-Feb. 1977, pp. 39-41.

7. Thomas Parkinson, *Hart Crane and Yvor Winters: Their Literary Correspondence*, Berkeley, 1978, p. 20.

8. Hugh MacDiarmid, "The Esemplastic Power," *Agenda*, Vol. 8, Nos. 3-4, Autumn-Winter 1970, p. 28.

9. Hans Robert Jauss, "Literary History as a Challenge to Literary Theory" in *New Directions in Literary History*, ed. Ralph Cohen, Baltimore, 1974, p. 28.

10. Donald Davie, *Ezra Pound: Poet as Sculptor*, New York, 1964, p. 244.

11. Charles Olson, *The Special View of History*, Berkeley, 1970, p. 29.

B · *PATERSON*

CHAPTER SEVEN · A LOCAL WAR?

1. Gertrude Stein, "Composition as Explanation" in *Look at Me Now and Here I Am*, Harmondsworth, Middlesex, 1967, p. 23.

2. Michel Foucault, *The Archaeology of Knowledge*, London, 1972, p. 114.

3. William Carlos Williams, *I Wanted to Write a Poem*, ed. Edith Heal, Boston, 1958, p. 5.

4. Ezra Pound, *The Instigations of Ezra Pound*, New York, 1920, pp. 243-246.

5. William Carlos Williams, *Paterson*, New York, 1963. All references are to the 1963 New Directions paperback edition, sixth printing, and are acknowledged in the body of the text. References are indicated by the Book in capital roman numerals, followed by the section in lower-case roman numerals, and then by page number.

6. William Carlos Williams, *The Selected Letters*, ed. J. C. Thirlwall, New York, 1957. All subsequent references are acknowledged in the text as: (*SL*:page number).

7. William Carlos Williams, "A Study of Ezra Pound's Present Position," ed. P. L. Mariani, *The Massachusetts Review*, Vol. 14, No. 1, Winter 1973, p. 119.

8. *Ibid.*, p. 119.

9. Pound's letter, dated 31 December 1916, was published in Daniel Pearlman, *The Barb of Time*, New York, 1969, p. 299.

10. Mike Weaver's study, *William Carlos Williams: The American Background*, Cambridge, 1971, contains an excellent

discussion of this aspect of the poet's career, as well as the best overall summary I know of Williams' relationship to the intellectual and artistic currents of his own day. On the rise of "the region" in American thinking see also: William Stott, *Documentary Expression and Thirties America*, New York, 1973.

11. William Carlos Williams, *Kora In Hell: Improvisations*, Boston, 1920, p. 26.

12. *Ibid.*, p. 28.

13. William Carlos Williams, "A Maker," *The Little Review*, Vol. vi, No. 4, August 1919, p. 37.

14. William Carlos Williams, *The Great American Novel*, Paris, 1933, p. 25.

15. William Carlos Williams, *In The American Grain*, New York, 1925, p. 112.

16. I have taken the phrase "trinitarian hero" from Richard Lane Denham, "William Carlos Williams' *Paterson*: An American Epic," unpublished Ph.D. thesis, U. of S. Carolina, 1974. Denham considers the creation of this figure Williams' principal solution to the problem of a modern verse epic, a view which, as the next chapter will make clear, I do not share. On the influence of Whitman upon *Paterson*, see also James E. Miller, Jr., *The American Quest For A Supreme Fiction: Whitman's Legacy in the Personal Epic*, Chicago, 1979.

17. William Carlos Williams, *The Autobiography of William Carlos Williams*, New York, 1951, p. 174.

18. William Carlos Williams, *Selected Essays*, New York, 1954. New Directions paperback edition, 1969. All references are to the paperback edition and are acknowledged in the body of the text as (*SE*:page number).

19. Hugh Kenner, *The Pound Era*, Berkeley, 1971, p. 515.

CHAPTER EIGHT · A DELIRIUM OF SOLUTIONS

1. Marsden Hartley, *Adventures in the Arts*, New York, 1921, p. 57.

2. John Dewey, "Americanism and Localism," *The Dial*, LXVIII, June 1920, p. 687.

3. William Carlos Williams, *I Wanted to Write a Poem*, ed. E. Heal, Boston, 1958, pp. 71–73.

4. James Breslin, *William Carlos Williams: An American Artist*, New York, 1970, p. 177.

5. William Carlos Williams, *The Wedge*, Cummington, Mass., 1944, p. 4.

6. William Carlos Williams, *A Novelette and Other Prose*, Toulon, France, 1932, p. 38.

7. William Carlos Williams, "The Descent of Winter" in *The Exile*, No. 4, Autumn 1928, pp. 46–47.

8. James Breslin, *op.cit.* p. 52.

9. Richard M. Sweeney, " 'Editur Ez' and 'Old Hugger-Scrunch:' The Influence of Ezra Pound on the Poems of William Carlos Williams," unpublished Ph.D. thesis, Brown University, 1969, p. 87.

10. William Carlos Williams, *The Autobiography of William Carlos Williams*, New York, 1951, p. 391.

11. Charles Olson, *Mayan Letters*, London, 1968, p. 30.

12. Sister M. Bernetta Quinn, "On *Paterson*, Book One" in *William Carlos Williams: A Collection of Critical Essays*, ed. J. H. Miller, Englewood Cliffs, New Jersey, 1966, p. 110.

13. I owe this phrase to my friend James A. Powell.

14. Quoted by Cid Corman, "The Farmer's Daughters: A True Story about People" in *William Carlos Williams*, ed. J. H. Miller, *op.cit.*, p. 167.

15. Leo Bersani, *Baudelaire and Freud*, Berkeley, 1977, p. 24.

16. The letter is now in the Humanities Research Center, U. of Texas, Austin.

17. Charles Olson, *op.cit.*, p. 27.

CHAPTER NINE · SPEED AGAINST THE INUNDATION

1. Paul Ricoeur, *History and Truth*, Evanston, Ill., 1965, p. 41.

2. J. M. Brinnin, *William Carlos Williams*, Minneapolis, 1963, p. 69.

3. James E. Breslin, *William Carlos Williams: An American Artist*, New York, 1970, p. 40.

4. J. Hillis Miller, *Poets of Reality*, Cambridge, Mass., 1966, p. 355.

5. Quoted by D. S. Carne-Ross, "The Sense of a Past," *Arion*, Vol. 8, No. 2, Summer 1969, p. 233.

6. Roland Barthes, *Mythologies*, London, 1973, p. 146.

7. William Carlos Williams, *The Embodiment of Knowledge*, ed. Ron Loewinsohn, New York, 1974, p. 149.

8. William Carlos Williams, "The Later Pound," ed. Paul L. Mariani, *The Massachusetts Review*, Winter 1973, p. 128.

C · *THE MAXIMUS POEMS*

CHAPTER TEN · THE OLD MEASURE OF CARE

1. Stéphane Mallarmé, *Correspondance*, ed. H. Mondor & L. J. Austin, Paris, 1959-1973, Vol. III, p. 67.

2. Paul Verlaine, "Art Poétique" in *Oeuvres Poétiques Complètes*, Paris, 1959, p. 206.

3. V. N. Vološinov, *Marxism and the Philosophy of Language*, New York & London, 1973, pp. 158-159.

4. I. R. Titunik, "The Formal Method and the Sociological Method (M. M. Baxtin, P. N. Medvedev, V. N. Vološinov) in Russian Theory and Study of Literature" in *Marxism and the Philosophy of Language*, pp. 198-199.

5. V. N. Vološinov, *op.cit.*, p. 158.

6. Charles Olson, *The Maximus Poems*, New York, 1960; *Maximus Poems IV, V, VI*, London, 1968; *The Maximus Poems*, Volume Three, New York, 1975. All subsequent references are to these editions and are acknowledged in the text itself. Where possible, I have listed the name or number of the individual "letter" followed by the appropriate page reference.

7. V. N. Vološinov, *op.cit.*, p. 159.

8. Eric A. Havelock, *Preface to Plato*, Cambridge, Mass., 1963, p. 69.

9. Charles Olson, *Mayan Letters*, ed. Robert Creely, London, 1968, p. 91.

10. Charles Olson, *Letters for Origin*, ed. Albert Glover, London, 1969, p. 130.

11. Charles Olson, *Mayan Letters*, p. 88.

12. Quoted by Julien Cornell in his book, *The Trial of Ezra Pound*, New York, 1966, p. 71.

13. Charles Olson, "I Mencius, Pupil Of The Master" in *The Distances*, New York, 1960, p. 62.

14. Catherine Seelye, ed., *Charles Olson and Ezra Pound*, New York, 1975, p. xvii.

15. Charles Olson, *Reading at Berkeley*, transcribed by Z. Brown, San Francisco, 1966, p. 32.

16. Olson's whole epistolary style, with its characteristic condensations, misspellings, and grammatical liberties, seems to owe its very existence to the prior example of Pound's letters. To me a far more irritating aping, however, is Olson's (very Poundian) habit of offering rigid, prescriptive reading-lists on every imaginable topic, choices that, although proclaimed in an absolutist and "totalitarian" rhetoric, are often quite arbitrary and narrow in their scope.

17. Marjorie G. Perloff, "Charles Olson and the 'Inferior Predecessors': 'Projective Verse' Revisited," *E.L.H.*, Vol. 40, No. 2, Summer 1973, p. 306.

18. Catherine Seelye, ed., *Charles Olson and Ezra Pound*, p. 18.

19. *Ibid.*, pp. 15, 17.

20. Robert von Hallberg, "The Poets' Politics: A View from the Archives," *Chicago Review*, Vol. 28, No. 1, Summer 1976, p. 149.

21. Charles Olson, "A Bibliography on America for Ed Dorn" in *Additional Prose*, ed. George F. Butterick, Bolinas, California, 1974, p. 8.

22. Charles Olson, *The Special View of History*, ed. Ann Charters, Berkeley, 1970, p. 29.

23. *Ibid.*, p. 18.

24. *Ibid.*, p. 17.

25. Maurice Merleau-Ponty, *Phénoménologie de la Perception*, Paris, 1945, p. 111. Translation mine.

26. Charles Olson, *Mayan Letters*, p. 90.

27. Charles Olson, "The Art of Poetry," *Paris Review*, No. 49, Summer 1969-1970, p. 198.

28. Charles Olson, *Poetry and Truth*, San Francisco, 1971, p. 64.

29. Charles Olson, *Letters for Origin*, p. 129.

30. Charles Olson, *Mayan Letters*, p. 26.

31. *Ibid.*, p. 29.

32. Lucien Goldmann, *The Human Sciences and Philosophy*, London, 1969, p. 29.

33. Charles Olson, *Mayan Letters*, p. 28.

34. Charles Olson, *Letters for Origin*, p. 129.

35. Charles Olson, *Mayan Letters*, p. 29.

36. Lucien Goldmann, *op.cit.*, p. 28.

37. Carl Ortwin Sauer, *Land and Life*, Berkeley, 1963, p. 326.

38. Charles Olson, *Mayan Letters*, p. 28.

39. Charles Olson, *Letters for Origin*, p. 131.

40. Charles Olson, *Additional Prose*, p. 40.

CHAPTER ELEVEN · THE NEW LOCALISM

1. Salvatore Quasimodo, *Il Poeta E Il Politico E Altri Saggi*, Milan, 1967, p. 130. "Man's body brings us close to history, not to aesthetics."

2. Donald Davie, *Ezra Pound: Poet as Sculptor*, New York, 1964, p. 244. See also: "Landscape as Poetic Focus," *The Southern Review*, Vol. IV, No. 3, July 1968, pp. 685-691.

3. Charles Olson, "The Advantage of Literacy Is That Words Can Be on the Page" in *Additional Prose*, ed. George F. Butterick, Bolinas, California, 1974, p. 51.

4. Carl Ortwin Sauer, *Land and Life*, Berkeley, 1963, p. 333.

5. Charles Altieri, "From Symbolist Thought To Immanence: The Ground of Postmodern American Poetics," *Boundary 2*, Vol. I, No. 1, Spring 1973, p. 631.

6. *Ibid.*, p. 632-633.

7. Charles Olson, *The Special View of History*, ed. Ann Charters, Berkeley, 1970, p. 25.

8. Charles Olson, *Letters for Origin*, ed. Albert Glover, London, 1969, p. 29.

9. Charles Olson, *The Special View of History*, p. 25.

10. John Cage, *Silence*, Cambridge, Mass., 1966, p. 108.

11. Charles Olson, *Reading at Berkeley*, transcribed by Z. Brown, San Francisco, 1966, p. 25. See also: Charles Olson, *Maps 4*, ed. G. Butterick, Shippensburg, Penn., 1971, p. 31.

12. Michael A. Bernstein, "Ezra Pound and Charles Olson: Towards an Inclusive Poetics," *St. Andrews Review*, Vol. v, No. 2, Spring-Summer 1979, pp. 77-88.

13. Charles Olson, "Equal, That Is, to the Real Itself," in *Human Universe and Other Essays*, ed. Donald Allen, San Francisco, 1965, p. 122.

14. Charles Olson, *The Special View of History*, pp. 35-36.

15. Charles Olson, *Letters for Origin*, p. 22.

16. *Ibid.*, pp. 59-60.

17. Charles Olson, "A Bibliography On America For Ed Dorn," in *Additional Prose*, p. 11.

18. Charles Olson, "Key West II," notebook entry, Feb. 13, 1945. Printed in *Olson*, No. 5, Spring 1976, p. 11.

19. Charles Olson, "The Carpenter Poem," *Olson*, No. 6, Fall 1976, p. 53. Emphasis is mine. In context the lines read ". . . Even though we know care, and can give maximum / attention, can saturate any given act so that the bottom / is as done as the top and all the parts, . . . /"

20. Charles Olson, "Again the sense . . . ," *Olson*, No. 5, Spring 1976, p. 45.

21. Georg Lukács, *History and Class Consciousness*, London, 1971, pp. 151-152.

22. Frank W. Davey, *Five Readings of Olson's Maximus*, Montreal, 1968. See also: Davey, "Theory and Practice in the Black Mountain Poets, Duncan, Olson, and Creeley," unpublished Ph.D. thesis, U. of Southern California, 1968.

23. Paul Harvey, *The Oxford Companion to Classical Literature*, Oxford, 1959, p. 154.

24. Charles Olson, *Letters for Origin*, p. 41.

25. Frank W. Davey, *Five Readings of Olson's Maximus*, p. 17.

26. *Ibid.*, p. 18.

CHAPTER TWELVE · POLIS IS THIS

1. Maurice Tuchman, *The New York School: Abstract Expressionism In The 40s and 50s*, London, 1971, p. 141.

2. Charles Olson, "Proprioception" in *Additional Prose*, ed. G. F. Butterick, Bolinas, California, 1974, p. 21.

3. For a very different interpretation of these lines see: Sherman Paul, *Olson's Push*, Baton Rouge, 1978, pp. 152-153.

4. My division of the poem into distinct rhetorical sections also corresponds to the publishing history of *The Maximus Poems*. See: George F. Butterick, *A Guide to The Maximus Poems*, Berkeley, 1978.

5. Charles Olson, "Variations Done For Gerald Van De Wiele," in *The Distances*, New York, 1960, p. 87.

6. José Ortega y Gasset, *The Revolt of the Masses*, New York, 1957, p. 151.

7. Martin Dodsworth, *The Survival of Poetry*, London, 1970, p. 26.

8. Charles Olson, *The Mayan Letters*, ed. Robert Creeley, London, 1968, p. 29.

9. Charles Olson, "Canto 3, January 24, 1946 . . ." in Catherine Seelye ed., *Charles Olson and Ezra Pound*, New York, 1975, pp. 52-53.

10. George F. Butterick, *op.cit.*, p. 83.

11. Paul Christensen, *Charles Olson, Call Him Ishmael*, Austin, Texas, 1979, p. 159.

12. Cf. Olson's interview with Herbert A. Kenny, printed in *Olson*, No. 1, Spring 1974, pp. 7-44. On migration, see especially pp. 19-20.

13. Quoted in Paul Christensen, *op.cit.*, p. 135.

14. Robert von Hallberg, *Charles Olson, The Scholar's Art*, Cambridge, Mass., 1978, p. 215.

CONCLUSION · REMEMBER THAT
I HAVE REMEMBERED

1. Friedrich Schiller, *Naive and Sentimental Poetry*, New York, 1966, p. 148.

2. Ezra Pound, "Pastiche: The Regional VIII," in *The New Age*, Vol. xxv, No. 17, August 21, 1919, p. 284.

3. James Joyce, *Ulysses*, New York, 1961, p. 34.

4. Walter Benjamin, *Illuminations*, New York, 1969, p. 254.

5. Hans-Georg Gadamer, *Truth and Method*, New York, 1975, p. 479.

6. Walter Benjamin, *op.cit.*, p. 255.

7. *Ibid.*, p. 254.

8. *Ibid.*, p. 263.

9. *Ibid.*, p. 4.

10. Eric A. Havelock, *Preface to Plato*, Cambridge, Mass., 1963, p. 80. The references in *The Republic* are to Book Ten, section 599c8 and 606e3.

11. William Carlos Williams, "Asphodel, That Greeny Flower," in *Pictures from Brueghel*, New York, 1962, pp. 160-161.

12. John Bayley, "The dynamics of the static," *T.L.S.*, March 3, 1978, p. 246.

13. Donald Davie, *Pound*, London, 1975, p. 90. Among the few genuinely helpful essays devoted to Pound's metrics is James A. Powell's "The Light of Vers Libre," *Paideuma*, Vol. 8, No. 1, Spring 1979, pp. 3-34.

14. See the chapter "Ideas in the Cantos," pp. 62-74, of Davie's book cited above, and my discussion in Section A, Chapter Three.

15. Thomas McKeown, "Review of *Ezra Pound* by Donald Davie," *Paideuma*, Vol. 5, No. 3, Winter 1976, p. 486.

16. As reported to Pound by Allen Ginsberg in 1968. See Michael Reck, "A Conversation between Ezra Pound and Allen Ginsberg," *Evergreen Review*, No. 57, June 1968, p. 28.

17. Robert Pinsky, *The Situation of Poetry*, Princeton, 1976, pp. 144-145.

APPENDIX · ON FOUNDING: A HISTORICAL SURVEY OF GLOUCESTER'S SETTLEMENT

1. Gloucester Association, *The Fisheries of Gloucester from 1623-1876*, Gloucester, Mass., 1876, p. 17.

2. James R. Pringle, *History of Gloucester*, Gloucester, Mass., 1892, p. 21.

3. William Hubbard as quoted in Frances Rose-Troup, *John White*, New York, 1930, pp. 89-90. Cf. also A. Johnson and D. Malone, ed., *Dictionary of American Biography*, New York, 1928-1937, Vol. 17, p. 500.

4. The information in this survey is intentionally schematic.

For a more detailed study of Olson's sources, and for a wealth of other information about the poet and his epic, George Butterick's *A Guide To The Maximus Poems* is invaluable.

5. Charles Olson, "MAXIMUS, Part II," an unpublished "letter" first printed in *Olson*, No. 6, Fall 1976, pp. 61-62.

INDEX

• • •

LIBRARY OF CONGRESS CATALOGING IN PUBLICATION DATA

Bernstein, Michael, 1947-
    The tale of the tribe: Ezra Pound and the modern verse epic.

    Includes bibliographical references.
    1. American poetry—20th century—History and
criticism.   2.   Epic poetry, American—History and
criticism.   3.   Pound, Ezra Loomis, 1885-1972.   Cantos.
4.   Williams, William Carlos, 1883-1963.   Paterson.
5.   Olson, Charles, 1910-1970.   Maximus poems.   I.   Title.
PS309.E64B4   811'.0309   80-129
ISBN 0-691-06434-2
ISBN 0-691-01372-1 pbk.